Chinese Economists on Economic Reform – Collected Works of Du Runsheng

This book is part of a series which makes available to English-speaking audiences the work of the individual Chinese economists who were the architects of China's economic reform. The series provides an inside view of China's economic reform, revealing the thinking of the reformers themselves, unlike many other books on China's economic reform which are written by outside observers.

Du Runsheng (1913–) has made major contributions to policy making on land reform, rural development and science policy. Politically active from the 1930s, when he served as a guerrilla leader fighting Japanese aggression, and in the 1940s, when he was involved in the War of Liberation (1945–49), he has held many Chinese Communist Party posts. He was secretary-general of the Chinese Academy of Sciences in the late 1950s, responsible for drafting the 1961 policy document which urged respect for intellectuals. Attacked and persecuted during the Cultural Revolution (1966–76), he was for most of the 1980s in charge of research on rural economic reform and rural development strategies.

The book is published in association with **China Development Research Foundation,** one of the leading economic and social think tanks in China, where many of the theoretical foundations and policy details of economic reform were formulated.

Routledge Studies on the Chinese Economy
Series Editor
Peter Nolan, Sinyi Professor, Judge Business School, Chair,
Development Studies, University of Cambridge

Founding Series Editors
Peter Nolan, University of Cambridge and
Dong Fureng, Beijing University

The aim of this series is to publish original, high-quality, research-level work by both new and established scholars in the West and the East, on all aspects of the Chinese economy, including studies of business and economic history.

Routledge Studies on the Chinese Economy – Chinese Economists on Economic Reform

Du Runsheng

Chinese Economists on Economic Reform – Collected Works of Du Runsheng

Du Runsheng

Edited by China Development Research Foundation

Routledge
Taylor & Francis Group

LONDON AND NEW YORK

First edition of *A Collection of Du Runsheng's Works on Economic Reform,*
written by Du Runsheng,
ISBN: 978-7-80234-197-5
published 2008 by China Development Press.

This edition published 2014
by Routledge
2 Park Square, Milton Park, Abingdon, Oxon, OX14 4RN

and by Routledge
711 Third Avenue, New York, NY 10017

First issued in paperback 2018

Routledge is an imprint of the Taylor & Francis Group, an informa business

British Library Cataloguing-in-Publication Data
A catalogue record for this book is available from the British Library

Library of Congress Cataloging-in-Publication Data

Du, Runsheng.
[Works. Selections. English]
    Chinese economists on economic reform. Collected works of Du Runsheng /
Du Runsheng ; edited by China Development Research Foundation. — First
edition.
       pages cm. — (Routledge studies on the Chinese economy. Chinese
economists on economic reform ; 4)
    title: Collected works of Du Runsheng
    1. China—Economic conditions—1976–2000.   2. China—Economic
conditions—2000–   I. Du, Runsheng. Du Runsheng gai ge lun ji. English.
II. China Development Research Foundation.   III. Title.   IV. Title:
Collected works of Du Runsheng.
HC427.92.D82613   2014
338.951—dc23   2013019579

ISBN 13: 978-1-138-59582-8 (pbk)
ISBN 13: 978-0-415-85767-3 (hbk)

Typeset in Times New Roman
by Apex CoVantage, LLC

Contents

Series preface

This series of books is authored by economists who were witnesses to and direct participants in China's 'reform and opening up' over the past three decades. Nearly three generations of Chinese economists are represented, for they include both older and younger economists. Articles that were selected display the characteristics of the period in which they were written. Most exerted a direct impact on China's economic-reform policies, whether they were policy recommendations, theoretical works, or research reports. Most of these works are being published for the first time.

The China Development Research Foundation organized and published this series in Chinese in 2008 to commemorate the 30th anniversary of the start of China's 'reform and opening up' and to further promote this historic social transformation. Authors and their descendants responded enthusiastically to the proposal. All the articles were edited and finalized by the authors themselves, except for those of the late Xue Muqiao and Ma Hong, which were edited and finalized by members of their families.

This series has been broadly welcomed in China. I am confident that this English edition will be helpful in giving foreign readers a better understanding of China's economic-reform policies.

I gratefully acknowledge the contribution of the World Bank, Ford Foundation, and Cairncross Foundation, who supported the translation and publication of this series in English. I would like to thank Justin Yifu Lin, Pieter Bottelier, Peter Geithner, David Dollar, and other experts for their valuable support and candid comments. My gratitude also goes to Martha Avery for her excellent translating and editing.

Wang Mengkui
Chairman
China Development Research Foundation

About the author

Du Runsheng was born in 1913 in Taigu County, Shanxi Province. He attended the Guomin Normal School in Taiyuan before going on to higher education at the Beijing Normal University. While still in school, he began to participate in revolutionary activities, joining the Student Union during the 'December 9 Movement' and serving as one of the student leaders. In 1932, he joined two 'peripheral organizations' of the Party, the Federation of Social Groups and the Grand Union of Anti-Imperialism. In 1936, he joined what was called the 'Vanguard for liberating the Chinese nation' as well as the Communist Party of China (CPC).

Du Runsheng served as a guerrilla leader in the early years of the War against Japanese Aggression in the central region of Shanxi Province, where he engaged in armed battles against the Japanese behind enemy lines. In the latter years of the war, he led work in democratic organization, mobilizing people, and setting up revolutionary bases in enemy-occupied areas. He served as head of the Propaganda Section of the Party Committee in the Shanxi-Hebei-Henan Region, a member of the government in the Shanxi-Hebei-Shandong-Henan Border Region, a commissioner in the 'second' and 'sixth' districts in the Taihang Mountains, deputy head of the Taihang Administrative Office, and secretary of the Taiyuan Committee of the Urban Work Department of the Taihang Party Committee.

During the War of Liberation [1945–1949], Du Runsheng accompanied troops led by Liu Bocheng and Deng Xiaoping in the march toward the south. His responsibility was to lead peasant movements to implement land reform in areas through which the troops were passing. He then served consecutively as secretary-general of the Central Plains Bureau of the CPC Central Committee, secretary-general of the Central China Bureau of the CPC Central Committee, secretary of the Party Committee of the Huaixi Region [west of the Huai River], and secretary of the Party Committee of the Fourth Prefecture of the Henan-Anhui-Jiangsu Region.

In the early years of New China, Du Runsheng served as secretary-general of the CPC Central Committee's bureau covering southern and central China. He was concurrently director of the policy office of the Central Committee, as well as deputy director of the Land Reform Committee of the Military and Political Commission of the southern and central region. In leading the land reform movement in what was called the 'new region' in southern and central China, he advocated that land reform be carried out in phases. Specifically, he felt that a number of steps should be carried out before land was redistributed, including mobilizing farmers, suppressing 'bandits and despots,' and setting up a reasonable structure for 'farmers' associations.' He further recommended that cadres who were 'sent into the countryside' to participate in rural land reform should actually eat, live, and work together with impoverished farmers so that the party's grassroots organizations could be established on the class basis of 'poor peasants.' Mao Zedong approved of his approach to land reform and, on behalf of the CPC Central Committee, transmitted written confirmation to that effect to all regions. This 'central authorization' stated, 'Doing things this way is absolutely necessary' and, 'The proper sequence in carrying out land reform should be as this recommends.'

In early 1953, Du Runsheng was transferred to serve as secretary-general of the Rural Work Department of the CPC Central Committee and concurrently as deputy director of the Agriculture and Forestry Office of the State Council. His responsibilities involved implementing what was called the 'socialist transformation of agriculture' and leading the agricultural 'cooperativization' movement. In the debate over how to conduct this movement, he was criticized for supporting Deng Zihui's recommendation that it be done in a stable way, and in stages.

In 1956, Du Runsheng was transferred to serve as secretary-general of the Chinese Academy of Sciences and concurrently as deputy secretary of the Party organization within the academy. He participated in the drafting of China's 'Twelve-Year Plan for developing science and technology.' In 1961, he chaired the drafting of what was called the '*Fourteen Guidelines on the current work of research institutions in the natural sciences (draft)*' (known commonly as the '*Fourteen Science Guidelines*'). This document was approved by the CPC Central Committee for nationwide trial implementation in July of 1961. The document affirmed that it was Party policy to treat intellectuals 'correctly'; it affirmed the policy known as 'double hundred.' These policies included 'respect for science' and 'respect for intelligence or human talent.' They 'rectified' [corrected] the prevailing attitude of deriding intellectuals and 'lording it over others.' They explicitly set forth the science policies and new developmental tasks of both Party and government.

During the Cultural Revolution [1966–1976], Du Runsheng was attacked and persecuted. He was sent to do manual labor at a May 7 Cadre School.

After the third plenary session of the 11th Central Committee of the CPC [December 1978], Du Runsheng was transferred in 1979 to the State Agriculture Commission to serve as vice chairman, where he was in charge of policy research on rural economic reform. From that position, he was able to advocate for what came to be called the 'contract system' in agriculture, also known as the 'household contract responsibility system with remuneration linked to output.'

In 1983, Du Runsheng was made director of the Rural Policy Research Office of the Secretariat of the CPC Central Committee (later renamed the Rural Policy Research Office of the CPC Central Committee) and also director of the Rural Development Research Center of the State Council. He continued to be in charge of research on rural economic reform and in charge of China's rural development strategies. He continued to provide policy recommendations to the Central

Committee of the Party and the State Council. The Central Committee and the State Council asked him to draft a number of policy documents on rural reform, specifically five of what are known as 'Number One' documents. These were important in terms of both theory and actual practice and made a very positive contribution to advancing policies that 'marketized' China's rural economy.

Du Runsheng has been a deputy to the 12th and 13th CPC National Congresses, a member of the Advisory Commission of the CPC Central Committee, a member of the 2nd National Committee of the Chinese People's Political Consultative Conference (CPPCC), a deputy to the 6th National People's Congress, and a member of the Financial and Economic Committee of the National People's Congress. In addition, he has served as a member of the Central Financial and Economic Leading Group, honorary chairman of the China Association of Agricultural Science Societies, chairman of the Chinese Association of Agricultural Economics, chairman of the China Society of Economists researching national land issues, a part-time professor at People's University of China, and an honorary professor of China Agricultural University.

Author's preface[1]

I am not sure how it is that I have lived to be 90 years old. Thinking it over, it may be due to the fact that the Communist Party really did create a 'new age' for people like me, intellectuals who came from the countryside. Our lives were indeed made better.

I joined peripheral organizations of the Party when I was 19 years old, more than 70 years ago. Glancing back, it seems to me I have not done much to be proud of. I was talking this over recently with some friends, and in the end I summed it up in a couple of statements. One was that I did more hard work [daily grind-type activities] than I did any work that really contributed. The second was that over time I seem to have been more of a 'right' than a 'left' deviationist. Yes, I was more right-leaning, but I was never declared a 'Rightist,' and the reason for that is that I was protected by Chairman Mao. In 1955, together with old Deng (Comrade Deng Zihui) in the collectivization movement, I committed the rightist mistake of 'walking like a woman with bound feet,' wanting to move ahead in a gingerly fashion. When Party Central called a meeting to deal with our case, Chen Boda said that Deng Zihui's mistake was in listening to Du Runsheng's advocacy and that Du Runsheng should be the one who was punished. Chairman Mao replied: 'Comrade Du Runsheng was firm on land reform. He said it should be done in three stages and the first should wipe out bandits and despots, which I completely agreed with. Where he went wrong may have been due to his not having enough experience in collectivization. This could be corrected by just sending him down to grassroots levels for a while.' Comrade Tao Zhu was preparing to send me on down to Hainan Island, and had even informed the local authorities there, when Comrade An Ziwen suggested that I be allowed to stay for a while. He said that as I was a university student, and the country was getting ready to prepare a Twelve-Year Plan for science and technology, I might be needed. So I was allowed to keep on working at the Chinese Academy of Sciences. Later, I voiced some views on protecting intellectuals when I was at the academy. Premier Zhou [Zhou Enlai] and Marshall Nie [Nie Rongzhen] were highly enlightened men. They personally chaired the discussions on the issue, and the talks became the Party Central document known as the '*Fourteen Science Guidelines.*' After the third plenary session of the 11th Central Committee, a National Agriculture Commission was established, and the first chairman of the commission was Wang

Renzhong, a close friend and comrade when we worked together at the Southern-and-Central Bureau. He transferred me out of the Chinese Academy of Sciences and enabled me to get back to work on the farming side.

In my years in the farming sector, I did a few things. This farming side of things has a very fine tradition and an excellent team. Both the old ones and the younger ones are highly capable and are pretty combat worthy. They include Wang Qishan, Chen Xiwen, Du Ying, Lin Yifu, Wang Xiaoqiang, Zhou Qiren, and other young people who have now formed the Rural Development Research Institute. We were also on good terms with other ministries and commissions, including the Ministry of Agriculture headed by Comrade He Kang, the Ministry of Water Conservancy headed by Comrade Qian Zhengying, and the Supply and Marketing Cooperative headed by Comrade Shi Lide. We've worked together well. People at the provincial level have also been very cooperative, and some of you are here today. This team, from top to bottom, speaks a common language despite our large number of people. The common message is that we are all willing to serve people in rural areas and be their spokesmen.

China's rural population has always been a reliable 'part of the allied forces' for the Communist Party of China. Rural people sacrificed hundreds of thousands of lives on behalf of the founding of the People's Republic. This was their first contribution. Their second contribution has been that, with 7 percent of the world's arable land, they have been feeding 20 percent of the world's population. Foreigners regard this as something of a miracle. Chinese farmers take care of the land. They use organic fertilizer, to preserve it. Their output is high – in southern China, grain output comes to over one ton per *mu*. Our people are extremely inventive. If we love our country, we must, first of all, love ordinary people, and in particular we must care for our farmers.

Two things are troubling me at the moment, two things in my mind that I can't stop thinking about. The first is how to enable our rural population to have the full rights of citizens in the country. This includes shifting around 200 million people who are currently farmers into other occupations by the middle part of this century. Right now, about 100 million people are transient workers, moving between cities and rural areas, and cities should make proper arrangements for these people. My second concern is that our farmers do not have a voice. They don't have their own spokesmen. Experience around the world shows that the best approach to this is to set up farmers' associations. We proposed this to Comrade [Deng] Xiaoping some time ago, and he responded favorably. He said it was an important matter and worth looking into. He said that we should wait for three years and if everyone agreed at that time, 'when you bring it up again, I'll approve it.' Three years later, we ran into the 'June 4 tempest,' and nobody had time to worry about this anymore. Now I am handing this task over to all of you. I hope that we can resolve it within 15 years.

My comrades have been very complimentary to me today, which I really do not deserve. Whatever positive work on rural matters that was done in the past really should be attributed first of all to our Central leadership and then to our team. I was just the point of reference for the team: when people say 'you did so much for agriculture,' what they are really praising is the work of you all. I am fully aware of it. After all, how much can one individual do? Nevertheless, I am very happy to represent the team, and I take all praise as encouragement to do more. I will do all that is possible on behalf of the people so that I may reach the end of my days with a clear conscience.

Note

1 This article was a speech made by Du Runsheng on the occasion of his 90th birthday party in July 2003.

1 On a responsibility system for agricultural production*

(September 14, 1980)

1

The main subject of this draft document is a responsibility system that emphasizes 'contracting production down to the household level.' The document was drafted by the State Agricultural Commission on behalf of the Central Committee of the Party. It is called, *Several issues on further strengthening and improving the responsibility system for agricultural production.*

We absolutely must adhere to a socialist orientation, but at the same time we need to take actual conditions as our starting point, connect with farmers, respond to their needs in order to guide them in a forward direction. When we allow the contracting of production to be done at a household level, we should take local conditions into account and not have a blanket policy, 'one knife trying to cut through all.' We need to change mistaken practices that for years were the norm and that were divorced from the masses. At the same time, we cannot reject and indiscriminately criticize everything, adopt yet another rigid approach. For example, we must differentiate between this policy and 'capitalism,' just as we differentiate between egalitarianism and socialism. We cannot rely exclusively on political struggle to resolve all economic issues. Coercion or forceful measures in dealing with farmers are forbidden; we must persuade, educate, and use economic motivation.

With regard to cadres, we must encourage them to emancipate their minds and think more broadly. They should dare to explore, conduct surveys, study things in a new light. Nobody should be taken to task for speaking his mind; both sides of any issue should be considered.

2

The draft clearly states that the unshakeable foundation for realizing 'modernized agriculture' is the collective economy [i.e., collective ownership of the land].

3

In confirming the direction of collectivization, the draft does not deny that our experience in this regard is far from mature. We still need to find ways to manage collective economies that embody the principle of 'distribution according to work' so that we get away from the old problem of 'no more pay even if you work more, and no reward for working better.' We still need to figure out how to motivate commune members to really care about the collective economy. Many aspects may be addressed by undertaking all kinds of trial projects and different kinds of experimentation.

Encouraged by the spirit of the '11th Third,' cadres and 'the masses' throughout the country have been liberating their way of thinking, carrying out bold experiments, and doing a great deal in setting up production responsibility systems. Statistics are not yet complete, but data on this year's wheat harvest indicates that 90 percent of production brigades across the country have established production responsibility systems of one form or another.[1] Among those, quota-based labor contracting accounts for 55 percent, while contracting production quotas to individual groups accounts for 25 percent. Other forms of responsibility systems include contracting production quotas to individual laborers as well as to individual households. Since June, 'household contracting' has gained momentum, and preliminary figures show that this form accounts for about 20 percent and is now spreading toward the central areas of the country. As a result, different points of view have come to the fore.

In fact, the range of things being debated over the past two years applies to far more than just this one issue. Debate on 'production responsibility systems' has begun to question the structure of people's communes. Many theoretical and practical issues have been raised that deserve attention. Issues include, for example, whether or not a unification of 'government and commune' in the same system is appropriate. Does 'publicly owned' mean the same thing as 'collectively owned,' and is it inevitable that a 'collectively owned system' will transition to a system of 'ownership by the whole people'? Will it be a 'transition to one system,' or will it be a 'merging of two systems'? How should we handle the question of 'individual economies' [private business] serving as supplementary to the State economy? These past two years have seen the most vital thinking on the rural front since the very founding of the country. And we should encourage this.

4

With its large and densely populated land mass, and with its uneven development, China's agriculture inherently has to have a diversified structure. For this reason, the structure of China's socialist collective economies must also be diversified. Premature determination of what forms economic organization should take, and especially determining these things in too subjective a manner, is not only detrimental but impossible. Only through diversifying can we find appropriate structures, and, when we settle upon structures, they will still be diversified structures.

Diversification will include some forms that are appropriate to areas that have relatively high productivity and some forms that are simply in transition in areas of lower productivity. Marxism never rejected the need to use forms of organization, as well as forms of struggle, that were appropriate to the needs of people and the level of development. Those could be lower levels of organizational structure and also diversified forms. Given the very nature of transition, such forms are unstable. Their 'nature' is not yet fixed, and they can always be improved upon. Some regions moved forward too quickly in the past [in moving toward idealized socialist structures], to the extent that people could not keep up. These places now need to modify their path, and even make an about-face in some cases, in order to galvanize the masses before moving forward again. In the end, this will help us to achieve our final goal.

In the very early stage of collectivization, we used mutual aid groups and other semi-socialist forms that were 'jointly operated' and based on private ownership. The 'general line' [policy] for the transitional period was set forth in 1953. The pace of collectivization accelerated at the end of 1955. Some places wanted to 'reach heaven in a single bound,' turn self-sufficient farmers into members of advanced cooperatives straight away. Today, the masses are voluntarily moving a step backward [in this process], only in a different way.

Over this past year, one could sum up what people wanted as follows. First, pay for work should be linked to output. Second, the scope of operations should be smaller, go from production team to group, to household and to individual. 'To household' means returning to household-based operations.

5

What is the 'nature' of this process of contracting production quotas to individual households, that is, is it of a 'socialist' nature or not? It is a responsibility system under a socialist economy. We confirm that the land is still collectively owned and certain links are maintained with collective operations, though to different degrees. Contracting *all* responsibilities down to the level of the individual household, total contracting, means that the household operates independently and is fully responsible for its own profits and losses, but the household is still linked to a collective through the '*cheng-bao* contract.' It remains part of the collective economy. This is different from the former style of self-sufficient farmer. It should be regarded as a mode of operation undertaken in the context of a socialist society, namely a form of responsibility system.

There are differing views on this subject that we can leave to be resolved in the future through actual practice.

6

The draft brought out the idea that, in contracting production at the level of individual households, different regions, communes, and production teams should take locally appropriate approaches. In remote mountainous areas and poverty-stricken areas that have long relied on the 'three dependencies,' and in places where the collective economies are in such bad shape they cannot survive, production may be contracted to the level of individual households. In more normal situations, production quotas may be contracted to specialized groups or specialized teams. [Note: the three dependencies means that rural communities 'depend on' the State for 'resold grain' (that the State 'sells' back to the producing entity in cases of dire necessity), for loans to carry out production, and for relief aid for daily survival.]

Nationwide, there are 5.066 million rural accounting units. Based on the 5.04 million accounting units for which there are figures, 16 percent have an average [annual] income per commune member of less than RMB 40. Another 27 percent have an average [annual] income of less than RMB 50, and 38 percent have an average [annual] income of less than RMB 60. At an income of RMB 50, there is nothing left after expenses are deducted for food and fuel. As for per capita grain rations, 19 percent of the dry farming areas get less than 150 kilograms per person while 18 percent of the paddy rice areas get less than 200 kilograms per person. With an average of 159 people in each production team, what we are talking about here is 151.48 million people who are subsisting at the minimum level. About 60 percent of the poorest production teams, with an annual per capita income of less than RMB 40, are in the nine provinces and regions of Yunnan, Guizhou, Henan, Shandong, Gansu, Ningxia, Inner Mongolia, Fujian, and Anhui. These account for 20 percent of the rural population. First, these places are poor. Second, their collective economies have no appeal, and the farmers have no confidence in the system. Third, at the leadership level all kinds of measures have been tried to change things, but there seems to be no inherent engine for change and nothing has been achieved. When introducing various forms of responsibility systems, this status quo should be taken into account. Contracting production down to the level of individual households should not be the only method for resolving fundamental issues of food and clothing, but it should help motivate people. When the masses put more into their labor and more into tending their fields, they will no longer have to rely on the State for resold grain and aid relief. When collective economies aren't doing well, people lose enthusiasm, and when that happens, collective economies get worse. It's a vicious cycle. To break it, contracting production quotas to individual households can be a fairly good option. Surveys indicate that output greatly increases after implementing the system. It may have some negative side effects, but these can be mitigated by guidance in how the system is implemented. In the places noted earlier, those communes and production teams that have been operating well should further improve their operations.

In other regions, about 20 percent of production teams can be regarded as fairly solid while the rest are fair to middling. If the masses in these regions do not want to contract production quotas to individual households, they should not be forced to do so. The strong suit of the 'solid' and the 'fairly solid' production teams is that they hold the dominant share of agricultural resources in the country. They have an overwhelming percentage of the RMB 80 billion in publicly held reserve funds, and they hold the lion's share of nation's 700 million *mu* of irrigated land and 180 million horsepower worth of farm machinery. This economic strength has a certain attraction for commune members. If the scale of production is too large to implement contract systems, it can be divided up. Teams should adopt responsibility forms that are appropriate to large-scale production (such as contracting production quotas for certain parts of the labor – in other words, using division of labor – and farm field management linked to output). As much as possible, methods should be adopted that address practical problems. There are all kinds of problems, and people should be proactive in finding solutions. If the masses are spontaneously contracting production quotas to individual households, they should be actively guided – they should not be obstructed, but they also should not be left to drift along on their own.

7

Production communes and teams that have contracted production down to individual households account for about 20 percent of the nationwide total so far. This is a rough estimate, not to be taken as a firm figure. Some production teams should not introduce this system or should be allowed not to do so. Those that should not introduce this system but have introduced it must not be arbitrarily corrected. There are others that should introduce but have failed to do so. In order not to set up confrontational situations with the masses, people should be allowed to choose on their own. An appropriate form of guidance should be offered if the masses in certain places want to proceed. The right moment should be selected for such guidance; it should not be forced. Stabilizing the overall situation and improving the overall outlook is the main goal. In terms of specifics, guidance should be tailored to different regions and different categories so as to prevent things from drifting along. Letting things drift along can lead to damage.

8

One major policy consideration must be addressed in the course of discussing production responsibility systems. How do we treat the individual laborers who operate independently in rural areas? As long as socialist public ownership remains dominant, rural areas should also allow the existence of diverse other forms of ownership. A whole series of policies should be worked out to deal with issues in this regard. The work is going to have to be done gradually over the course of future reforms.

Notes

* This is the author's speech at a meeting convened by the Party Central Committee and attended by the first secretaries of the party committees of all provinces, autonomous regions, and centrally administered municipalities. After this meeting, the CPC Central Committee issued the Notice on Printing and Distributing the Several Issues on Further Strengthening and Improving the Responsibility System for Agricultural Production (namely the Central Document No. 80–75). This document was drafted by the former State Agriculture Commission on behalf of the Party Central Committee, and this speech was an explanation of the draft text.
1 The diverse forms of production responsibility systems at the time can be roughly classified into two major categories: contracting with remuneration linked to output and contracting with remuneration unlinked to output. Contracting with remuneration unlinked to output mainly refers to the piece-rate labor contracting for quota

remuneration, namely quota-based labor contracting. In general, a production team contracts its farm work to working groups or individuals according to farming seasons. After tasks are fulfilled according to qualitative, quantitative, and time requirements, the production team gives them work points according to their quotas. If remuneration is linked with output, the main form at the time is contracting production quotas to individual groups. In general, a production team fixes land, labor, farm animals, and farm tools to working groups and contracts the three targets of output, labor, and production cost to these groups. After tasks are fulfilled, the contracted portions are handed over to the production team for unified distribution, and the production team gives them production cost and work points according to set targets. While contracting production quotas to individual groups, some places contract production quotas to individual laborers or households, hence the forms of contracting production quotas to individual laborers or households. Some other places contract farm field management responsibilities to individual persons with remuneration linked to output, which is called the farm field management system with remuneration linked with output. Land contracting also takes diverse forms. In places where division of labor is undeveloped and planting is a predominant occupation, land is generally contracted to individual persons on an equal basis. Some other places also contract grain ration farm field according to the number of persons and contract responsibility farm field according to the number of laborers. In places that have certain forms of division of labor and relatively more items of production, they contract production quotas according to the lines of specialization, namely the output contracting system based on specialized division of labor or the specialized contracting system with remuneration linked to output. In distributing labor fruit, some places contract all responsibilities for individual households, in which distribution based on work points is abolished. This is commonly called contracting all responsibilities for individual households. In other words, the contractor retains earnings and surplus products after handing over a certain amount in kind or in cash to the collectives and fulfilling the task of selling products to the state according to the terms set between the contractor and the collective economic organization.

2 Some opinions on rural economic policies*

(February 1981)

From January 1 to 8 this year, I accompanied Comrade Zhao Ziyang on a visit through the three provinces of Hubei, Henan, and Shandong. We toured the five prefectures of Yichang, Jinzhou (the worst-hit disaster area), Nanyang, Kaifeng, and Heze (one of the more difficult areas). During the trip, we inspected rural conditions, heard reports from regional cadres, and visited with some rural households.

1. Implementing a system of contracting production down to the household level for a few years will help stabilize the situation in hardship areas

Lankao County in Henan Province and Dongming County in Shandong Province are chronically backward and impoverished areas. They are representative of 'three-dependency' counties that depend on State reallocations of grain, State loans, and State relief. Lankao County started contracting production to households in 1978, and by now 80 percent of its production teams have adopted the system. Dongming County now contracts out some 90 percent of its production, and the results are striking. Grain output in Lankao County typically stayed around 100 million kilograms over the past decade or so but reached 155 million kilograms in 1980. In 1978, the county consumed 4 million kilograms of State-resold grain. In 1979, it posted a grain surplus, and in 1980, it sold 16 million kilograms to the State. Production of cotton and peanuts has also gone up sharply. The per capita income from collective distribution rose from RMB 49.7 in 1979 to RMB 80 in 1980, but if personal income from above-quota production is included, the total comes to RMB 140 or even more. Some of the poorest households in the worst production teams had incomes that reached RMB 300 to 400, and 'rich' households have now emerged that are making on the order of RMB 1,000 per year. By 1980, the accumulated debt that communes and production teams in the county owed the State was RMB 15 million. That same year, farmers repaid RMB 1.8 million of the debt and were still able to realize an increase in their own incomes. In the 20 years between 1958 to 1978, Dongming County consumed 225 million kilograms of State-resold grain and spent RMB 78 million in State relief and State loans. Now, the county has gone from being grain-deficient to having a surplus. So far, it has sold the State 30 million kilograms of grain, 1.5 million kilograms of cotton, 3.7 million kilograms of peanuts, and 2.35 million kilograms of sesame seeds. The per capita income from collective distribution was only RMB 31 in 1979 but exceeded RMB 100 in 1980 if the above-quota income was included. The county's per capita savings rose from RMB 3 in 1979 to RMB 17 in 1980.

Dengfeng County in Kaifeng Prefecture and all counties in Heze Prefecture have contracted out production quotas to individual households, and their situation is broadly similar to Lankao and Dongming Counties.

Basic subsistence in terms of food and clothing has been resolved for most commune members in these regions. Farmers are smiling all over when they say that they used to worry about having enough to eat and now they worry about where to put all the grain. They feel they are no longer going to have to go out begging. They are also saying, 'When you link pay to output, production turns around within a year. We're now eating buns made of flour instead of sweet potatoes, and the young men are beginning to go out and find themselves wives.' In rural markets, such consumer goods as wrist watches, bicycles, sewing machines, radio sets, and Dacron are in demand. About 10 percent of rural households have built new brick houses with tile roofs. The demand for the means of production has increased at the same time. Many households have purchased domestic animals, handcarts, double-share plows, cotton gins, mini-threshers, and high-quality walking-tractors. They say, 'After more than twenty long years, we are finally our own masters. Now we have both the freedom and the energy to do what we want to do. We watch enough plays, go to enough markets, visit enough relatives, do enough work, and harvest enough grain.' We heard the same message wherever we went: this policy should remain unchanged for at least three to five years. 'If it doesn't change for a year, we'll have enough to eat. For two years, we'll have some money to spend. For three years, we'll be somewhat prosperous. The government had better start building grain bins pretty fast.'

How could chronically backward and impoverished regions see such tangible results in just two years? There are a variety of reasons including, naturally, weather. But the weather was plenty good enough under the ultra-leftist line, and yet it failed to bring about the kind of change we saw last year. It looks as though the dominant factor was Party policy. According to what the Heze Prefecture Party Committee is saying, in keeping with the spirit of the Central documents that came out of the Third Plenary Session of the 11th Central Committee of the Party, they have implemented 11 new policies to date. The three main policies are as follows.

1. Respect the right of the communes and production teams to decide what to farm according to local conditions. In the past, you were not allowed to plan peanuts on sandy soil, you couldn't plan cotton on saline-alkaline land, and you couldn't plant soybeans on silt deposits.

2. Offer preferential purchase prices. The State mostly does not levy grain requisition requirements on these poor regions, or the base figures are low. Therefore most of the grain, cotton, and oilseeds that they sell to the State can be sold at purchase prices that have 'preferential treatment' and so are higher.

3. The production teams have introduced various production responsibility systems and have allowed individual households to contract directly for production.

It is an undeniable fact that the system of contracting production quotas to individual households has greatly motivated farmers. For a considerable time in the past, things that we extolled as the virtues of the collective economy, such as concentrating labor and giving equal pay to all, actually worked against any positive initiative. This 'everybody's in it for all' and 'one big pot of rice' were in fact sapping everyone's vigor. Commune members worked 'collectively' under the supervision of Party cadres, and no matter how much or how little they worked, or how well, the pay they got was exactly the same. And, at the end of the year, what you got was not enough to keep body and soul together. When things became so bad that people really could not survive and tried to find a way out by making a living on the side, this was criticized as 'capitalist behavior.' It was 'struggled against' and stopped by forceful means. There was no margin for any freedom at all. As a result, commune members showed up for work but did not exert themselves. The more tightly cadres tried to control them, the more ways the people found to deal with the cadres. 'When the team leader is around, I dawdle over my work; when he goes away, I stand up and do nothing at all.' People summarize their situation in the three words: dawdling, poverty, and dependence. People faced the poverty together, and when it became too much to bear, they relied on the State for relief. Relations between cadres and 'the people' went from bad to worse. A Party branch secretary told us, 'I am like a dragon or a tiger in spring, summer, and autumn, but I turn into a bear in winter.' What he meant was that he tried to 'rectify' the masses and pull them into line in the three seasons of spring, summer, and autumn, which offended some people. In winter, he therefore became the target of struggle sessions, since winter was usually the time for political campaigns. Upper levels of leaders looked over the poor performance of the collective economies and always attributed it to the 'devilish workings of capitalism,' so they ordered 'rectifications' year after year. The more rectifications they ordered, the more 'leftist' they became and the more divorced they became from the masses. Collective economies were originally meant to 'liberate the forces of production.' Instead, the ultra-leftist approaches as mentioned earlier suppressed the initiative of commune members and began to shackle the forces of production. If we understand these things, it is not too hard to see why the system of contracting directly to households has had such appeal and success in the very poorest and most backward regions. The fact that the people welcomed the system so warmly, but also the fact that cadres took certain risks to advocate it, only goes to show that 'production relationships' must be in line with the nature of the 'forces of production.' Behind everything, that law plays an irrefutable role. In his talks with cadres, Zhao Ziyang advised them to go with the flow. He said, 'This system of contracting to households cannot be dammed up and stopped, for that will only fail. All one can do is guide it. If the people want the policy to remain unchanged for three years, we should do as they wish. In places like this, the system of contracting production quotas to individual households should stay stable for quite some time.' His approach was in line with the actual state of affairs in these localities, and it helped stabilize the overall situation.

About 150 million people live in poverty-stricken areas similar to Lankao and Dongming. If we pull back [our collectivization] to a system of contracting production quotas to individual households, and keep it up for three or five years, it is entirely possible that communes and production teams will overcome poverty and increase per capita income to RMB 100 (counting both collective income and family income). This will also lighten the State's burden of having to deliver billions of kilograms of 'resold' grain each year. Although contracting production quotas to individual households, and in particular contracting *all* responsibilities to individual households, does indeed have an 'individual-enterprise' nature, it is set within an overall socialist structure and so is quite different from small-time farming as practiced under feudalism. It can be said with certainty that considerable potential remains to be tapped in the future. It is an invalid argument to claim that farmers stayed poor over the course of two thousand years precisely by practicing this kind of smalltime farming, and it is invalid to deny the potential of the contracting system. Of course, contracting production quotas to individual households has its own undeniable limitations and negative aspects. Many problems are coming to the fore in places that have contracted production quotas to individual households and contracted all responsibilities to individual households. They include arrangements for planting, the use of farm machinery, the maintenance and use of irrigation systems, the fragmentation of land into dispersed lots, the question of who supports servicemen's families and 'five-guarantee' households, and who pays for community-supported teachers and barefoot doctors. Nonetheless, experience shows that so long as the organization and leadership of the production teams can continue (this is vitally important), solutions can always be found. For example, farm machinery can be contracted to a mechanized plowing group or a household for paid plowing. A community-supported teacher can contract for a share in a field and at the same time receive 100–200 kilograms of 'rationed grain' and RMB 180 in an annual publicly paid salary, which is not all that bad. There are also ways to handle the issue of paying for dependents of soldiers and martyrs. In addition, it should be recognized that as production grows after contracting begins, farmers' needs for secondary production items will increase, and then they will form new alliances. Some farmers are very clear in their own minds about not wanting to contract, however. They say, 'Contracting production quotas to individual households is a poor way to do things. After a few years of it, I'll again have to do what I'm told to do. It will be collectives again.' Some communes and production teams that started contracting fairly early are already seeing income disparities, since some commune members perform better than others for various reasons. In other places, to deal with production issues, some farmers have begun to form small-scale cooperation by sharing animals, swapping labor, and adjusting land plots among themselves. Some people with slightly more funding are linking up with four or five others to start specialized technical services such as well drilling, tractor plowing, seed raising, and grain and rice processing. They are fully responsible for their own profits and losses. In the future, contracted plots will gradually be concentrated in the hands of those more adept at farming, while sideline occupations will gradually be done by people more skilled in those areas. Specialized operations will develop, and further alliances will grow on the basis of this initial foundation. The evolution is inevitable, from contracting production quotas to individual households to forming alliances, but it is an evolution that does not at all travel along the same old road. We are not undertaking this in response to one 'overriding order,' one 'organizing everyone altogether,' but rather voluntarily, in response to economic needs. Forms of cooperation are set up that gradually expand, but all of this is something that comes later. Right now, we need to keep things stable and seek change that arises out of a stable situation. We don't want to be too hasty and plan out too far in advance.

2. A responsibility system that is suitable for the average commune and production team: Unifying operations and linking output to labor

Around 20 percent of China's communes and production teams belong to the category called 'three dependencies' – in other words, they are dependent on the State for their needs. These should be allowed to contract production quotas to individual households. Another 25 percent of our communes and production teams have fairly advanced 'forces of production,' diversified operations, and fairly solid collective economies. These communes and production teams have the means to institute specialized responsibility systems as recommended by the Central Committee's Document No. 75, issued in 1980. These systems feature specialized contracting and linking pay to output. The remaining 50 to 60 percent of communes and production teams are pretty much in the middle. They are not terribly well managed, and the emerging contract systems might pose a new challenge for them. Improving the way labor is organized and compensated in these places is a pressing problem.

Zhao Ziyang said, 'The problem of suppressing productivity [through the old system] exists even in the more advanced regions and needs to be reformed. We can't just carry on with the status quo.' This view is very important. We must be concerned with stability, but we can't simply keep in place 'stable systems' that bind productivity to a degree that is unbearable to the masses. We must reform. Karl Marx himself noted that without the use of machines and natural forces, a communal economy cannot on its own become a new force of production. Without any material basis whatsoever for change, such a 'communal economy' will simply become a kind of monastic economy.

A number of average-level communes and production teams in Henan Province are implementing production responsibility systems that 'unify operations' and 'link output to labor.' The Zengzhuang Production Brigade in Jinhua Commune in Nanyang County is one example. The cotton fields are contracted to commune members according to labor (not according to the number of people and not separating out a portion of the land so that people can provide for themselves). These contracted cotton fields are called the 'responsibility area.' The brigade sets the output (output value), quality, cost, and 'rewards and penalties' (across-the-board rewards and penalties, or proportional rewards and penalties) and unifies planning, plowing, growing, supply of seeds, pesticides, and chemical fertilizers, as well as accounting and distribution. All farm operations that can be decentralized are contracted out to individual commune members, including preparation of seedlings, planting, pesticide spraying, fertilizer application, weeding, and harvesting. This maintains the benefits of operating the collective economy in a unified manner but also mobilizes individual initiative by contracting production quotas to individual households. In 1979, this brigade's per capita income from collective distribution was RMB 94. By 1980, it rose 36 percent to RMB 128. In Nanyang, we saw that this method was being used not only for cash crops but also for wheat production. It incorporated all the features of a production responsibility system that was still under 'unified operation.' For years, cadres had been called upon to participate in manual labor, which never happened. Now, cadres are suddenly transformed, and relations between cadres and masses are much improved. People are saying, 'When one man contracts, the whole family cares. People work voluntarily from dawn to dusk, try to use improved seeds, learn better methods. The three summer jobs [planting, harvesting, field management] are carried out in all kinds of weather; weeds aren't given the chance to sprout even in the rainiest periods.'

This method is now being experimented with in other parts of the country, but these experiments are still limited to minor cash crops and crops for which harvesting and threshing can be done individually, such as rape, cotton, tuber crops, soybeans, and corn. In Anhui, these are called the crops that don't use stone rollers [for leveling the ground, which has to be done with collective labor]. Henan's experience indicates that this method can also be used for growing wheat. Whether or not it can be used for growing rice in places south of the Yangtze River remains to be seen.

3. A recommendation to increase the number of privately managed plots in places that are not yet contracting production to households

The Party Committee in the province of Hubei made this recommendation last year. It allowed the amount of land used for private plots to be increased to 12 percent of all land. Zhao Ziyang said, 'The proper line between the collective and private sectors of the rural economy is something we have to evaluate carefully. We have to figure out what the right percentage is for each, so as to achieve the greatest social and economic efficiency and create the most material wealth for society.' Speaking overall, family-operated noncommunal farming currently constitutes a tiny fraction of our rural economy. The experience of the past three decades shows, however, that more product gets to market whenever family operations are encouraged. Last year, we had major natural disasters, and private plots were important in making sure people had enough to eat. Therefore, in appropriate measure, not only should communes and production teams in 'ordinary' rural areas expand the acreage of private plots, but places where collectivization is highly entrenched should also consider doing so. For example, private plots for raising food as well as land for raising fodder may be expanded from 5 percent to 10 or 15 percent. The surplus of rural labor in China has long been a problem, with our huge population and limited amount of arable land, but the problem was obscured in recent years by how we organized labor. Our practice of 'eating from the same big pot' and our 'mass movements' meant that we failed to focus on this problem. It has become far more pronounced with the introduction of various production responsibility systems. In solving this problem, not only should different operating methods be developed for the collective economy, but private plots might be increased in proper measure so as to absorb part of the surplus labor into labor-intensive operations. This will both increase people's income and provide more products for market demand. It can meet multiple objectives. We asked Party comrades in Jingzhou Prefecture why they did not take action as suggested by the Provincial Party Committee. They said they were afraid that individual commune members would begin to compete with collectives for labor and fertilizer. In fact, labor is undeniably in surplus. So long as production teams implement responsibility systems properly, such concerns are manageable; nothing presents an insurmountable barrier to increasing privately managed plots. Of course, matters should accommodate local conditions and be handled through consultation with the masses. We cannot resolve everything with one policy, in one fell swoop.

4. Regarding the problem of stabilizing relations between cadres at the county and the commune levels

In our discussions, we discovered that there are misgivings and concerns among cadres at the two levels of county and commune. These fall into three categories.

1. The 'three-in-one' policy fails to give adequate consideration to the existing composition of cadres. The idea is that promotion of cadres should depend on the 'three qualifications' of 'young, knowledgeable, and professional.' Many older cadres at the county and commune levels do not meet these three requirements, however. They mostly started work back in the time of land reform and collectivization and therefore call themselves the 'three fives' cadres: they started work in the 1950s, are now 55 years old, and earn only 50 RMB. They say that as a result they are faced with 'three ineligibilities': ineligible for promotion, ineligible for becoming 'advisors,' and yet also ineligible for retirement. Since they see no future for themselves, they put little effort into their work. They hear this news that policy is requiring commune cadres to be under the age of 40, and county cadres to be under the age of 45, and so they look around for any way to make enough to be able to live out a decent life.

2. Everywhere we are seeing a great move to move children into their parents' jobs. Many grassroots cadres recognize that they themselves will not be able to meet the 'three requirements,' while their children, living in the countryside, face little in the way of a future. They therefore are opting to retire early and allow their children to assume their positions. Once they retire, however, their children will become entitled to the 'commodity grain' that their previous status accorded them, while they themselves will now be forced to eat 'rural grain.' This is a major grievance of these cadres.

3. About 60 percent of these older cadres will have no chance for wage raises. Not only do they recognize that their wages will not be increased, but their performance will be rated as 'nonmeritorious' [not making a contribution]. In addition, rural cadres are one grade lower than their urban counterparts in the local benefits that they receive. Cadres engaged in Party, political, and mass work receive a de facto amount that is two grades lower than cadres working in enterprises. Rural communes also have people who are known as 'bag-bearing cadres' [cadres who 'carry' specific responsibilities]. Numbers vary, but these include people who guard forests, veterinarians, irrigation tenders, agro-technicians, and operational managers. These cadres receive pay from operational departments, eat 'rural grain,' and have worked for over 20 years without being converted into regular workers. In short, our current policy with respect to wages and travel allowances encourages people to want to become urban dwellers and receive urban cadres' benefits.

The problems noted here are pervasive and therefore require the following approaches.

1. We must organize study sessions for cadres so that they understand the Central documents put forth in 1981 called 'No. 1' and 'No. 2,' and particularly the report of Comrade [Deng] Xiaoping. We must make sure they comprehend the strategic significance of the 'three qualifications' for cadres and the 'in first and out second' policy.

2. Henan Province has introduced a relatively good solution that might be adopted elsewhere that features 'two liberalizations [relaxations] and one restriction.' The solution relaxes strict limits on the number of allowable county and commune cadres and broadens their age range by three to five years. Meanwhile, it limits the substitution of cadres' children for those cadres who are ineligible for retirement. Henan also proposes that if cadres who began their career in the early years of New China have families in rural areas, they can continue to be entitled to commodity grain after they retire (specific conditions may be worked out).

3. Every means should be adopted to offer professional training to those cadres who are 'Jack of all trades and master of none.'

4. The wage system should be reformed. At present, transitional methods should be adopted to improve the benefits of rural workers. Zhao Ziyang noted, 'The benefits officially given to rural cadres in both production brigades and teams are too low.' He advocated 'reducing the number of cadres somewhat and raising their officially-allotted income.' I am very much in favor of this idea. This approach can help rectify [straighten out] Party behavior and keep cadres from seeking special privileges.

5. Public security is poor in rural areas

Social reaction is intense in Hubei, and the situation is similar in Henan and Shandong, though to varying degrees. Poor public security can be attributed to many factors but particularly to the mentality of rural cadres. While we should carry out the work noted earlier in stabilizing the situation of grassroots cadres, we should also make sure they understand what is and is not part of governmental policy so that they do not step across the line. We should encourage them to study legal practices, try to boost their morale, and make them improve their ideological and political work among the masses. We should support them in daring to counter illegal 'elements' when that is in accord with the law.

Note

* This is an inspection report submitted by the author to the CPC Central Committee and issued by the General Office of the CPC Central Committee.

3 The historic transformation in [the Party's] rural work*

(September 4, 1982)

After the Third Plenary Session of the 11th Central Committee of the Communist Party of China [December 18–22, 1978], the Central Committee of the Party successfully initiated a historic transformation in China. The work of the Party in rural areas was among the major changes. I would like to share some of my feelings here in that one regard.

In his report to the 12th Party Congress [1982], Comrade Hu Yaobang [then head of the Party] pointed out that, in terms of economic work, the Third Plenary Session of the 11th focused on agriculture and emphasized the importance of correcting 'leftist' mistakes that had long existed in the Party's guiding ideology. This brought about a swift and very noticeable change in agriculture, from a near standstill to active growth. Comrade Hu Yaobang's estimation fully conforms to the facts.

1. 'Leftist' mistakes have plagued agriculture for over 20 years, as seen in the many different problems that have arisen. Some are known to all, such as the arbitrary and impractical 'commands,' the high State levies required, the 'scissor-nature' of price differentials between industrial and farm products, and the abolition of minor freedoms. Consensus over these problems has been relatively easy. Consensus with regard to other problems such as what form the operation and management of communes and production teams should take, or how responsibility systems should work, has not been easy. Since 'leftist' approaches were regarded as correct for so long, what we now see as 'correct' approaches are being thought of as 'rightist.' It is hard to distinguish right from wrong and correct from incorrect in this particular climate. It was only in the last two years that 'leftist' mistakes on the issue were thoroughly corrected. For two years after crushing the Gang of Four [1976], we still carried on the campaigns to 'Learn from Dazhai' and to 'Realize basic mechanization of agriculture by 1980.' These were seen as the fundamental route to solving agricultural problems, while the key issue of production responsibility systems was not given sufficient emphasis. Responsibility systems were indeed advocated, but the contracting of production quotas to individual households was forbidden. Experience over the past few years has shown that such contracting is precisely the most effective approach to cracking the ice of 'leftist' thinking on the agricultural front. A very entrenched and powerful 'leftist' tradition built up over the years on this issue. Indeed, the synonym for 'revisionism' in the rural context of Party work was a phrase that essentially defined contracting production quotas to individual households (*san zi yi bao*, meaning private plots, free markets, self-responsibility for profits and losses). When some places spontaneously introduced responsibility systems after the Third Plenary Session of the 11th, the masses preferred the form that contracted production quotas to individual households. The saying in these places was that 'linking pay to output is better than not linking, and contracting by household is better than contracting by group.' Certain regional leaders discovered this, and Comrade [Deng] Xiaoping, as well as certain other Central leaders, supported it. Experiments were carried out, and it was discovered that wherever there was such an experiment, output went up. Based on the practical experience of the masses, the Central Committee of the Party issued Document No. 75 in October of 1980, which advocated various forms of responsibility systems and allowed the masses to decide for themselves, on a voluntary basis, whether or not they wanted to adopt a contracting system that links pay to output. (At the time, this was called 'contracting production quotas to individual households,' while the 'contracting system linking remuneration to output' was the general term describing various forms of responsibility systems.) The most powerful policy is one that embodies and consolidates the correct desire of the masses. Such a policy has the greatest ability to mobilize energy. Document No. 75 released a long-suppressed initiative on the part of rural masses to increase production. Basic agricultural infrastructure that had previously been created, including irrigation projects and fertilizer plants, now began to have a greater effect. Agricultural production moved out of a long period of stagnation. The most important result of the policy, however, was that the Party won the warm support of 800 million farmers and was able to consolidate its political base in rural areas. The Central Committee of the Party adhered firmly to the mass line and to the principle of seeking truth from facts. Its revolutionary courage in upholding truth and correcting mistakes naturally won the praise and the trust not only of the entire Party but of all the people.

2. Why are farmers so supportive of a responsibility system that links remuneration to output? It meets their two primary demands. One is that it takes into account their personal material interests and is able to unite the mutual interests of both public and private, thereby overcoming the defects of 'eating from the same big pot.' The second is that it grants them autonomy, the right to make decisions by themselves. They directly manage their own production and income distribution. This prevents the ability of a few people to assert control over all, to issue blind edicts without a basis in reality, to behave in ways that are unfair and incorrect in various other ways. These two points brought into being a new kind of economic impetus that also proved to play a major role in developing commodity production, building up human resources, and accumulating funds. When production develops and income increases, farmers are naturally happy. Of course, the system of contracting all responsibilities to individual households should be improved. Educating farmers about the future of socialism must be strengthened, and the

Party's leadership and principles must be upheld. But these two points can in no way be abandoned. Otherwise, we shall return to the old road, which is something we cannot afford to do.

China has about two *mu* of arable land for each rural inhabitant, which means that people cannot grow enough to eat unless they engage in intensive farming. If intensive practices are widespread, however, and aided by appropriate science and technology, not only can there be enough to eat, but people can eat well. In the past, privately operated plots were all well managed. The contracting system linking remuneration to output is designed to encourage people to tend their contracted fields in the same way that they once tended their [tiny] allocations of 'private plots' and to boost the output of average-yield and low-yield fields as well. We have had a succession of natural disasters over the last few years, but output has remained stable or even increased, and this is the reason.

China's agriculture traditionally produced a diversity of projects. In the future, the utilization of surplus labor, the development of natural resources, and the accumulation of investment funds will depend on this same practice. In the recent past, farmers were prevented from carrying on 'supplementary production' by methods that were known as 'cutting off capitalist tails.' [The phrase referred to eliminating the remnants of capitalist practices in China's economy.] The monostructure of agriculture that resulted, however, led to less income, insufficient funds, and a decline in the rate at which products are exchanged as 'commodities.' China's urban industries have been developing vigorously, and market capacity has greatly expanded. China's rural economy must now accelerate the process of moving from primitive self-sufficiency to a commodity economy. This not only should happen but is altogether possible.

Today, China's rural populations have the autonomous right to utilize labor and spare time more efficiently for family sideline occupations. These are already generating one-third to one-half of their family incomes. Based on this, large numbers of specialized households have also emerged that are run by people skilled in various crafts, people familiar with technology, 'returned educated youth,' decommissioned servicemen, and retired cadres. These people have technical or operational talents and are trusted by their communities. Alliances are forming on a voluntary basis, centered around these people. The basic method is to distribute income in proportion to a person's contribution of capital, labor, or technical expertise. The newly expanded fixed assets belong to the public in the sense that they belong to the collective. These specialized households and alliances are the embryonic form of what will become specialized and socialized agriculture.

3. The pressing and fervent hope of farmers is that policies will stabilize so that they can carry on their work. Our Party must satisfy this urgent need. Comrade Hu Yaobang announced in his report that the various production responsibility systems would be maintained consistently on into the future. In no way would they be changed lightly, transgressing the desire of the masses, and policies certainly would not return to the 'old path.' This should encourage farmers to increase production with greater confidence and greater care.

The Party's consensus on the issue of responsibility systems is the primary guarantee of the stability and continuity of correct policies. Even today, however, a few comrades still question contracting systems that link remuneration to output and especially systems that contract production quotas to individual households. They feel that such systems do not look like collective economies under a socialist system.

Neither Marx nor Lenin provided us with any concrete description in their writings of what a socialist collective economy actually looks like. All they said was that in economically backward countries with many small-time farmers, once the working class had seized power, it could guide the farmers in a transition to socialism through cooperative systems. They said that farmers should in no way be deprived of their private property and that the principle of free will must be upheld. The State should allocate loans from social funds for the purchase of machines, fertilizers, and so on in order to gradually replace the old means of production, expand the amount of secondary production, and use practical results as the means to persuade farmers. In his work *On Cooperative Systems*, published before his death, Lenin said that under the dictatorship of the proletariat in Russia, supply and marketing cooperatives might be used to guide the farmers in the transition to socialism. This could only be achieved, however, on the basis of accommodating their individual benefit.

In his opening speech at this Party Congress [September 1982], Comrade Deng Xiaoping said that China's matters should be handled in light of China's own national conditions. Indeed, they can only be handled in this way. China's vast territory, uneven economic development, and low levels of industry and culture dictate a very long and incremental process of transitioning to a socialist transformation of agriculture. This has been shown by our own historic experience and means that the process will be one in which diverse forms of cooperation develop as alternatives. Specific methods have to be clarified only after repeated practice and exploration. It is unfeasible and self-defeating to proceed in rigid fashion from abstract principles. It is equally wrong to adopt a model borrowed from 'outside' and try to use it indiscriminately on a nationwide basis in China. Any transitional form that can help farmers move toward socialism should be employed, not rejected. The current household contract responsibility system represents a stage in the development of China-style socialism. It conforms to the level of the forces of production in most regions; it is beneficial in promoting the development of production. This realization is the product of experimentation by hundreds of millions of people. Its emergence, existence, and development are the result of historical necessity.

Other comrades fear that household contract systems may impede modernization. We shall respond to this view with explanations, but practice is also providing an answer. Household contract systems contract publicly owned land to farmers, for farming operations. Farmers are obliged to fulfill contracted quotas, amounts they 'hand up' to the government as well as amounts for reserves. They are allowed to keep what is left over for themselves. What ought to be unified is unified; what ought to be separated is separated. Household contracting is different from the small-time farming economies of the past. In places in which manual labor predominates, land is contracted to farmers for decentralized use, which is more efficient than centralized use. Putting on airs about large-scale production but actually never realizing it, while simply waiting for mechanization, results in nothing more than 'one big pot.' Seeking empty fame often leads to real misfortune. Even in the future, with the household as the basis, when households form alliances for large-scale production, such alliances must be able to develop the forces of social production. Purely man-made elevation of a concept that is unconnected to reality does not work. Agricultural production involves the re-creation of living things, whether animal, plant, or microorganisms. If the operators and producers unite with each other, they can achieve good results despite being on a small scale. If dozens, hundreds, even thousands of people in a production unit have to obey the commands of one or two people, instead of making their own voluntary decisions, it is a certainty that mistakes will be made. Even in the midst of floods and droughts over these past two years, we can see the benefits of contract responsibility systems and recognize the collective wisdom in adopting this new approach.

China's 'collectivization movement' has already been under way for 30 years. The State has constantly increased its level of fiscal support for cooperative economies. If various forms of cooperative economies are allowed to coexist, develop, compete with each other, draw on each other's strengths, integrate, eliminate what doesn't work, and improve, as Comrade Hu Yaobang has noted, we can anticipate that 'in the near future, more diverse, improved, cooperative economies will appear that have the advantage of being locally appropriate and that help spur the adoption of advanced technologies for production.'[1] These will accelerate agricultural development. We should be able to fulfill the tasks as specified by the 12th Party Congress, and China should become 'moderately prosperous' by the end of this century.

Notes

* This is a speech delivered by the author at a group discussion during the 12th Party Congress and published later in the *People's Daily*.

1 Hu Yaobang, "Comprehensively Create a New Situation for Socialist Modernization Drive," a report delivered on September 1, 1982, at the 12th CPC National Congress.

4 The household contract system linking remuneration to output represents a new development in the rural cooperative economy

(November 23, 1982)

Economic restructuring that implements production responsibility systems in rural areas has already been going on for over four years. Practice proves that the form of the system that links remuneration to output is the most appropriate; it has produced excellent economic efficiencies and has been warmly received by farmers. Some comrades once had misgivings. They questioned whether or not the system conformed to the principles of socialism and to the goals of agricultural modernization. Based on practical experience over recent years, we can now make a fairly explicit response.

1. Ways in which the contract responsibility system linking remuneration to output has improved the cooperative system

1. The system has combined centralized and decentralized operations in an appropriate way. It allows individual households or groups to contract for using public land and other items of production according to specified, agreed-upon terms. Matters that cannot be handled by individual households or small groups can be handled in a unified way by cooperative organizations. Here, we have both centralization and decentralization integrated by 'contracting.' This system draws on the strengths of advanced agricultural producers' cooperatives while overcoming their defects, and it also gets around the limitations of family economies and retains their advantages. It takes advantage of the superiority of public ownership and the flexibility and initiative of farmers.

2. The system has led to specialization and economic alliances. Specialization in production processes will inevitably accompany the development of a commodity economy. When there is social division of labor, there will be social alliances, including production alliances and the alliances between preproduction and postproduction services. This can involve alliances in which the degree of public ownership is quite substantial or alliances that are not a matter of property rights at all. Based on grassroots labor alliances of all kinds of producers, multilevel alliances can be formed both vertically and horizontally. This then forms the structure of a diversified cooperative economy; through this structure, the entire socialist economic system of the country is tied together.

3. The system has led to a combination of accounting tied in to contracted distribution. In keeping with these trends, the more specialization occurs and division of labor develops within a cooperative economy, the more we must consider how to preserve a balance among the interests of producers in different sectors. We have to ensure that the principle of more pay for more work and less pay for less work can be honoured among members of any given unit. In addition, a balance should be struck between consumption and accumulation and in the distributions made to the State, collectives, and individuals. This requires that unified accounting, though in different degrees, should be maintained within a specific scope. In the meantime, contracted distribution should be used for each contracting unit in order to directly manifest the link between rights, responsibilities, and interests and to encourage farmers to care more about production. In the language of farmers, 'contracted distribution' means to 'ensure sales to the State, reserve enough for the collectives, and allow farmers themselves to keep the rest.' This gets rid of the need to assign work and allocate work-points every day. It enables 'direct benefits, clear responsibilities, and simplified methods.' It has become the main distribution system for collective economies today. Of course, some items cannot be handled by contracting, but those can be solved by other methods.

We can see from this that cooperative economies, which combine centralized and decentralized operations in keeping with the contract responsibility systems linking pay to output, have inherited the positive elements of our previous form of collectivization and overcome some of its defects. These cooperative systems are better, and they are irrefutably of a socialist nature. It is obviously inaccurate to regard the situation purely from the standpoint of the decentralized labor associated with household contracting and its superficial similarity to private economies. It is inaccurate to doubt the socialist nature of the system by not taking into account the overall structure of collective economies and their links to the entire national economy.

2. The nature and role of family-style operations at the current stage

In the process of collectivization, one highly significant issue was how to treat family operations in a correct manner. Small-scale family operations have a long history in China. The feudal system in our history was different from the manor system in some other countries. In China's landlord economy, land was divided into small plots and rented out to farmers, known as 'tenant farmers,' for cultivation. At the same time, certain farmers themselves owned small plots of land that they farmed. The common feature of the two categories was that the family was both the operator and the producer. These decentralized small agricultural economies constituted the foundation of feudal rule. The primitive 'natural economies' remained at a low-level equilibrium, forces of production hardly developed at all, and farmers generally remained impoverished over long stretches of time. Viewed from an overall perspective, however, these agricultural economies were very resilient. They persisted under extremely unfavourable conditions. They endured an unending stream of natural calamities, human disasters, and exorbitant taxes and levies yet recovered enough to survive to the next series of ravages.

This tragic history was brought to an end by the Liberation of the country. The process of land reform removed feudal constraints, allowing small-time farmers to achieve a pure form of small, private ownership and to have room to develop freely. Small, private ownership is intrinsically at odds with the trends of agricultural modernization, however. Under the conditions of a commodity economy, the wish to perpetuate small, private ownership was but a backward-looking illusion. It was clear that small-time farmers were either to be eliminated by a capitalist economy, or, under the leadership of the working class, to transition to socialism through the intermediary of cooperative systems, or, under wholly new conditions, to expand their scale of operations and enter modernized operations. History determined that Chinese farmers would themselves choose a noncapitalist path. Collectivization was an objective historical process in which one economic form moved on to another and labor and the means of production were gradually socialized. The length of this process was determined by many factors and could not be terminated by a singular change. In China where economic development is uneven, cooperative systems that represent a whole new mode of production must evolve out of the original mode of production and must necessarily pass through an extended and diverse process of development. In this process, the tradition of family operations cannot be abolished overnight. Instead, over a certain period of time, the tradition should be utilized and its substance reformed while taking advantage of its potential. The aim is to fully mobilize the considerable means of production scattered in individual families and the traditional techniques and knowledge that people have. Moreover, we want to mobilize the initiative and energy of the direct operators. One principle of Marxism is that changes in the relations of ownership are the inevitable result of the development of new forces of production that no longer conform to the old relations of ownership.[1] The role of an old relation of production cannot automatically vanish before the forces of production it has contained are brought into full play. Family-style operations are exactly the same.

In the stage of history called 'socialism,' a certain amount of 'family-style business' should be preserved for a long time as a kind of supplementary economy. At present, Chinese farmers still want to utilize family operations within collective economies. The system of contracting production quotas to individual households that was introduced in the late 1950s was a method that the masses themselves created in order to realize this desire. The method unavoidably had many defects as evaluated at that time, but it finally found a rational form of self-expression in the 'contract system linking remuneration with output.' The reason the system is rational is that it has broken away from the narrow confines of small, private ownership, has left room for future scientific and technological applications, and has preserved the advantages of family operations. Family operations today have undergone a fundamental change. They are based on public land ownership and are subject to the constraints of collective economies in many respects. They represent one operational level in collective economies and are neither the individual-economy model, as practiced after land reform, nor the small-farmer economy model as practiced in the old society. After the commodity economy further develops, a small number of individual operators will separate from their former collective economies. They still have to maintain links with the socialist economy or enter into new economic alliances, however, and so are no longer the small, private, individual operators as understood in the old days.

3. Will a household contract responsibility system that links remuneration to output become an impediment to agricultural modernization?

Judged by traditional concepts, family operations seem to contradict modern large-scale production. Here we need to clarify one concept, namely the relationship between modernizing agriculture and the scale of farming operations.

What is agricultural modernization? It refers to using modern science and technology to arm agriculture for highly intensive operations and highly socialized [mass] production. Modernization and the amount of land under operation are interdependent to a degree. Large-scale production replaces manpower with machinery and other natural forces and undoubtedly requires an appropriate scale. Both capitalist large-scale production and socialist large-scale production are superior to small-scale farming economies – this stands as a general rule. But the scale of production cannot be judged by land acreage alone. Lenin once said that, in the course of agricultural intensification, a reduction in the amount of a farmer's land often does not mean a reduction but rather an increase in output. He also said that the future course for capitalist agriculture is to change from operating on the basis of how much land is farmed, which is still a small-scale mode of operating, to how much production results from the land, given developments in animal husbandry, amounts of fertilizer applied, and amounts of machinery put to use.[2] From this, it can be seen that the scale of production is not strictly equivalent to the amount of land. The key factor is the degree of capital formation and operational intensification. The experience of the modern world also indicates that modern industry has provided farm machinery, fertilizer, and other agro-industrial inputs, which can be used by farmers in a decentralized way. When production processes are highly specialized and socialized, modernization can be realized irrespective of whether one is farming one hectare or 1,000 hectares of land and irrespective of whether one engages family operations, hired operations, or collective operations. Family operations are not incompatible with modernization. Different regions can employ different optimal values for size and economic efficiencies. Larger is not necessarily better, nor is smaller necessarily better. Local conditions must be taken into account.

Given China's actual conditions, relatively small-scale intensive operations are expected to become the primary mode of operation, instead of either intensive or extensive large-scale operations. Note that operations will be small-scale on an individual basis, but not overall. China is noted for its huge population, scarce arable land, and vast territory, all of which contribute to dramatic regional disparities in economic development. Transforming agriculture in a comprehensive way, with new technology, will require a fairly long time, especially with China's constraints of energy, transport, and surplus labor. Extensive hilly areas and topographically variable paddy fields mean that China's farming systems and techniques are complex. They also include double-crop farming, triple-crop farming, and inter-cropping. In view of these diverse factors, it is imperative that China pursue intensive operations and focus on productivity. For the present, small-scale intensive operations are most effective. In the future, when surplus labor is transferred off the land to a large extent and we have a higher degree of mechanization, the scale of operations will increase. Operations and the use of machinery will vary, depending on the region. In the great-plains areas, with fewer people and more acreage, the size of operations will increase, while they may be somewhat smaller in other places. The masses themselves, through practice, will determine the most effective ways to concentrate land and to service agriculture with machinery. We can be certain, however, that collective ownership is a fundamental advantage to the way we concentrate and employ machinery and agricultural services. Collective ownership mitigates the problems that arise in Japan and Western European countries from private ownership of land. Currently, the contracted alliances between the specialized land-operating households, the specialized groups, and the machine service contractors are providing us with some useful ideas. It is not unrealistic to imagine that we can achieve rational allocation of land and machinery under a system that allows for contracted production.

People worry that contracting land to families may encourage a conservative way of thinking that is in favor of private property. One cannot deny there may be some basis for this, but we must also recognize the other side of things, which is of greater importance. Our farmers today are different from what they were in the past. They have become new-style laborers in socialist cooperative systems. The reason they have accepted contract systems is in order to break from practices such as 'eating from the same big pot' and being subject to 'blind commands.' They wish to establish a better and sounder socialist mode of operation. At the same time, they enjoy the support of State industrialization and government finance. They have better conditions for agricultural development and higher levels of income and culture. Farmers today are already living in a socialist environment that grows stronger by the day. Such prevailing conditions were unavailable in the past and are decisive in guiding the direction of their behavior.

In our country, the socialist sector already accounts for an overwhelming part of the economy. Although China's agriculture does not possess abundant new and advanced technologies, its efforts over the past three decades or so have created a certain material basis in rural areas for the forces of social production. The horizons of rural inhabitants are now far broader. They have personally witnessed and comprehended that new means of production, farming techniques, and scientific knowledge can help them increase productivity. In the North China plains, a field used to be considered high yielding if it could produce 100 kilograms of grain per *mu*. Nowadays, it is considered low yielding if it produces anything less than

200 kilograms per *mu*. Farmers also recognize that many things cannot be handled by a single family and require joint and collaborative effort. Therefore, they support the two fundamental policies of the Central Committee of the Party: land and other means of production must be publicly owned, and the function of communes and production teams as indispensable unifier of operations must be preserved. A few farmers and even cadres at one point misinterpreted responsibility systems as being the divvying up of land for private operations. They came to a correct understanding after it was explained. When put into the concrete form of contracts, it is clear that farmers are more than willing to operate irrigation systems in joint fashion, develop improved seeds, prevent pests, unify farming systems and plans, and contribute to public reserves. It seems that the necessary unified operations are similarly in farmers' common interests. The masses prefer responsibility contracting to private operations. This is a fact. Farmers want both centralization and decentralization. However, centralization must be done correctly, in conformity with economic requirements. What farmers fear is a return to 'one big pot.' The 12th Party Congress report reflected this desire of the masses when it said that China should never return to the old path.

As division of labor occurs in the future and large amounts of surplus labor are transferred off the land, farming operations will become more centralized and capital accumulation will allow for greater and more economically justifiable mechanization. At that point, the masses will require that current forms of contract systems be improved in keeping with these changes. Today, certain communes and production teams that are more modernized and employ more intensive farming methods are already focussing on large-scale production facilities when they select their forms of responsibility systems. They are combining unified operations with various forms of contracting, including specialized contracting, family contracting, and contracted distribution, and this is working well. Currently, the total power of farm machinery in China has reached 200 million horsepower, irrigation facilities are extensive, and assets owned by the 'three levels' of communes, production brigades, and production teams are in excess of RMB 100 billion. All these must be protected and utilized with great care. While reforms should accommodate the features of different communes and production teams, and allow flexibility, reforms must be carried out. Reforms are designed to stimulate the initiative of farmers. Only when farmers are being proactive can advanced technology be fully utilized. Otherwise, technologies will not be adopted and will not lead to greater productivity even when available.

In short, we have to distinguish between the concept of 'small-time farmers' and what we are advocating. We want to move to modern large-scale production, instead of perpetuating small farming economies, and we need to recognize that contracting to family operations should not be equated to small farming economies that by nature are closed and 'natural.' Although the contracting units of our cooperative economies are small, to the degree that they use modern science and technology, pursue intensive operations, and socialize production on the basis of division of labor, they can be regarded as modern large-scale businesses.

4. Do contracted distribution and cash dividends violate the principle of public ownership of the means of production and the principle of distribution according to work?

The principles of public ownership and distribution according to work are the socialist ideal. They cannot be encompassed solely by some imaginary concept of rationality, however, that is divorced from actual circumstances of a particular time and place. In realizing these principles, different countries must pass through different historical and economic processes. These natural processes cannot be arranged by people according to their own will. In undeveloped countries that are experiencing the primary stage of socialism, economic activity inevitably retains vestiges of relationships left over from the old society. These remain to varying degrees. Public ownership in China, for example, includes 'ownership by the whole people,' 'collective (cooperative) ownership,' but also individual ownership. Furthermore, collective ownership can take many forms. The 'nature' of a country's social system is generally only determined by the 'ruling' and 'leading' economic forms. Nationwide, economic components are not limited to pure forms but rather exist in combinations that include dominant and supplementary, guiding and supporting. The leading forms govern all other forms, however. The 12th Party Congress explicitly said that the State-owned economy will continue to play the leading role, with other forms of economic structure coexisting. This basic system or economic structure conforms to China's national conditions. In the past, China lopsidedly focused on what it called 'first: large, second: public.' This referred to the large scale of people's communes and the high degree of public ownership. That experience has already informed us that we must never again subordinate the richness of actual practice to abstract concepts and schemes.

In his work *The Peasant Question in France and Germany*, Engels discussed how to treat small-time farmers after the proletariat seized political power. He said that the first step was to turn their private production and private ownership into cooperative production and ownership. This process must not use force, however, but be done through demonstrations and provision of social assistance. In discussing specific forms of cooperation, he introduced a plan put forward by the socialist party in Denmark. 'The peasants in a village or a parish . . . should combine their land into a large country estate, farm it together, and distribute income in proportion to their share of contributed land, advanced capital, and contributed labor.'[3] In this instance, land and capital are still privately owned, but Engels does not therefore reject the use of the form. Instead, he recommends this cooperative modus operandi as a realistic way to proceed. In the 1950s, China's 'elementary agricultural producers' cooperatives' were organized in a similar way. The 'Documents' on mutual-aid groups and cooperatives issued at the time by the Central Committee of the Party also affirmed the positive role of this way of doing things in the collectivization campaign.

Today, still based on the foundation of public ownership of land and other basic means of production, we are implementing contract systems that link remuneration to output. Farmers may put investment into improving the land and may purchase some means of production. With regard to the means of production, public and private are mixed: some are publicly owned and publicly used, some publicly owned and privately used, some privately owned and privately used, and some privately owned and publicly used. This ownership structure seems 'impure' but is willingly accepted. It is economically efficient and enhances social productivity, so the feeling is that it can't be all that bad.

The same rationale applies to the principle of distribution according to work. The intent of this concept is to give an equal amount of pay for an equal amount of work. For many reasons, it is impossible to be absolutely accurate in achieving this, however, so it can only be done in an approximate way. In this respect, we must educate farmers not to be too calculating. However, we should never confuse this kind of education with our existing primary policies. Most importantly, we must not advocate egalitarianism, for this runs counter to the principle of distribution according to work. The 'equal rations' system introduced in the period of the people's communes benefited lazy people at the expense of industrious workers and was very clearly a failure. Calculating pay according to labor quotas sounds good in theory but runs into many practical problems in terms of setting quotas, verifying performance, and calculating results. Labor quotas are indeed useful only as reference. They cannot be accurate, and therefore few are continuing to use them. Most places use the 'work-points' method instead. Work points are based on persons, and pay is based on work points. Those who work harder cannot receive more pay, however, and those who receive more pay do not necessarily work harder, so this system still suffers from the fundamental defect of egalitarianism. What's more, people compete for work points instead of trying to get the work done, which naturally impedes the rational flow of labor. The system also makes rural production ever more singular in approach, reduces opportunities for people to seek employment on their own, and blocks their way to wealth. Today's contract systems that link remuneration to output conform to the principle of distribution according to contract responsibilities: ensure sales to the State, reserve enough for the collective, and allow farmers to keep the rest. 'The rest' here includes remuneration arising from privately invested funds. In the formal sense, this system cannot be called 'distribution according to work' in its purest sense, but those who work harder and invest more can receive more pay. Moreover, 'investment' is still a materialization of one's personal labor, which is different from exploiting the surplus labor of others. Compared to the egalitarian method of distribution, this labor remuneration system is in fact closer to the principle of distribution according to work and is certainly more suitable for China's current level of rural productivity.

5. Trends in the development of cooperative economies

As reported by the Fifth Session of the 5th National People's Congress, contract responsibility systems that link remuneration to output have now spread throughout China. They have gone from a few regions to nationwide coverage, from rural to urban areas, and from agriculture to other sectors. This proves that the model is a very effective way to tap into the advantages of China's socialist economic system in rural areas. Since diverse forms of the system have been introduced to most parts of the country, our current task is to gather our forces and make sure we improve upon various aspects of the process. A key question facing many regions is how to manage the relationships between centralization and decentralization and between specialization and alliances in a correct fashion. Most communes and production teams across the country should focus their current efforts on encouraging initiatives for decentralized development. They should keep current policies stable and allow households who are contracting out land, households who are contracting for specialized services, and self-employed specialized households to increase production and 'get rich' through the efforts of their own labor. Only in this manner can we enable productivity to reach a new level. Then, on a new material basis, these communes and production teams should gradually strengthen collective operations and economic alliances. This will be helpful in beginning to address the problems of 'eating from the same big pot' and beginning to release economic dynamics that have been suppressed. Only then can we enable agriculture to move from self-sufficiency and semi-self-sufficiency to large-scale commodity production, and from a traditional to a more modern mode of operations. As production develops and technology improves, rural cooperative economies will advance according to the will of the masses themselves and through the mechanisms of economics. We will thereby be able to avoid the harmful consequences of relying exclusively on administrative measures.

Diversified operations in rural areas have already brought forth swift new developments and large numbers of specialized households. Enterprises that are managed by communes and production teams are also seeing new growth. When their operations develop even further, they will face the need for improved operational conditions, expanded operational scale, and greater alliances in production, supply, marketing, transport, processing, and technical services. Such needs have already appeared in some of the more developed regions. In most parts of the country, they are still in a formative state and will only grow when certain conditions are available. We must warmly support them and create conditions for their healthy development, but we should not be too eager for success, try to 'pull at the young shoots in order to make them grow faster.'

The system that combines government administration with commune management in one body should be changed. It should become a system that separates out 'government' from 'management.' Grassroots governmental authority should be established in a way that conforms to constitutional requirements. The original basic accounting units of what were communes and production teams will be implementing 'contract responsibility systems that link remuneration to output,' but after this is accomplished they will still have responsibilities. They will still be responsible for contracting out land, for managing irrigation projects, for accumulating public funds, for signing contracts, and so on, as well as for providing all kinds of necessary services. It may be that the size of the resulting units will conform to the natural topographic areas of farmland. In the future, as a commodity economy develops, higher-level alliances will develop among the different 'basic cooperating units' and cooperating units of different types. Economic complexes made up of agricultural, industrial, and commercial units will be the result. A commodity economy requires cities and therefore stimulates the creation of cities. Some rural towns will therefore become urban centers of secondary and tertiary industries and also the links in urban and rural economic networks. Other supplementary forms of economic activity will also appear. This outlines a rudimentary forecast for the development of cooperative economies. In the course of developing commodity production and commodity exchange, the factors of production will inevitably flow in a multitude of directions and enter into diverse combinations. This is a phenomenon that is in line with logic, and it should be guided adroitly instead of being deliberately obstructed or artificially fostered.

A large-scale reform is under way. There are many problems. When old contradictions are resolved, new ones emerge. Whatever the contradictions are, those who are in control of political power can consciously adjust and try to resolve them. This is impossible in a capitalist society. We are advancing into the future with full confidence. One basic tenet governing our work is that we must always uphold the 'mass line' and respect the free will of the people. Objective economic demands will be manifested directly or indirectly in the will of the people. The moment we act against the will of most people, we also betray objective economic laws. We must have some preconceived concept of what we are doing when we carry out reforms, but we should never regard our ideas as something unchangeable and impose them on the masses. On the contrary, we should learn from the masses, respect their creativity, respect their practical experience, and constantly modify our own views.

Mistaken practices will not be accommodated by the people. Such things as great movements ['blasts of wind,'], getting everyone to jump on the same bandwagon ['rising up with one shout'], or applying one solution to all problems ['one knife cutting through all'] are incompatible with the 'mass line.' In our current reform, the Central Committee of the Party is not advocating coercing anyone, criticizing anyone, or sticking them with a label ['hatting' them]. Instead, it is emphasizing investigation and study and proceeding from practical conditions. It is emphasizing acting according to local conditions, diversification of forms, democratic elections by the masses, gaining experience through experimentation. It cautions against compulsions and inflexibility. In keeping with the instructions of the Central Committee of the Party, comrades in various regions have adhered to the practice of appropriate action for local conditions, offering guidance depending on type of problem, conducting experiments in advance of policy recommendations, and moving forward incrementally by providing leadership. Advances may be somewhat slower when adopting these means, but they allow both cadres and masses time to deepen their understanding, distinguish right from wrong according to their own practical experience, and handle matters effectively and efficiently. This is the voice of experience speaking. In the future, as we continue to move into the resolution of even more complex problems, we should adhere firmly to these methods.

Notes

1 *Selected Works of Marx and Engels*, Volume 1, People's Publishing House, 1972, p. 218.
2 *Selected Works of Marx and Engels*, Volume 22, People's Publishing House, 1958, pp. 58–59.
3 *Selected Works of Marx and Engels*, Volume 4, People's Publishing House, 1972, p. 310.

5 Explanations on some issues regarding current rural economic policies*

(December 31, 1982)

In line with the 'spirit' of the 12th Party Congress, both farmers and cadres are hoping that the Central Committee of the Party can issue an agricultural 'document' that affirms achievements and points the way to where they should be putting their energies next. For this purpose, I am now submitting a draft document for review and adding to it explanations on some issues.

1

Conditions of the countryside are better than expected. Certain changes can even be described as a leap forward. In the words of cadres, 'they were previously unimaginable.'

In 1981, farmers' income reached RMB 223 [for the entire year], an increase of RMB 110 over a span of three years. Annual income had risen only RMB 45 over the entire previous 20 years.

Regions that are classified as dependent on government aid [the 'three-dependents'] and low-yielding regions have caught up with other areas. In 1981, harvests of Huaiyin in Jiangsu Province overtook those of Suzhou in the same province, producing 4.5 billion kilograms of grain. The four regions in the northwest part of Shandong Province, the northern part of Shanxi Province, Ji'an and Gannan in Jiangxi Province, Yudong in Henan Province, and Yan'an and Yulin in Shaanxi Province, previously grain deficient, all now have a surplus. Nationwide, most of the 231 counties with a per capita income of less than RMB 50 for three consecutive years now have enough to eat and wear. Currently, low- and medium-yielding regions account for two-thirds of China's total cultivated acreage, and we estimate that the percentage is likely to change considerably. Only transformational change of a revolutionary nature could have caused these things. Since the Third Plenary Session [December 1978], the 11th Central Committee of the Party has formulated several major policies on prices, grain imports, diversified operations, free trade at market centers, and the responsibility system. The last two policies appear to have had the greatest effect, for they changed the nature of the relationship between collectives and individuals in terms of benefits. This had the effect of amplifying the impact of other policy measures, and it enabled the past conditions of production to play greater roles. It is evident that without such systemic reform, even if prices were raised and subsidies were granted, they would not be effective.

The most important change to the responsibility systems is that contracts linking remuneration to output have been used to preserve family operations within the cooperative economies so that they can become independent operating units. The families [households] can at their own discretion allocate labor and determine inputs into the means of production. Land is publicly owned, however, and it is necessary to maintain certain indispensable centralized operations. The combination of centralized and decentralized operations represents a new type of family economy and also a new type of cooperative economy. These are completely different in 'nature' from the individual economies of small-time private owners and from the collective economies of the past.

Peasant family economies have existed in China in the form of small-time private ownership for several thousand years. [Immediately] after land reform, they had the opportunity to develop freely. 'Advanced' [high-level] agricultural producers' cooperatives then abruptly abolished small-time private ownership, and the means of production that had been scattered throughout millions of peasant households, together with their traditional techniques, all became useless. This occurred despite the fact that socialized means of production had not yet been developed to replace them. Seen from today's perspective, the move seemed to be somewhat hasty. Things would have been far better if the first document relating to collectivization had been enforced for a few more years. Later on, household contracting systems emerged several times. This time, it reappeared in Anhui Province. It was no accident that the system spread rapidly to all parts of the country after being approved by the Central Committee of the Party. As people were saying, 'When land is contracted, output goes up; when mountains are contracted, they become green; when water is contracted, ponds are full of fish; and when factories are contracted, they take on a whole new look.'

People [cadres] initially had two fears. One was that things would return to small-time private economies, or so-called 'go-it-alone' economies. The concern was that things would return to pre-Liberation conditions, despite 30 years of laborious work, and public assets would all be divided and 'eaten up.' The other fear was the planned economy would be damaged to the extent that it would plunge 800 million peasants into a sea of chaos. The 500,000 households of the past have now grown into 170 million to which goods must be distributed; the fear was that market supply to them could not be guaranteed. In fact, events over the past two years have proven that people's fears were groundless, and, indeed, things changed for the better.

'Cooperative economies' with both centralized and decentralized operations allow the masses to combine their own decision-making autonomy with the use of new technologies, all integrated with the requirements of the plan. People are still using irrigation facilities and mechanization.

As to State purchases, grain is now exceeding the plan year after year. Over the past four years, the [State] purchasing of pigs has gone up by 35.9 percent, while sugar, tea, and other products are similar. Purchased amounts rose to RMB 95.5 billion in 1981, which was 71 percent higher than in 1978 (directly purchased by the State and urban residents).

This year, the State urged the peasants to cut the planting of oilseed crops, and farmers responded by decreasing land planted to such crops by 11 million *mu*. This was evidence of the quick reactions of farmers; our 1980s farmers are a new breed. The response also proved that the Party's rural policies and especially the policies on economic restructuring are correct. This has been affirmed by documents.

2

In the future, our work on these cooperative [economic] systems should focus on a period of stabilization and improvement. Suggestions [indications] on future directions should be made.

Our work in making 'improvements' involves many aspects, but one particular aspect of the work is extremely important. I just mention it in passing, due to the lack of thorough research. That aspect relates to the land issue.

Currently, farmers all hope that land they have contracts to work will be stabilized and will continue so that they can tend it properly. From this perspective, we should indeed emphasize that the current situation is not going to change.

However: 1. Movements [migrations] of the rural population, and increases and decreases, may trigger a need for readjustment. 2. Greater specialization of labor – i.e., division of labor – may mean that some farmers leave their contracted farmland while specialized farming households that only contract land may appear. This will result in land transfers and concentration of land in fewer hands, which is both beneficial and logical. In order to ensure that land is publicly owned, it is quite right that the Constitution prohibits the transfer, leasing, and buying and selling of land. This leads, however, to a contradiction: as mechanization is encouraged in the future, the scale of farming operations will be a problem. Too large is not right. Too small, on the other hand, forever five *mu* per household, is also not feasible.

We have made the following estimate. Given China's huge population and scarce land, land must be intensively operated. With socialized services (specialized households or teams can be formed for mechanization), one solution would be to turn 30 percent of the labor into specialized farming households. That means that 110 million laborers would take on responsibility for farming 1.5 billion *mu* of grain-producing land. Land is bound to be adjusted, and there are really only two ways to do this. One is to have everything go through the management institutions of cooperatives. The other is to allow the peasants to subcontract their contracts. They do not transfer the land itself; we separate out surface rights from underlying rights to the land itself. No matter which method is used for contract transfer [via the cooperative or individual farmer], the labor input and fertility created by the operators should be recognized, which is in fact the differential rent. At present, we should continue to tap the potential of small-scale operations. Small adjustments should be made bit by bit; major moves should be avoided.

'Cooperative economies' in the future should take into account the need for diversified operations and commodity production and gradually move into specialized and socialized production so as to form specialized production cooperatives and service cooperatives.

Once people's communes have separated out government administration from commune management, and begun to implement contract responsibility systems that link remuneration to output, the structure of the overall system will have been reformed, but certain rural economic organizations are necessary and must be retained. Publicly owned land still requires management. We cannot abolish service systems that are based on land cooperation and require unified management (this is irrespective of whether they are called production teams, production brigades, or any other name).

The direction in which cooperative economies are developing is as follows.

This document explicitly provides that cooperative economies represent an inevitable path for agricultural development. However, the substance, forms, and scale of economic alliances and cooperation cannot be as monolithic and rigid as they were in the past.

First, the means of production of cooperative economies should be publicly owned but allow diversification. Independent operating units can form alliances, and farming households can pursue independent operations. Within the cooperative entities themselves, the mode of operation can be both centralized and decentralized.

Second, the principle of distribution according to work should be upheld, and, at the same time, a certain degree of share dividends should be allowed. While labor alliances can be formed, capital alliances can also be formed.

Third, alliances can be formed in production but also in other fields, such as supply, marketing, processing, and technical services.

Fourth, cooperation can be organized within regions or between regions, industries, and forms of ownership.

3

Regarding commercial circulation: Rural areas currently find it very difficult to sell or buy products, which impedes the development of commodity production. This relates to both the pricing system and the fiscal system, and a thorough solution to the problem is going to require great efforts. This document recommends the following measures as ways to improve the situation.

1. The policy on buying and selling farm and sideline products should emphasize 'macro planning' and 'micro liberalization,' which means 70 percent should be purchased by the State according to plans, while the remaining 30 percent can be regulated by the markets. (Currently, the State's purchases at fixed or negotiated prices account for some 90 percent of production.)

At present, the departments of the Central government control 132 products of the first and second categories, which are purchased at fixed prices. Local governments [provincial on down] add to the quotas, but in fact the third category is small. Preliminary estimates indicate that grain, cotton, and pork purchased at fixed prices account for 53 percent. If sugar, wool, beef, and mutton are added, the percentage goes over 70 percent. How to adjust the specific numbers will have to be decided by the relevant departments.

There is still debate on whether or not grain operations should be allowed to be [contracted out]. It seems preferable to allow such operations. The more grain is sold, the more grain will be produced. If grain is not allowed to sell, farmers won't plant it.

Amounts above and beyond State purchases should be allowed to be operated through various channels. At present, eleven specialized State-owned specialized companies operate in the related sectors. They have only limited outlets, but if they had more, they would have no business to handle. This is one reason why selling and buying are difficult. The prevailing opinion is that the amount above State purchases should be allowed to be bought and sold by the supply and marketing cooperatives, other rural cooperative commercial units, and individuals.

2. Private long-distance transport of goods for sale should be allowed. Long-distance transport of goods for sale already exists (for example, most of the vegetables and fruits sold in Xining City in Qinghai Province are transported by private individuals coming from Sichuan, Shaanxi, and other provinces, with some aquatic products being transported from Zhejiang Province). This is beneficial but is opposed by some people, or these people think that private persons should only be allowed to engage in short-distance transport or in transport of self-produced products they have produced themselves. They should not be allowed to transport as well as to resell.

This document says 'allow it.' It poses three restrictions. One, products can be transported for sale only after the State purchases are fulfilled. Two, the private persons should complete their business registration and pay taxes according to law. Three, market regulation should be strengthened, and illegal behavior should be dealt with in a timely manner. With these three restrictions, there should be no big problems if the State-owned commercial units properly handle goods throughput and control prices.

3. Rural cooperative commerce should be developed. The commercial nature of supply and marketing cooperatives should be restored. They should be responsible for their own profits and losses and should pay taxes according to law.

4

Regarding the issue of doubling the value of total agricultural output: The 12th Party Congress said the value of total annual agricultural and industrial output should double by the end of this century. How much should agriculture increase?

1. The general idea is that doubling the total output value will not be difficult as long as integrated growth is emphasized. Integrated growth means the comprehensive development of agriculture, forestry, animal husbandry, sideline occupations, and fishery. If agriculture, industry, and commerce are operated in an integrated fashion, doubling agriculture should not be a problem.

Doubling is not difficult for cotton, oilseeds, sugar, and other cash crops, but it is difficult for grain. We hypothesize that per capita grain consumption goes from over 300 kilograms at present to 400 kilograms by the end of this century. On the basis of a population of 1.3 billion people by that time, the total output should be slightly higher than 500 billion kilograms, of which 100 billion kilograms will be used for the development of the livestock industry.

In light of these targets, China should increase grain output by 10 billion kilograms each year over the next 20 years. But the statistics for the past 28 years (since 1952) indicate that average annual growth has been only 5.5 billion kilograms. If cultivated land expands by 100 million *mu* per year, that is only sufficient to make up for the land lost each year. Therefore, grain increases must be achieved solely by raising output per unit.

It is estimated that 1.5 billion *mu* of China's 2 billion *mu* of arable land can be used for grain production. High-, medium-, and low-yielding lands each constitute around one-third of all arable land. In the best areas such as the Taihu Lake, the Dongting Lake, and the Pearl River Delta, the output per unit is as high as over 600 kilograms for some counties. In other counties of superior districts, output currently is only 300–400 kilograms but can be raised to over 500 kilograms. In the medium-yielding regions, the unit output should reach 300–400 kilograms. If the low-yielding regions are transformed, a total grain output of 500 billion kilograms is possible.

3. The conditions of production must be improved so as to provide a material stimulus for farmers. These conditions mainly include three major areas: science (mainly seeds), fertilizer, and irrigation projects.

According to statistics from such countries as the United States, the Soviet Union, and Eastern Europe, increased chemical fertilizer application can contribute 50 percent to a rapid increase in grain output (China's unit output for the major grain crops is 30 to 70 percent lower than in agriculturally developed countries, and its chemical fertilizer use ranges from only one-fifth to one-half that in the United States, Britain, France, Japan, and other countries).

Over the past 10 years, nationwide use of chemical fertilizers increased by 20 percent. The 13 large chemical fertilizer plants that were imported played an important role in this and lay a foundation for the future.

According to existing plans, chemical fertilizer production will increase less than 10 percent by 1985 and less than 30 percent by 1990. We recommend that plan targets be adjusted upward.

According to scientists, chemical fertilizer does not necessarily hurt the soil if it is not overused. Scientists believe that increased chemical fertilizer application can produce more crop stalks, which can either be returned to the soil or used to raise livestock, the manure of which can be returned to the soil. This process uses inorganic fertilizer instead of organic fertilizer; it turns the nitrogen in the air into plants that are then returned to the soil. This has been proved to be an effective method in many parts of the world. In the past, the Punjab State in India was not self-sufficient in food. Over the past 20 years, its total grain output has risen by 2.7 times, and it now contributes half of India's commodity grain. This is attributed to improvements in chemical fertilizer, seeds, and irrigation. The experiment throughout India shows that chemical fertilizers can be used to increase organic matter in soil. At the same time, our traditional agronomy based on organic fertilizer should never be abandoned. We are going to have to find mechanisms for encouraging farmers to use these traditions, for as the cost of labor goes up, the old practices may be thrown out.

The mutual conversion of fuel, feed, and fertilizer should be achieved by scientific means. China should develop forestry (for use as fuel) and feed industries and should take the path of combining livestock industries and agriculture.

5

Regarding the hiring of labor: Labor hiring has been occurring throughout China in recent years, though more in the southern coastal provinces. Labor is hired either by collectives or individuals. Individuals hire labor after contracting to produce items for the collectives, and labor hiring is also done among collective units.

This has been a very hot topic in recent years, triggering divergent views. This conference believes that hiring labor for exploitation should not be allowed as a system. Nonetheless, labor mobility within a certain scope is inevitable and therefore should be adroitly guided and treated according to the situation. Under current conditions, few people hire labor in the way that it was done in the old society. Labor hiring by some major contracting households is different in nature from being in the business of labor hiring. In Yiwu County in Zhejiang Province, for example, labor hiring is limited to individual operations, which means one or two hands and three or five apprentices can be hired. Labor hiring beyond this limit should neither be publicly promoted nor banned. It should be guided to move in the direction of cooperative economies.

6

Personal purchase of motor vehicles and tractors began in 1979 and increased every year after that. By the first half of 1982, individuals owned about 500,000 tractors (one-sixth of the total number of tractors in rural areas) and 7,000–8,000 motor vehicles. Actual figures could be higher.

Opinions on this subject differed greatly just one year ago. Different regions and departments viewed it differently, but all came to a consensus at this conference. That consensus was that individuals should be allowed to buy small tractors because they are needed for rural production and transport and that individuals should not be prohibited from purchasing large- and medium-sized tractors and motor vehicles. The social demand is huge, while State-owned transport companies are noted for their poor services. Collectives still have to depend on government loans for managing their farm equipment.

By now, rural areas have been revitalized, but many problems still exist. Once the whole concept of 'contracting' reared its head, a host of follow-up policies became necessary. Innovations have to be made in organizations and systems, and technologies must be promoted. What problems could this new method trigger? Some people say we should guard against the potential for one 'tendency' to conceal another, meaning that a rightist tendency might appear in the course of battling against a leftist tendency. No one can say that that is absolutely impossible. But if rightist tendencies were to arise, what would we do? We certainly do not want to correct rightist tendencies with 'leftism.' As farmers say, 'We fear neither heaven nor earth. What we fear are yet more changes in policy.' We cannot repeat these changes any more. [We do not have the luxury of making any more abrupt switches in policy.]

Hundreds of millions of farmers are looking to the Central Committee of the Party for indications [of policy]. They say, 'We owe our emancipation to Chairman Mao, and we owe our wealth to Deng Xiaoping.'

Note

* This is a brief report made by the author when the Political Bureau of the Central Committee discussed the Several Issues of Current Rural Economic Policy (central document no. 1983–1).

6 Explanation of the CPC Central Committee's notice on rural work in 1984*

(December 18, 1983)

1. In accordance with the decision of the Central Committee of the Party, a national conference on rural work was held from November 29 to December 15 this year, at which the participants heard the report of Comrade Wan Li and the speeches of Comrades Yao Yilin and Tian Jiyun. The conference examined the implementation over the past year of the Central Committee's No. 1 Document in 1983 and also drafted, on behalf of the Central Committee, the Notice of the CPC Central Committee on Rural Work in 1984. This document is now being submitted to the Central Committee for examination and approval.

2. Nationwide, agriculture reaped an unprecedented bumper harvest in 1983. A total of 21 provinces [including centrally administered municipalities and autonomous regions] had record grain outputs. In particular, five provinces had increases in grain output over the previous year of at least 2.5 billion kilograms, namely Henan, Shandong, Liaoning, Jilin, and Heilongjiang. The provinces of Jiangxi, Hunan, Sichuan, and Guangdong had higher grain results than 1982 levels despite serious natural disasters. Only four provinces and municipalities reported a drop in grain output – Anhui, Hubei, Tianjin, and Shanghai.

Farmers' income nationwide continued to rise slightly. The National Bureau of Statistics estimates that, in 1983, net per-farmer income nationwide will be RMB 304 – RMB 34 or 12.6 percent higher than in 1982. Besides, an investigation of the 1,700 agricultural cost estimate sites under the Ministry of Agriculture, Livestock, and Fisheries indicates that farmers' income went up by RMB 24 on average.

3. The emphasis of our cadres' work in 1984 should be placed on stabilizing the responsibility system and developing commodity production. The reason for this is that rural development has scored great achievements and brought forth new contradictions and problems. When the contract system linking remuneration to output was introduced, most farmers, except in a few regions, refused to accept our recommended contracting according to the number of *mu* [a Chinese measurement for land, equivalent to 0.667 square kilometers] and preferred to do contracting according to the total number of people. This meant that everybody was entitled to his share of responsibility lots, including those with both good and poor soil fertility. The result was that land was divided up into small, fragmented parcels, which was found to be highly inconvenient. Farmers now have woken up to this fact and are asking for readjustments, as well as long-term stability. This is the first problem. The second problem is that agricultural production has developed faster than expected, while transport and storage facilities are lagging behind and can't catch up. In addition, prices are upside down in the sense that purchasing prices are higher than selling prices, which is blocking up circulation. The commercial system and its operations cannot cope with this situation. In addition to the products of oil, flax [or hemp], soybeans, rabbit, tea, and wool, grain has also become difficult to transfer and sell this year.

In light of these problems and in order to continue to implement the Central Committee's No. 1 Document in 1983, work in 1984 should focus on the central task of developing commodity production and should cover the following areas:

1   Properly solve the issue of land contracting [*cheng bao*] and raise the quality of farming
2   Remove certain factors that impede circulation
3   Improve production in areas that are of a 'development' nature (mountain and water, grass and wood and feed industries)

4. The term for land contracting and the issue of personal subcontracting: Since the issuance of the No. 1 Document in 1983, the household contract system linking remuneration to output has spread to all rural areas and industries nationwide. It is quite apparent that this step released the energies of the forces of production. It looks now as though the issue of land contracting must be tackled if the forces of production are to be further emancipated. Two policies are proposed. One is to extend the term of contracting so as to encourage farmers to operate land with more freedom and greater care. Two is to overcome the problem of having plots that are too small and fragmented by allowing individuals to subcontract their land so as to form proper economies of scale.

With regard to the term of land contracting, the masses are requesting that it be neither too short nor too long. If it is too short, they will not accept because they cannot recover investment, but if it is too long, they will not have faith that this is really going to work. They say they will use chemical fertilizer if the term is 1 year, manure if it is 2 years, phosphate fertilizers if it is 3, and convert dry fields into paddy fields if it is 8 or 10 years. After taking into account differing conditions in various regions, this document sets the term for contracting land at 15 years.

Many places have found that their responsibility plots in many places are too small and fragmented, which makes farming them inconvenient and a waste of labor. When one family has over 20 plots, some lose out while others are poorly farmed. Farmers hope that each family can be allocated one larger plot, or two, but no more than three.

Transfer of *cheng-bao* contracts should be allowed. As social division of labor processes, some households may let go of their land and allow it to be concentrated in the hands of people who specialize in farming. Land will gradually be operated on a more cost-effective basis, which is a process that should be encouraged. An investigation covering 192 production teams in Siping Prefecture in Jilin Province indicates that 2.2 percent of total households have subcontracted their *cheng-bao* contracts, and 1.3 percent of the total land area has been subcontracted. In Yichun County in Jiangxi Province, the figures are 2 percent and 1 percent respectively. The economics of subcontracting are that some households are compensated (mainly with fair-priced grain rations and some additional pay) and some are not. But subcontracting with or without compensation is first agreed upon by the two sides through consultation.

5. Remove some obstructing factors and enliven commodity circulation. Many farm and sideline products are in a situation of supply not being able to meet demand and yet supply also being greater than demand. There are two reasons for this anomaly. One relates to pricing that is [artificially] topsy-turvy: purchasing prices are higher than selling prices. Since fiscal subsidies are insufficient, the only solution is [for the government] to restrict buying and selling. The other reason relates to the fact that material conditions [for handling grain] can't keep up with production: storage, transport, and processing capacities are inadequate. Changing either of these two requires money. They touch upon a vast area of other considerations as well and so are hard to fix. There are some things that can be improved without more State spending, however. For example:

Fish and fruit: Would it be possible to 'open these up' a bit [i.e., have less restrictive controls]? Right now, there is a wide margin between the State-listed prices and the market prices of these products, so the State purchase plans are difficult to fulfill. In order to fulfill the plans, some places erect barriers and impose blockades [to prevent goods from being sold off to markets], which strains cadres' relations with farmers. In the discussions at this conference, the participants are unanimous in feeling that State quotas should be maintained on vegetables. But views differ widely on fruit, aquatic products, and fresh eggs. After Guangdong Province liberalized its policies on fish, pond fish output rose from 160,000 tons in 1978 to 320,000 tons in 1982, and the price dropped from RMB 4 to RMB 2 per kilograms. Fish is now in plentiful supply.

Grain: After a bumper harvest, we have run up against the 'three problems' of grain being difficult to sell, store, and transport. Eight provinces have asked to transfer out 15 billion kilograms of grain. In the first quarter, the request was for transferring 6.2 billion kilograms, but arrangements for transferring and storing only 2.8 billion of those could be made. Jilin Province asked to transfer 4.15 billion kilograms, but only 935 million kilograms can be transferred out this winter and next spring. Because of these 'three problems,' grain-growing areas have become reluctant to grow grain. Farmers have begun to indicate that they would grow no more than what is required for rations and for the State quota, which they refer to as the 'Emperor's grain.' In the Dongting Lake area, farm fields have already been converted into fish ponds, and in Chuxian Prefecture, they have been converted into lotus ponds. Some places have already switched from two-crop farming to single-crop farming.

Could we therefore consider a further reduction in grain imports by five billion kilograms, which would save around two billion RMB? The two billion could then be used to build warehouses, construct docks, and buy vehicles.

Pork: Pig raising has also shown signs of decline. In recent months, both the number of mature sows and the price of piglets have fallen. The total amount on hand in 16 provinces is expected to drop by 2.4 percent (4.9 million head) by the end of the year. The main reason is that the bonus grain for pig selling has been reduced, the price of feed grain has risen, the former collective subsidy has been abolished, and the price of tuber crops has gone up. This problem can be solved by stabilizing our original policies.

Wool: A 3.27-fold increase in wool imports over the past four years has led to excess inventories of 53,000 tons of locally produced wool. Many places find it difficult to sell wool. After rising for five consecutive years, the total output dropped to 1,339,000 kilograms in 1983. The price of imported wool is RMB 14 per kilogram, while that of locally produced wool is only RMB 10. We suggest that wool imports be reduced in favor of protecting local producers and that the RMB 100 million import subsidy be used to support and improve locally produced wool.

Supply and marketing cooperatives: Converting these from State commercial institutions into farmers' commercial institutions requires no money at all but invigorates circulation and promotes production. After the supply and marketing cooperatives in Wangdu County in Hebei Province were converted into farmers' commercial institutions, for example, they have helped farmers develop hot pepper production in eight different ways, from providing information to technical guidance to help with organizing processing. This one action alone increased per capita income by RMB 60 and doubled the profit of these cooperatives. In Wuzhi County in Henan Province, the supply and marketing cooperatives purchased fallen apples in time for processing. As a result, hundreds of thousands of kilograms of apples did not go to waste, and there are many other examples.

Warehouses and cold storage: There is also a great potential for farmers to raise funds to build warehouses and cold storage facilities. In Dacheng County in Hebei Province, the farmers in two production brigades raised RMB 260,000 and built a 100-ton cold storage facility in half a year. The investment was 40 percent less than it would have been using State investment. The building of this facility spurred a rapid development of the livestock industry in surrounding areas – cattle raising went up by 20 percent and poultry by 84 percent.

6. Properly develop small-scale rural industries and increase the added-value component of farm products. Developing small-scale rural industries is an important way to absorb rural surplus labor. Rough estimates indicate that, by the end of this century, China's rural areas will have 450 million laborers. Among them, 30 percent will continue to farm, 20 percent will be engaged in forestry, animal husbandry, and fisheries, 10 percent will enter major industrial cities, and the remaining 40 percent will have to shift into working in rural industries and town service industries.

In some countries, the production value of the food industry is multiples that of agriculture. It is two times the value of agriculture in Japan and the United States and nine times the value of agriculture in Britain. The total output value of China's food industry reached RMB 75.55 billion in 1982 (of which the food industry owned by communes and production teams accounted for 7 percent, or RMB 5.3 billion). This output is only equivalent to one-third of China's agricultural output. China's food exports account for only about 1.5 percent of the world's total food exports. The food items consumed by people are mainly semi-finished and roughly processed products. Rural residents are not even producing their own soy sauce and vinegar – they have to go into cities to buy them.

The number of households that specialize in breeding livestock grew vigorously over the past two years but is now losing steam. The reason is that the feedstock industry can't keep up with the growth. Incomplete statistics of Jiangsu, Zhejiang, Hunan, and Guangdong indicate that about 6.5 million tons of rice is used to raise pigs every year, even though 5 million tons of corn could do the same job. Feed resources are far from being rationally utilized. Bean pulp is protein rich, and China now produces over 10 million tons a year, but over 80 percent is used directly for fertilizer. China produces 350–400 million tons of crop stalks of various kinds every year, and more than two-thirds is used as fertilizer or for fuel for cooking. Experts estimate that due to limited number of feedstocks raised in China, we use more than 8 billion kilograms of grain over what is really required for raising pigs and egg-laying hens. This amount is close to the country's annual increased grain output in recent years.

China's rural areas have a solid basis and favorable conditions for developing the building materials industry. Right now, 4.2 million people are engaged in construction in rural areas, accounting for more than one-third of China's total construction force of 11.94 million people. Of the building materials produced in the rural areas, lime and sand account for 90 percent of the national total, bricks and tiles for 75 percent, concrete housing components for 70 percent, and cement for 13 percent. Since raw materials for the products are sourced locally and local labor is used, their prices are rather low. In 1982, completed housing constructed in China's urban and rural areas totaled 740 million square meters, of which 81 percent (600 million square meters) was in rural areas. The output value of the rural construction enterprises reached RMB 20 billion, and construction has become the largest industry among rural enterprises.

Based on a representative investigation made by the urban and rural construction department in 1981, in every year before 1990, a total of 7.5 million farmers will need to renovate their homes or build new ones. Based on an average 80 square meters per household, the total floor space required will be 600 million square meters. Since rural towns will be developing in the future, we anticipate that the area used for housing will increase.

This future development of rural towns is inevitable given the impetus of rural industries, so it might be good to consider allowing some farmers to move into these towns, make their own arrangements for food [grain], and settle down into a trade. I realize there are different viewpoints on this issue.

7. Regarding the income of farmers and their ability to save and raise funds for investment: Since 1978, farmers' income has risen quickly, by RMB 34 per year on average. As the growth in agricultural production is still of a 'recovering' nature, however, the increase in farmers' incomes is still getting back to normal. During the 1957–1976 period, the annual increase in farmers' income was just RMB 2 per year on average. Moreover, unlike workers, farmers have to spend part of their income on investing in the next year's production. In 1981, this took up 15.1 percent of income, in 1982 it was 16.7 percent, and it is expected to be higher in 1983.

Farmers' income varies radically among different regions. Between 10 and 20 percent of all farmers still earn less than RMB 100 per year and face the problems of inadequate food and clothing.

The income disparity between workers and farmers remains roughly at the level it was back in 1965.

One component of farmers' income derives from State subsidies. These subsidies are exceeding the State's ability to pay as a result of ongoing annual increases in production. In this respect, adjustments are going to be required both to reduce the State's fiscal burden and to help streamline market circulation.

Over the 28-year period from 1953 to 1980, State investment in agriculture accounted for 11.9 percent of the State's total investment in basic infrastructure. In the Sixth Five-Year Plan [1981–1985], the percentage is expected to be only 6.5 percent.

If agriculture is to expand secondary production [increase value-added], it will need to use funds sourced primarily from farmers' savings. Farmers should retain part of their income as retained earnings. At the end of October 1983, the sum of total 'rural' savings was RMB 66.9 billion, of which RMB 35.5 billion was the savings deposits of farmers. This is a considerable sum, and if these funds could be pooled, they could be put to many useful purposes. About 30 percent of the wealthier farmers own 70 percent of the funds.

Various places have created some new methods for increasing liquidity. One good experience has been to establish investment shareholding companies – farmers become investors in these companies and receive dividend payments.

With regard to the issue of grain, the price of State-resold grain [resold by the State to the place of production in order to supplement its local needs] should be raised, the State-purchasing price should be run at 70/30 – that is, 70 percent fixed and 30 percent negotiated. Prices that are 'mixed' should be stabilized. These measures have both advantages and disadvantages and will have tremendous impacts, so we should put off considering them right now and address them later.

8. The situation with regard to hired labor in rural operations:

(1) Representative surveys are showing that less than 1 percent of all rural households hire labor for their operations, while hired laborers account for 1 to 2 percent of the total labor force engaged in agriculture. These percentages vary widely among different regions. Wenzhou City in Zhejiang Province hires more:

rough estimates indicate that around 120,000 laborers are hired in the city's rural areas, accounting for 6.4 percent of the total labor force engaged in agriculture. In Shanxi Province, the percentage is 5 percent province wide, but it is 19 percent in Shanxi's Hejin County. The percentage is only 0.6 percent in the suburbs of Shanghai, however, and only 0.58 percent in Hubei Province.

Of the units hiring labor for operations, most hire less than 10 people, and the employers generally participate in the work as well. Some enterprises are also appearing, however, that hire dozens or even hundreds of people. The employers' income can be more than 100 times that of the employees. Investigations in certain counties of Shanxi and Guangdong Provinces indicate that 60 to 80 percent of units hire less than 10 people. Only some 10 percent of units hire more than 50 people.

'Commune and production-team enterprises' are generally the result of one person or a small group of partners getting together and 'contracting' with the commune or team to make products. These generally operate with hired labor, and they are increasing. To give an example, in 1980, only 30 such enterprises in Pucheng County, Shaanxi Province, used this method, which was 2.6 percent of all the enterprises in the county. By the second half of 1983, 86 percent of all enterprises were operating in this way.

A very substantial percentage of the people hiring labor, i.e., the employers, are cadres. They are cadres in production brigades and production teams, leaders of enterprises in those communes, or they are in charge of sales and purchasing. Statistics covering 103 employers in Shaanxi Province indicate that such cadres account for 46.6 percent. In Liaoning Province, the percentage is about 70 percent (including retired cadres).

Statistics on how many of the employers of hired labor are Party members are not available. Only Shaanxi's investigation mentioned that six people, or 5.8 percent, of the 103 employers were Party members. Beijing's investigation noted that 15 people (including 8 cadres with Party membership), or 17 percent of the 88 employers, were Party members.

(2) Reasons behind the hiring of labor. The main cause is that because private-person operations are being allowed to exist, labor, capital, and technical personnel are being allowed to circulate. Still, certain people are taking a wait-and-see attitude toward cooperative economies and alliances.

Under China's existing conditions, many factors serve to limit the hiring of labor. Existing operations with hired labor are highly flexible, and it is not possible they will develop much further. For example, if a 'rectification' were to occur with regard to the contracting system of the enterprises run by communes and production teams, many of these operations would not be regarded as operations with hired labor.

(3) There are different opinions about the question of hiring labor. Everyone [each of you cadres] is just in the process of conducting 'internal democratic discussions' on it right now, and no clear-cut conclusions can be reached at this moment. This conference suggests that the 1983 No. 1 Document should continue to be implemented for some time so as to allow time for observation and research. We should return to the issue next year.

9. Regarding the extra burdens that farmers have to bear: According to surveys and estimates in various regions, farmers have to cover around RMB 25 per person in 'social burdens' as levied by the State and collectives. Some of the levies are reasonable, some are unreasonable, and some are reasonable but overcharged. A substantial sum that is not part of this calculation includes overly wasteful costs of entertaining and increases in the prices of things used in production and in daily life.

(1) Levies that are assigned by departments and borne by the masses total over RMB 10 billion. Specifically, RMB 3.2 billion for birth control, RMB 2 billion for compulsory highway construction and services, RMB 1.6 billion for nongovernmental education (i.e., education organized by people themselves), RMB 1 billion for supporting the 'five-guarantee' households, RMB 500 million for subsidizing families of servicemen and martyrs, and RMB 2 billion for militia training, relief for families in difficulty, and subsidies for barefoot doctors and anti-epidemic personnel.

With regard to militia training, in addition to levying the basic costs to localities of compensation for missed work and food expenses, such things as ammunition beyond a certain quota, gun-cleaning fees, arsenal construction and fees for guarding the arsenal, and shooting-range construction are charged to localities.

In promoting birth control, farmers are required to cover all procedures, with extra payments for such things as 'health care' in assuring one-child families and wages paid to birth control teams.

(2) Institutional and staff redundancies: Costs for a total of 30 million people have to be covered every year, coming to some RMB six to seven billion. This is to pay for cadres in production brigades and teams but also various 'support' staff, in addition to which 'temporary' staff of all kinds and descriptions have to be supported.

(3) Then there are the 'extrabudgetary' fees and arbitrary charges that cadres in many localities and departments are ingenious at dreaming up. In order to cover their fiscal deficits, some counties mandate that farmers purchase tens of thousands of pigs, at nonnegotiable prices. Some counties change bicycle plates and household-registration licenses twice in three years in order to reap the fees; some have also introduced tree licenses and dog licenses. Some units are forcing farmers to pay negotiated prices for their inputs rather than the lower State-fixed prices that should be applied.

The solutions put forward by various places are as follows. A. Resolutely streamline administration. Most localities can get rid of all production team cadres. B. Have township governments control expenses in a unified way. They should keep legitimate expenses within reasonable limits and not have to undertake projects that they don't have the means to undertake.

I believe that we can cut the burden on farmers by RMB 5–10 per person.

10. Regarding our policy on forestry: According to investigations done in Guangdong Province, the operating, felling, and transport costs per cubic meter of timber come to RMB 138, whereas the official State purchasing price is only a little over RMB 60 per cubic meter. Investigations in Lingxian County in Hunan Province show that the official purchasing price of pine is RMB 69, while the cost is RMB 105. The response of the masses is to switch to more profitable lines such as firewood and growing grasses. The purchase price of pine for boards is RMB 60 per cubic meter, but it is RMB 80 per cubic meter when that pine is cut into firewood and sold at RMB 10 for 100 kilograms. In Guizhou, the income from growing *bamao* grass is five or six times that from growing trees. Since we can't really adjust timber prices right now to any great degree, we need to adopt other policies to encourage farmers engaged in forestry to grow more trees. A certain amount of timber should be left to them for their own purposes when implementing the 'one account book for timber felling,' which they can then, in proper organized and unified [collective] fashion, exchange for grain and materials with other places. That will give them a little more incentive.

11. A suggestion: China has around two billion *mu* of arable land, which comes down to 'many people, little land.' Other than Heilongjiang, only Xinjiang has appropriate conditions for large-scale land reclamation. We suggest formulating a long-term investment plan and transferring several hundreds of thousands of people to Xinjiang for land reclamation. This will help stabilize frontiers, unite local ethnic groups, and lessen the pressure on the State to transport grain over long distances.

Note

* This is an explanation made by the author when the Party Central Committee discussed the Notice of the CPC Central Committee on Rural Work in 1984 (namely the central document No. 1984–1).

7 Several 'social objectives' behind developing a rural commodity economy*

(December 20, 1984)

There are two sides to every coin and, similarly, different ways in which the consequences of policies can be interpreted. Our decision to develop a commodity economy is a good example. The growth of a commodity economy is going to help stimulate productivity and raise efficiency. If we ever want to accomplish socialism, we must proceed with developing a socialist commodity economy. On the other hand, the process contains its own contradictions. It is not conducive to a healthy society in the sense of equity and harmony, and therefore these are things that we have to focus on through appropriate adjustments and the proper handling of various relationships. One particular problem is the relationship between rural and urban areas. Others are the economic relationships among different regions and the relationship between the 'commodity economy' and the 'cooperative economy.' Failure to address these relationships may lead to imbalances in the overall situation and even deviation from our socialist orientation. For this reason, we should define some of the social objectives that we should be paying attention to and striving toward.

1. We must assure that rural and urban areas are cohesive and prosper together

When the commodity economy begins to develop, it may lead to excessive prosperity in urban areas and temporary stagnation in rural areas. This is what has happened in many capitalist countries and even in some third-world countries. The initial consequence of the spontaneous action of the market is that rural funds and human resources flow toward urban areas. The rural labor force declines dramatically, supply and demand of agricultural goods becomes imbalanced, and funds and labor then begin to flow back to rural areas. This is a long and painful process, so the question is how to avoid it in the context of a socialist system. Comrade Mao Zedong long ago noted that agriculture should be the 'foundation' and industry the 'guiding' factor. He later instructed that planning should follow the sequence of first agriculture, then light industry, and then heavy industry. Despite this, our rural development has been retarded for years. Because of the 'scissor' nature of price differences in industrial and farm products, rural funds still continue to flow toward urban areas, and the income disparity between farmers and urban workers is considerable. Very few intellectuals live in rural areas, especially those who are at higher level, while any middle school students who can test into higher education then stay in cities. This makes transfer of technology into rural areas difficult. There also aren't many channels through which funds can flow into rural areas, so the only alternative is State aid and bank loans.

Since we are well aware of the problem of the scissor relationship in pricing, why has this not long since been resolved? The reason is that it is beyond the power of human beings to control directly. In cities, technology is constantly being upgraded and labor productivity is constantly improving, both at a higher rate than the situation in the countryside. The scissor differential therefore continues to exist, in line with the changes in comparative costs. Moreover, China's industrialization has been funded mainly through the country's own accumulation of financial resources, and these have come not just from retained earnings from industry but also from funds earned by the agricultural sector. In order to maintain the proper relationship between accumulation and consumption, the State has often had to prevent prices of farm products from rising too fast. For a certain period of time, there was no alternative but to use various means to requisition a portion of farmers' income and put it in the service of building up industry for the socialist system. If the levies on farmers go beyond a reasonable limit, however, it impoverishes rural areas and influences the solidarity between workers and farmers. In the future, as the urban–rural exchange is completely marketized, things may worsen in the sense that the technological gap will widen and rural areas will be even more disadvantaged in their competitive position. The question is: How we are going to keep the urban–rural gap from growing to a degree that is beyond control? We obviously can't accomplish it purely through pricing, since the prices of farm products cannot be raised through the roof. It is also unrealistic for the State to drastically increase investment in agriculture, since our fiscal resources are limited.

If the urban–rural gap is to be narrowed, the following two interrelated conditions must be met.

1. Labor productivity in agriculture must be greatly increased. China's total grain output is currently a little over 400 billion kilograms, or over 400 million tons, which ranks it first in the world. Output per laborer is only a very low 1,200 kilograms on average. The grain produced by one agricultural laborer in the United States can feed 52 people. We are very far from achieving this level. When productivity is too low, it is hard to increase per capita income.

2. The structure of employment must be changed. We must increase those employed in nonagricultural sectors in rural areas and reduce those working in agriculture. Comrade Mao Zedong said long ago that no wealth would be generated if China's 800 million farmers just kept on growing grain. Nonetheless, despite years of effort, solutions to the problem elude us. All advanced countries in the world have developed by growing their cities and encouraging a migration of the population into those cities. We too have implemented a shift in population, but due to the international climate of affairs, which was unfavorable, we first had to develop capital-intensive and technology-intensive heavy industries, and these were not able to provide many jobs. In addition, it was necessary to place restrictions on the free flow of rural labor. The experience over the past few years has provided one solution: develop diversified operations. In addition to the primary industry of farming, rural areas should also develop secondary and tertiary industries so as to absorb surplus labor, allow an in situ shift of the labor force to new occupations, and thereby realize full employment. In recent years, the nonagricultural population in China's rural areas has increased to nearly 100 million people, and in 1984, the output value of rural enterprises came to RMB 150 billion. This opens out the chances for common prosperity of both urban and rural areas in the future.

The secondary industry in rural areas can be roughly divided into two major categories.

1. The processing of farm products and sideline products: In the past, both pre-processing and final processing of farm and sideline products was concentrated in urban areas, including the handling of grain, cotton, oilseeds, livestock products, aquatic products, fruit, vegetables, sugar, flax, tobacco, and silk. In the future, new processing projects should be mainly located in rural areas. If individuals are unable to handle the size of some, they should be run by collectives, and if collectives are not up to the task, then they should be run by local governments, and by the State if local governments don't have the resources.

Some comrades look down on the small profits they see deriving from value-added of agricultural products. This is short-sighted. The more the processing of farm and sideline products develops, the brighter the prospects for this kind of processing will become. Although China has long since gone beyond a primitive state of agriculture and entered the stage of intensive farming, still the 'commodification rate' of produce is low, and we are still basically at a level of self-sufficiency, or semi-self-sufficiency. Today, we must, and we should, be able to carry out large-scale commodity production by moving into more intensive operations and getting far more results from slightly more investment. Large-scale commodity production will rely on large-capacity markets, and the growth of those markets depends to a large extent on the processing of farm products. Only through processing can farm products form new qualitative conditions and expand both the amount supplied and the range of products supplied. Milk is an example: If milk is not processed, only local people can drink it, and the profits will be insufficient to generate larger business. If dairy processing plants are built, the market can be much larger. A host of other industries will also develop to serve the processing, including storage, packing, and transport. Processing of farm products is not merely designed to increase value-added, therefore, but also to create the underlying conditions for expanding the entire scale of commodity circulation and for creating demand. Without a corresponding large market capacity to absorb product, mass production simply won't work.

We can also anticipate that a whole new stage of agriculture will be appearing, namely one in which the industry is armed with new technologies – i.e., the stage of a 'knowledge-based' agriculture. In the future, when genetic engineering, recombinant gene technology, cell fusion, and other scientific results are utilized, mankind will be able to produce new animal and plant species depending on need. These newly developed species can be made highly resilient and have various qualitative attributes. When this happens, a new industrial revolution will occur in agricultural production. Scientific results have long been applied primarily to industry, and not to agriculture. Microelectronics, microorganism technologies, mathematics, physics, and chemistry, together with other cutting-edge technologies and materials sciences, have failed to shift toward agriculture. A shift began in the 1970s, however, and will certainly achieve breakthroughs as time goes on. Solar energy and photosynthesis are the cause of much energy transfer among matter in the world, and the combination of solar energy, via photosynthesis, and earth produces plants and animals. In geologic time, plants turned into coal and animals into petroleum, and petroleum and coal can produce tens of thousands of new products today. The existing plants and animals are regarded as useful for little more than eating, wearing, and using. In the final analysis, however, mankind will acquire renewable energies, food, medical materials, and other valuable organic materials from agriculture. That planting, breeding, and scientific processing will form whole new industries is a certainty, and the size and scope of those industries will be vastly greater than anything today. The era in which agriculture has no wasted material is soon coming.

2. General processing: Most industries of this type are currently in urban areas, but they can just as easily be developed in rural areas. Labor is abundant there, and wages are low. Some urban industries, especially those that are labor intensive, may not develop as fast in the rural areas, but in the interests of the whole society, they can offer employment to hundreds of millions of people. Solving this longstanding difficult problem will be a tremendous social efficiency in itself.

Urban–rural exchange should not be limited to industrial and farm products. In addition, the secondary and tertiary industries should begin to play a role, spurring the transfer of technologies, the exchange of human resources, and the mutual flow of funds. This will stimulate the growth of small cities and help to form a more balanced mix of industry and agriculture, with a growing symbiosis, more coordinated interaction, and common prosperity between urban and rural areas.

2. Combine market competition with cooperation

Over these past few years of implementing the household contract system with remuneration linked to output, a two-level form of operation has been underway with both the collective operations and restored family operations working in tandem. The results have been good, and we should maintain this situation for a long time to come. The 'basic nature' of family operations is that farmers are themselves producers of commodities, operating in a relatively independent way.

Independence and autonomy help to motivate them to work harder and get rich through their labor. Removing the myriad unnecessary yokes and burdens from the backs of farmers, allowing them to have free choice in what they produce and what they do with the product, has greatly stimulated their great creativity and initiative and has vastly accelerated rural development. The key issue is that, with political power led by the Communist Party of China, once the commodity economy begins to accelerate, that power should emphasize both efficiency and equity so that social and economic development will advance on a socialist track. We should be very explicit about this – farmers must be educated and organized to take the road of cooperatization.

The goals of developing a commodity economy and improving cooperative systems are identical, as are the processes. The common aim of the two is to develop productivity. We know from experience that when productivity is low, imposing collective systems that feature a high degree of public ownership on farmers inevitably leads to the practice of 'eating from the same big pot.' Put the other way around, the development of productivity requires the socialization of production and the development and improvement of cooperative systems.

As the commodity economy develops, farmers will soon encounter the limits of individual and family operations as they try to enter competitive markets. They will then ask to expand the size of their operations, and they will need certain types of social services. The commodity economy may itself exhibit two tendencies at that point. One is alliances and various forms of cooperation. If this trend is not properly guided, a second tendency may develop – namely, concentration of the means of production in the hands of a few private businessmen. Poor families will have no alternative but to turn to these businessmen for their livelihoods and to rely on them. The second trend is already highly visible. For now, the development of private services is beneficial rather than harmful, but it is necessary to point out the overall direction. It is not good to be hasty in setting policy, but neither is it good to lag behind the will of the masses. Farmers' requests for alliances first appeared in the areas of supply and marketing, processing, irrigation, and farm machinery. In the 1950s, collectivization first began in the realms of supply and marketing. Later, collectivization of land and production was done a little too precipitously. Now we come back to emphasizing that farmers should organize themselves in voluntary fashion, building links of supply and of marketing, as well as processing and other technical services. We must take advantage of existing already-reformed cooperative organizations, such as regional cooperative organizations, to make sure *cheng-bao* contracts are performed properly, to provide such services as irrigation improvement, mechanized farming, and pest prevention, to improve the environmental quality for agricultural production, and to support how farmers can develop altogether. On the other hand, new economic alliances should be developed in light of the trend of specialization. In recent years, farmers have created some forms of cooperative economies themselves. On the basis of family operations, they are making use of shareholding systems to jointly operate various services. Distribution according to work is combined with dividend distribution according to the number of shares that are held. Companies and farming households are also jointly coming together to form supply, production, and marketing chains. These forms do not affect the existing property rights of farmers, but rather can create new forces of social production and accumulate public assets, which are an advantage. Even though distribution of dividends is not done according to work, it can help develop the forces of production. On the principle of voluntary participation, it helps resolve the problem of farmers not otherwise being able to accumulate enough funds or reach economies of scale. Since advantages outweigh disadvantages, dividend distribution should be allowed. We can also use this method to operate factories, build highways, construct warehouses, and establish breeding operations and other enterprises in rural areas. But we should resolutely oppose coercion – that is, making farmers participate if they are not willing. No matter how good a thing is, it can be spoiled if the wrong methods are used. We must ensure that good things are properly done.

Any cooperative organization should have its own bylaws, or articles of association. For the time being, we do not advocate nationally unified articles of association. These documents should be formulated from bottom to top and according to local conditions. This is a new working method: first diversify, then later standardize.

3. Economic assistance among regions

Given the stimulus of a commodity economy, certain regions will be developing faster than others. Making slower regions keep up is beyond our control since economic development is done on the basis of what came before, and what came before was already quite uneven given different social, economic, cultural, and natural conditions. Our ultimate goal is to eradicate poverty and enjoy common prosperity. While we should encourage those who are further along, we cannot forget to support the many who lag behind. Grain has always been inadequate in mountainous areas, and so people there mainly depend on forestry, medicinal herbs, and native products for living, yet it was precisely in these areas that our 'unified control' in the past stifled any initiative. Therefore, the Central Committee of the Party and the State Council have decided that while tree felling should be controlled in mountainous areas, timber prices should also be liberalized so as to allow these areas to develop production by tapping their own advantageous resources.

The eastern part of our country enjoys the greatest advantages in capital and technology, while the western region is strong in resources. Our most pressing task is to reform price-formation mechanisms so as to streamline the prices of resources and form unified markets for commodity exchange. Therefore, we must promote 'east-west' mutual support, encouraging the two regions to establish horizontal ties on a voluntary basis and to organize entities that undertake development together. The State should adopt policies that provide incentives for the transfer of technologies and capital to more backward regions.

We should improve the use of State funds that have been allocated for supporting backward regions. Instead of spreading them indiscriminately, 'peppering them' over too many projects, we should organize priorities and focus capital, technology, and human resources on key projects. In terms of the structure of production, backward regions should first choose such labor-intensive industries as planting, breeding, mining, highway construction, and initial processing of native products. Practice proves that projects that do not conform to the current stage of development will not only fail but will lose money. Wenzhou Prefecture in Zhejiang Province began to enliven the local rural economy by using family industries, since family operations had unique advantages there. Other poor mountainous areas should similarly choose proper industrial structures, rather than simply imitate what developed regions are doing.

As for developed regions, they should begin to set up bases for the export of commodities. They should attract foreign investment and technology in the area of agriculture with an aim to improving their technology. Areas around the Pearl River Delta, the Yangtze River Delta, the Jiaodong Peninsula, the Liaodong Peninsula, and the Beijing-Tianjin-Tangshan region should be oriented toward international markets and gradually establish an industrial structure of trade, industry, and agriculture. To meet the demands of international markets, they should organize export trade. Through production in the areas of agriculture, forestry, animal husbandry, and fisheries, and through the value-added processing of products, they should commercialize and modernize their rural economies. As they attract in foreign investment and technology, they should also make alliances with inland provinces so that capital can flow to the hinterland to develop the processing of primary products. Successful technologies should also flow to the hinterland to accelerate the development regions that are 'later to develop,' but that should not be done at the cost of sacrificing the interests of more advanced regions.

Note

* This is a speech delivered by the author at the national conference on rural work convened by the Party Central Committee and published later by the *Red Flag* magazine.

8   Getting rich first, later, and together*

(December 20, 1985)

1. Adhering to the policy of allowing some people to get rich first

1. Common prosperity has always been the goal to which our Party adheres and something we struggle to achieve. But practical experience over the past three decades tells us that it is pure metaphysics to think of having all people achieve prosperity at the same time, to the same degree, and in the same space. 'Equal distribution' by trying to 'suppress the rich and help the poor' inevitably leads to common poverty instead of common prosperity. Actual practice in the course of modern Communist movements has proven that once the proletariat seizes power in any developing country, establishing socialist public ownership and realizing distribution according to work are goals that require a certain process. A purely socialist society cannot be built, and disparities in social distribution cannot be eliminated, all within a short period of time. In keeping with the spirit of seeking truth through facts, since the Third Plenary Session of the 11th Central Committee of the Party [December 1978], our Party has adopted a new policy advocated by Deng Xiaoping on behalf of the Central Committee. This new policy allows some regions and some people to earn more income and get rich first through hard work as a way to stimulate greater wealth for more people. The greater wealth comes about through economic transmission and stimulus mechanisms. This policy was first implemented in rural areas, and results over the past few years have been highly apparent.

In the 25 years prior to the Third Plenary Session of the 11th Central Committee of the Party, per capita net annual income of Chinese farmers rose by only RMB 70, from RMB 64 in 1954 to RMB 134 in 1978. With the new policy, per capita net income of Chinese farmers rose by RMB 221 in six years. The percentage of low-income households fell, and that of high-income households went up. Farming households with a per capita net annual income of less than RMB 200 went from 85 percent in 1978 to 14 percent in 1984. The percentage of farming households with a per capita net annual income of more than RMB 500 rose from 0.6 percent in 1978 to 18 percent in 1984. This is an indication that the growth in rural prosperity has been steady and healthy. Surveys of actual practice also indicate that the policy to 'allow some people to get rich first through hard work' is entirely correct in that it is conducive to overall economic development and to the realization of common prosperity. The policy must be firmly adhered to for a long time and should not be allowed to change.

We should recognize that, as farmers' income grows, disparities will exist in the amount that people make. According to estimates of the National Bureau of Statistics, the disparity between high- and low-income households was 1.9-fold in 1978 and widened to 2.6-fold in 1984, an increase of 0.7-fold over six years.

2. Objective factors are the cause of disparities in personal income in the course of economic growth. China's socialist public ownership system provides the basic living conditions and development opportunities for all 'laborers.' It ensures that social and economic development continues to move toward the goal of common prosperity, and it helps to avoid the polarization that arises from a commodity economy that is under the system of private ownership. However, given that our society still distributes income according to the principle of 'pay for work done,' since different people have different skills and abilities, they will inevitably have different incomes. Income disparities will continue to exist until society begins to distribute income according to need. Currently, China pursues an economic system that features 'public ownership of the means of production as primary, while diverse other forms of economic activity develop in tandem.' Since individual economies, in particular, are allowed, different individual farmers possess and use means of production that are unequal both in quantity and in quality. Moreover, units engaged in production also have access to different resources, in terms of both nature and quantity. As capital accumulates and technology develops, gaps will widen even further between different industries in terms of access to resources and the efficiency with which they are used. In the course of economic growth, the equation of supply and demand is constantly changing, providing opportunities to those who can take advantage of them. Excessive profits can be made, and high incomes can result. Differing conditions will therefore inevitably lead to income disparities. Recognizing this, and using proper regulatory tools to keep it within bounds, is the proper course in order to encourage the development of a commodity economy at the same time. Not recognizing this, denying the reality, is tantamount to denying development itself.

In the process of developing a commodity economy, some people will look for loopholes and use illegal means to convert public into private wealth and in so doing damage the interests of both producers and consumers. These people, small in number but extremely high in income, have already triggered widespread social opposition. While this too is a phenomenon that is hard to avoid in the course of developing a commodity economy, we must control and prevent it by legal means and through taxation.

3. Given our vast territory and the uneven economic development among regions, it is natural for our country to have a range of economic and technological circumstances. Western and border regions are underdeveloped due to various historical reasons but enjoy a wealth of natural resources. Most inland regions are moderately developed. Relatively speaking, coastal regions possess more advanced technologies and economic resources and therefore are positioned to benefit most from international expertise, in terms of both production and management. These areas will develop first and then, through economic transmission and stimulation, will be able to shift the emphasis of economic development on to the middle and western regions. We agree that in certain instances more backward regions can use their natural advantages to leverage themselves, such as by importing advanced technologies and creating economic advantages. Still, nationwide, the general trend over dozens of years to come will be development that progresses from east to west. Another factor favoring coastal regions is the way prices of primary products have long been relatively low and those of finished products relatively high. It is still impossible to form an average profit rate. The situation has created a better environment for capital accumulation in developed regions, where most processing industries are located. Regional unevenness in economic development has exacerbated the disparities in income distribution. The State can try to adjust these with macro-regulatory measures; still, we have to admit that income disparities are an inevitable result of developing a commodity economy.

This is not to say that western and central regions of the country will never be developed. Economic differences in themselves create opportunities for the mutual dependence of different regions in terms of demand and supply; market opportunities lie in mutual utilization of resources. As long as these regions can seize opportunities, pool their limited human, material, and financial resources, tap their local advantages, and cultivate the growth points for economic development, they will create some of the basic conditions for a shift in national economic development strategies and be able to improve their own economic status.

2. Regarding the debate about efficiency versus equity

1. The debate on economic efficiency and social equity has been going on for a long time in Western countries. Social equity refers to equalizing income among members of society, while economic efficiency refers to organizing means of production and modes of economic operation in a way that favors economic growth. On the basis of economic efficiency, the market rewards producers who have invested capital, labor, and technologies, and this remuneration constitutes the income of those people. Frequently, in order to increase economic efficiency, remuneration must retain different levels; if income is equalized, society will be unable to maintain high efficiency.

This contradiction between production and distribution and between efficiency and equity cannot be fundamentally resolved under the capitalist system. The reason is that distribution of interests and profits rests upon the exploitation of hired labor. Private ownership of the means of production and of capital means that hired labor is exploited in order for private gain. Our socialist country is based on public ownership. It attempts to ameliorate the contradiction between efficiency and equity by creating conditions that serve both. The people's political power has the ability to create the maximum amount of equity through minor concessions in efficiency by using appropriate wealth distribution and redistribution policies. Our economic reforms are being designed to create the practical conditions for realizing this assumption.

2. For some time, we have mistakenly taken 'social equity' to mean 'absolute equality,' and we have disregarded the whole issue of economic efficiency as a result. We resorted to administrative tools in economic management that featured what was known as 'one: equal, two: transfer.' This meant utter egalitarianism and indiscriminate transfer of resources to meet that end. Our purely administrative measures sacrificed efficiency as the presumed necessary cost of maintaining equity. This rejected the idea that a commodity economy could develop under socialist conditions and denied the objective law that income distribution is subject to regulation by the market. It used noneconomic tools to enforce mandatory interventions. It cut the tie between equity and a sequenced process and undermined the mutual stimulus that equality and efficiency can provide in a socialist society. This form of arbitrary intervention served to foster an even greater social awareness and insistence on egalitarianism among small farmers. Today, this awareness continues to be a major ideological obstacle to the development of a commodity economy. People do not correctly understand that the overall level of social income has improved, even though certain disparities exist, so they focus exclusively on those disparities and insist that they be eliminated as soon as possible. Although the living conditions of some people are greatly improved, they still feel that they are less well off than some others or that others have improved even more. They point to abnormal cases for comparative purposes in order to reject the policy of allowing some people to get rich first. This is a way of thinking that we must do our utmost to overcome.

3. Create conditions that will help realize our common prosperity

1. The material conditions for realizing common prosperity can only be created through economic efficiencies. We need to exercise proper control over income disparities, but we should also be very careful to protect the development of the forces of production. We should recognize the positive role that income disparities and farmers' material interests play in growing those forces of production. When disparities arise as a result of differing abilities of producers and operators, then it is best to avoid intervention. Specific and appropriate adjustments can be made when there are excessively great disparities, and they affect specific consumption items that are within the scope of the overall social consumption fund. High incomes arising from differences in how much capital and resources a person has can be regulated through the progressive income tax and the resource tax. High incomes that arise from operators' taking advantage of market deficiencies and the opportunities that arise in the course of changing tracks from one system to another should, first, be regulated through tax adjustments, but at the same time we should improve the market and improve the system so as to block these loopholes as soon as possible. As to those who gain exorbitant profits through illegal activities – the legal system should be improved, and those engaging in illegal activities should be prosecuted according to law. Rural Party members and cadres who are proactive in leading the masses in allowing everyone to 'get rich together' should be praised. Party members and cadres who are the first to get rich through hard work should be protected. Those few Party members and cadres who abuse their power for selfish gain and get rich by illegal means should be punished according to law. The policy of 'allowing some people to get rich first through hard work' should be upheld for a long time and should not be subject to change. At the same time, we should encourage farmers to invest in developing production and create an atmosphere that emphasizes long-term steady growth so as to prevent people from excessive consumption and wild speculation. Economic development has led to a social division of labor, which has in turn created a large number of specialized households in rural areas. These should be protected, encouraged, and supported and should be allowed to use their advanced science and technology and operations and management expertise to 'get rich first.' The artificial creation of 'high-income households' in rural areas is something quite different from allowing some people to get rich through hard work. The creation of 'high-income households,' at the cost of development opportunities for the public, runs counter to Party policy. It cannot be regarded as a proper phenomenon.

2. China has the basic conditions to prevent polarization and to provide the guarantee of pursuing common prosperity. As far as rural areas are concerned, upholding public ownership of the basic means of production and improving and developing cooperative economies can provide equal development opportunities to all laborers in the most fundamental way. Places with highly developed cooperative economies are places where more farmers are getting rich at a faster pace. The main impetus to cooperative economies comes from the demand of farmers for developing commodity production – namely for preproduction and postproduction services – which leads to the need for larger scale of operations. Therefore, we should meet the various needs of different regions by allowing the formation of all kinds of economic alliances. The starting point should be services, and the alliances should be formed on top of a foundation of family operations and in conformity with local conditions.

Implementing cooperative systems is not, however, going to eliminate the extent and speed at which income disparities are growing. Within cooperatives that are implementing unified operations, the system of distribution according to work naturally preserves income disparities. Within the cooperatives that have introduced two-level operations, disparities are even more unavoidable because of the difference in the underlying production conditions among different households. Differences in standards of operation and management, geographic conditions, and ownership of product inputs are other important factors contributing to income disparities among farming households. Therefore, cooperative economic systems pursue common prosperity in the sense of promoting common development and preventing class polarization. They absolutely are not intended to pursue simultaneous and egalitarian prosperity. For this reason, we should take proactive measures to improve and develop these cooperative systems, while avoiding absolute egalitarianism and guarding against taking the old path of 'eating from the same big pot' and 'turning farmers' private property into collective property.' By so doing, we assure that 'getting rich first' is inherently consistent with 'getting rich altogether.'

3. In order to enable low-income earners to get rich, we must find ways to raise their levels of education and 'human quality,' increase their production skills and operating abilities, so as to help them adapt to the needs of developing a commodity economy. It will be even more important for us to open out opportunities for them, allow the development of diversified forms of operation in terms of ownership structure, and recognize that a shift in rural labor away from farming is going to be the basic prerequisite for realizing long-term prosperity for all. In particular, under the condition that sufficient labor for agriculture must be a given, realistic measures should be taken to promote the movement of rural labor from agriculture to secondary and tertiary industries and from countryside to cities. Labor mobility can occur between different sectors, or regions, or between the different social strata of urban and rural areas. Allowing such mobility will help enable equal opportunity, thereby encouraging people to be enterprising and enhancing economic efficiency. This is a form of social potential that is still waiting to be tapped.

Generally speaking, we can create the necessary material basis for common prosperity only when steady growth in our gross national product is guaranteed. In eliminating disparities, it will be more important to focus on greater production than it will be to focus merely on distribution. The task of our rural reform is to create a favorable economic environment for developing the rural forces of production, and that means, first of all, creating favorable market conditions. Market conditions in which technology does not advance, operations are too small, and labor productivity is low cannot be turned to advantage for economic development. The basic Marxist view is that production determines distribution and the relations of production determine the relations of distribution, hence distribution itself is a product of production. Accordingly, when we talk about the goal of common prosperity, we necessarily have to talk about developing the forces of production. The general level of material wealth in society determines the total amount of distributable income. Common prosperity can only be achieved when production is highly developed, social products are abundant, and public ownership is firmly assured. If the goal of common prosperity is to be achieved, we must raise the standard of the forces of social production in rural areas and gradually develop cooperative economies that develop the forces of production as per the will of the masses.

Note

* This is part of a speech delivered by the author at the Central Conference on Rural Work and published later by the *People's Daily*.

9 Raise the economic standing of agriculture through reliance on science and technology*

(April 11, 1986)

China's natural resources rank among the top few, worldwide, in terms of absolute amount. Per capita, our resources are far below the world's average – they are stringently inadequate. They are not enough to feed and clothe our one billion people or to enable our 800 million farmers to improve their standard of living.

Of course, there is no absolute standard for measuring the degree of 'stringency.' Indeed, I believe that improved resource utilization can mitigate this condition and turn it into abundance. We can overcome our scarcity of natural resources and open up far more optimistic prospects for the future if we increase our fiscal support for agriculture in a gradual manner and begin to rely more on science and technology to improve our utilization of resources. This path has been well traveled by countries that have already modernized their agriculture. We too not only should take this route, but we should be able to do remarkably well by it. The key factor is recognizing the role that scientific advances can play in promoting economic development of rural areas. The reforms we are currently undertaking are designed to add new vitality to our economic systems. They will not be enough, however, to achieve sustained growth without employing scientific advances and improving our material base.

1. Meeting the needs of commodity production will require widespread adoption of scientific results

Advanced science and technology typically benefits developed parts of the world first, before spreading to more backward regions, and it benefits industry first before spreading to agriculture. This appears to be the pattern in world economic history. Agriculture was born many thousands of years ago, and rural civilizations existed long before urban civilizations appeared. Industry began to propel the world in the direction of 'urban civilization' over 300 years ago. By today, 'rural civilization' lags far behind urban civilization, particularly in terms of its lower utilization of science and technology.

The progress of history also seems to indicate that widespread use of advanced technologies is intimately connected to the development of a commodity economy. Science is transformed into technology, and technology is transformed into the forces of production. Technological transfer from developed to undeveloped regions and from developed to undeveloped sectors moves in step with the development of a commodity economy. Sectors with higher profits and enterprises with more capital have a better chance of taking advantage of advanced technologies. Sectors and enterprises with low profits and less capital have a harder time, find they cannot plow retained earnings into investment in technology, and so are caught in a vicious cycle. The backwardness of rural science and technology is a reflection of this condition.

It is simply a fact that advanced regions and sectors are the recipients of greater benefits; this is not something that human intentions can change. Does this then mean that backward regions will forever be backward, caught in that perpetual state? Not at all. One of the requirements for growth in a commodity economy is that science and technology also move in the direction of opportunity. As the relationships of benefits change, science and technology seek new viable regions for growth; our underdeveloped regions can provide precisely this opportunity. A number of historical examples show the process in action. The United States replaced certain European countries as global leader in science and technology. The Japanese economy was rejuvenated through use of technology after World War II. A number of other countries and regions have attained moderate levels of development or notable progress in certain sectors through use of technology. We can draw forth two general principles from evaluating these transitions. One is that the development of science and technology depends on an economic foundation. It develops faster in more developed places. The second is that advanced technologies tend to shift from developed to undeveloped regions and from advanced to more backward sectors.

From the first principle, we can recognize that developing science and technology requires certain basic conditions, but if we simply acquiesce in that conclusion and do nothing, we will be succumbing to what Marx regarded as fatalism. We must also recognize that there is promise in the second principle, and we should employ that principle to further economic development, especially in the agricultural sector. This is partly because it is the sector on which the predominant share of our laborers rely for a living, and it is also the most backward of all our industries.

2. Select proper priorities and emphasize practical efficiency

The most important consideration, when we think of accelerating the transfer of science and technology to rural areas, is to know precisely where to focus our energies. We should not simply increase the number of our projects or have excellent aspirations. Instead, we must thoroughly understand where scientific inputs will have the greatest and most efficient impact, where they will become an impetus to agricultural development. In this, we need to be clear about which technologies are both advanced but also suitable for local economic and social conditions. Once we identify the key links, we must grasp hold of them and be utterly persistent in making sure we achieve practical efficiencies and avoid work practices that are not effective.

Given China's current rural conditions, priorities might be evaluated from the following four perspectives.

1. Raw materials: Major products such as cotton, flax, silk, sugar, fruit, livestock, and aquatic products still enjoy a relative price advantage and strong market demand. Light industry requires these raw materials, and the textile sector in particular cannot live without them, so the State must allocate financial resources toward production of these products. All are badly in need of advanced technologies and deserve utmost attention.

2. Agricultural products that earn foreign exchange: While the State has over 40 major 'projects' in this regard, various regions also have minor projects underway. Different regions should tap into their own strengths in particular products.

3. Rural enterprises [also known as town-and-village enterprises]: This is the most profitable sector in rural areas. The sector is urgently in need of expanded production and improved quality so as to maintain its competitiveness. Rural enterprises are 'collective economies' that are responsible for their own profits and losses and that therefore are strongly motivated to pursue profits through technological improvements. The 'Shooting Star Program' launched by the State Commission of Science and Technology was aimed precisely at this need and is bound to be a great success. These enterprises serve as growth nodes in rural economies and in the future are going to have a major impact on China's overall situation.

4. All kinds of rural units that are engaged in intensive operations: Coastal areas along China's southeastern region and the outskirts of major cities are already showing the budding signs of spearheading the development of a commodity economy. In the future, production alliances of specialized households will be forming that incorporate many rural enterprises into businesses of a certain economy of scale. These production alliances, which have already accumulated a sizeable amount of fixed assets, will become the medium for absorbing and utilizing new technologies. For example, in the southeast coastal region, several large 'planting households' may appear in a given natural village where each farms between 30 and 40 *mu* of farmland [around 6 acres, at one *mu* = 0.1647 acres]. Instead of relying on an increase of labor, they use inputs of machinery, fertilizer, and new technologies to increase yields. As their fixed assets increase every year, their labor requirements are reduced. They increase production mainly through technological advances.

These four items represent certain areas in which we can determine our priorities. They are also entry points for the transfer of advanced technology into rural areas. Of course, we still need to keep in mind other overall considerations. For example, although technology may be used to support poverty-stricken mountainous areas, this does not mean other support to those areas is not needed. Nonetheless, we need to set priorities.

5. Selecting products that have low costs and bring in high profits: Production technologies naturally incur production costs. Trying to implement and popularize them necessarily comes up against this issue. In modern agriculture, improved varieties often have the lowest costs; yields are enhanced by improving biological properties. Improved varieties, and I include breeding stock in this category, do not require heavy investments for cultivating crops or raising livestock and are more acceptable to farmers. Our country is a socialist state and so has covered most of the costs of developing advanced breeds or advanced seed. User costs are very low. Once a fine variety is bred, it can have excellent economic efficiency. With a long history of developing better varieties and a large reservoir of species, China has the ability to grasp modern breeding technologies very quickly. Tapping into this advantage to improve varieties in a sustained way will be of inestimable value in the future.

3. Rely on science and technology to enhance the comparative return on agriculture

A constant decline in comparative returns off agriculture is almost a worldwide phenomenon. The same dollar will make less off agriculture than it will off industry, and the same person's labor invested in agriculture will make less than it does off industry as well. That is why the farmers always want to 'bolt out of the gate of agriculture' and are unwilling to increase their investment in land. In 1985, farmers in some places became less inclined to grow grain, to put investments into their land, to purchase chemical fertilizer, and even to apply organic fertilizer. Some were unwilling to raise pigs. Herein lies an economic law. When the level of investment reaches a certain level, laborers will make choices, be more selective among money-making opportunities and even in the choice between labor and leisure. This phenomenon is an expression of social progress and shows that our economy truly has improved quickly over the past few years.

Raising grain currently gives the lowest returns in rural areas. Grain is necessary for life, and its practical value is apparent, yet its exchange value is not very high. It is a highly self-contradictory commodity. Consumption of grain is tremendous, but its price cannot be too high since it affects the national economy and people's standard of living. Every government on earth is very conscious of its nation's grain production and carries out protective policies in order to maintain stable living standards. One reason for this is to ensure that farmers receive above-cost income from raising grain and thereby in so doing safeguard national interests. Another is that subsidies, and even stockpiling grain, help shield consumers from the risk of price hikes that they might otherwise not be able to bear. China's government is no exception. We subsidize RMB 0.1 for each 0.5 kilograms of grain so farmers can sell their grain at higher prices and urban residents can buy it at lower prices. When selling prices are lower than purchasing prices, the State has to offer a subsidy. Even so, raising grain is not as profitable as other forms of production. When one *mu* of land yields 750 kilograms of grain, which is a very high level, if each kilogram is sold at RMB 0.14, the total income is only RMB 300. Net income, not deducting the cost of labor, is only about RMB 180. Since a total of 100 labor days are required for two crop seasons, a farmer's income for his labor alone is RMB 1.8 per day. In many places, this income is lower than one might make in any other occupation. If the grain sells RMB 0.3 per kilogram, raising grain is even less profitable. Grain prices were raised in 1979, and farmers were happy at the time, but now prices of other products as well as the costs of raising grain are higher, and the comparative advantage of raising grain is lower. Can we again raise grain prices? That would affect the prices of other products and put pressure on the ability of incomes to withstand the hikes, as well as on overall social psychology. Trying to provide State subsidies for a grain price hike is similarly not affordable right now. The chief solution is to rely on science and technology for increased yields. Spending money on science and technology and infrastructure construction for a specific period of time can be the most efficient way to develop agricultural production. We must work hard to enhance the level of technology in rural areas and make greater breakthroughs in the production technologies of some farm products so that they can become more competitive on international markets. We can turn a low-income industry into a high-income occupation, and a low-profit industry to a high-profit one. Another way is to expand the production processes applied to farm products, by introducing advanced technologies, carrying out preprocessing, in-depth processing, and integrated utilization, and encouraging agricultural labor to move into processing and value-added. Surplus labor will then become an economic advantage, resources will have new methods for utilization, and farmers' income will go up sharply. In the United States, only 2 million people are engaged in planting and cultivating, but 20 million people are involved in pre- and postproduction services and processing. If we can gradually develop all these sectors in the rural areas, we can resolve many of our current problems.

4. Align with laws of nature as well as economic laws

Agriculture has to bear the 'double risk' of both natural conditions and economic constraints, unlike industry.

China's agriculture still bears the vestiges of a 'natural economy' in that its level of technology in many places is not much different than it was 1,000 years ago. A single family, or a single household, is largely unable to combat natural risks. Without advanced technologies or a solid infrastructure, it is impossible for a family to overcome natural calamities when they occur. In the course of agricultural production, capital and labor are idle for a long time, and the operator loses money if he doesn't handle all inputs with great care. When inputs into land reach a certain level, returns from that land begin to tail off if not backed with technological advances. For every unit of investment put into the land, the farmer sees diminishing returns. Industry is quite different, for it can be done anywhere and does not face the same environmental risk.

We have put considerable effort into land reclamation of salinized land, and certain small areas are showing returns, but in general the effort has not worked.

Trying to reclaim large stretches of land is clearly too costly for China right now. Can we change our avenues of approach and look for crops that can withstand relatively harsh environments so that a higher percentage of our 9.6 million square kilometers of land can be utilized? Nature presents the evidence that this should be possible. Beaches have long since had salt-resistant plants, deserts have had drought-resistant plants, and penguins and krill can breed and grow in hyper-cold Antarctica. Clearly, many biological species can adapt themselves to extreme environments through variation. The development of modern science and especially genetic engineering has already begun to make utilizing the adaptability of species a possibility. Strengthening research in this respect will definitely be able to break through the limits of nature.

China currently classifies its arable land into three categories: high yield, middle yield, and low yield. Middle- and low-yield land accounts for two-thirds of all our arable land. It is very difficult to turn low-yielding fields into high-yielding ones, so one important avenue of research is how to find better planting methods. In the past, we dismissed the traditional experience of farmers and how they went about making decisions, and as a result we made terrible mistakes through 'blind' issuing of orders. Nonetheless, the wisdom of farmers is not unlimited, and it is moreover based on small-scale production. Large-scale farming arrangements made to utilize and adapt to the environment must be based on modern science and technology, instead of merely on the experience of farmers. For example, we can use computers for analysis and comparison in order to work out better farming methods for existing arable land, with existing technologies. Computers can calculate the 'shadow prices' of all the basic factors of production and put forward various options through optimized designs. Such modern decision making has gone beyond the limits of the traditional methods of farmers.

Things that farmers are incapable of doing for themselves, or researching for themselves, should be done by our scientists and institutions. Introducing modern science and technology to rural areas and gradually eliminating the technological gap between urban and rural areas should be important historic tasks for them to pursue. For this reason, our comrades working in science and technology and in propagating applied technologies should know more about economics and society in general. In addition to scientific know-how, they should have a head for economics. Science has a vast sphere of application in rural areas. One vitally important area, first and foremost taking environmental protection into account, is improving the efficiency with which we use natural resources. We must find better ways to conserve and find ways to substitute for our precious and diminishing stock of natural resources. This is not only a technological issue; it is also an economic issue. Only when an advanced technology can produce economic efficiencies above a certain level will it be embraced by society at large.

Note

* This is a speech delivered by the author at a national conference on the exchange of experience in scientific work and published later by the *People's Daily*.

10 Foreign-oriented development strategy for coastal regions*

(December 3, 1987)

1. Foreign-oriented strategy

In line with the 'opening up' policy that we have already established, China will gradually be implementing a development strategy in its coastal regions that 'faces towards the outside.' That means China will be tapping into its cheap and abundant labor resources by building up a cheap and well-qualified labor 'army' to produce labor-intensive products for trade with foreign countries. The producers will primarily be town-and-village enterprises. By importing raw materials, exporting finished products, earning wages for processing, and using products as the medium for exporting labor, China can participate in international economic circulation and accelerate its own development.

This strategic concept reflects objective trends in China's economic development. In recent years, the call has been for 'export-earning' products from town-and-village enterprises. Prior to this, coastal areas in Guangdong Province were already integrating trade with industry and agriculture to develop foreign-oriented economies. Since certain dilemmas continued to appear in the course of economic development, a number of comrades analyzed the problems and put forth proposals. Comrades at the National Bureau of Statistics in particular said that the export of farm products and sideline products faced the problem of being unable to satisfy both foreign and domestic markets. Selling internationally pushed up domestic prices and aggravated market shortages. At the same time, given the poor quality and low price of exports, enterprises had no way to fulfill their exchange-earning quotas other than increasing the amount of their exports. To solve this dilemma, people at the National Bureau of Statistics recommended that we focus on modernizing our agriculture, that we develop processing industries so as to produce high-quality, high-value-added products with enhanced ability to earn foreign exchange. Another researcher at the State Planning Commission suggested that cheap and abundant rural labor be utilized to produce labor-intensive export products. By importing raw materials and exporting processed products, China could participate in the great flow of international goods and ease our own problem of a shift in surplus labor and yet an inadequate supply of capital. Their suggestions received careful attention.

The foreign-oriented strategy has brought the opening-up policy together with the realization that we should use the advantage of our labor resources. This has enhanced the substance of our opening up policy and made it into a specific component of our economic strategy. This has been a major step of vital importance to the overall situation; all signs indicate that the time is now ripe for pursuing this strategy.

2. Necessity

Labor ranks first among all of China's abundant resources. Capitalizing on our labor advantage should be elevated to high consideration from a strategic perspective. China's rural areas have huge amounts of rural surplus labor that will be an increasingly heavy burden if these people cannot be allocated to a rational structure of production. China will not be able to modernize its society if it continues to carry this burden on its back. Conversely, proper use of this advantage will mean that moving into a moderately prosperous society is not at all beyond reach. Suzhou has been able to shift so much labor into secondary and tertiary industries that its per capita GDP reached US $1,000 in 1986, evidence it can be done. No country in the world has ever shifted the employment of such a massive number of people, however, and various difficulties and contradictions will certainly appear. In some productive sectors, we are already seeing that town-and-village enterprises are becoming an indispensable complement to large industries. Rural enterprises already account for over 50 percent of the building materials sector. Since resources for building materials, such as mountains, stones, and coal, are abundant, contradictions are not as sharp there as in some other industries, and the same is true of smaller commodities. In manufacturing sectors that require the supply of wool, cotton, steel products, and timber, however, rural enterprises are now in competition with large industries for raw materials. In addition, 60 percent of China's rural enterprises are located in the southeast developed regions. Development of rural enterprises is far slower in the west, so products flowing in from eastern China only serve to further impede development there.

We absolutely must find job opportunities for surplus rural laborers, but we recognize that shifts in employment are constrained by resources and capital. This is indeed a contradiction. Turning some enterprises into foreign-oriented entities can ameliorate this contradiction and turn an overly large population into an advantage.

The interconnecting of global economies is now an inevitable trend as all countries, no matter whether they are socialist or capitalist, try to expand markets for their domestic production and take advantage of international division of labor to accelerate their own development. It is not only necessary but also beneficial for our own country to uphold the policy of opening to the outside world and combining international and domestic ways that complement each other. Participating in international circulation will train our enterprises to compete, thereby to learn, and to shorten the time it takes to catch up with foreign counterparts in all forms of technology. We particularly need to learn international marketing methods and corporate operations and management. Marking out areas along the coast for fairly large-scale adaptability experiments should produce the desired results.

Our coastal regions have dense populations on very little land. Their resources are not well distributed, and as a result they are very hard to manage. Farmers in these areas cannot be forced to grow grain since the real costs of doing this are constantly increasing and it doesn't pay. If a foreign-oriented strategy can be implemented, local farmers can instead export processed products and specialty products. With the foreign exchange, we could import grain, or we could also purchase grain for the coastal regions from inner provinces, employing import-substitution methods under conditions of mutual benefit to both sides. This would ease the pressure on coastal regions to grow grain themselves. Instead, they can grow cash crops that conform to local conditions for processing and export, accumulate retained earnings, and in time be able to start using economies of scale that take advantage of modernized agricultural techniques.

China's very rapid economic growth recently has begun to trigger inflation. We are experiencing foreign exchange shortages due to importing large amounts of raw materials, which means we must export more primary products. The cost of those primary products, however, when calculating in the exchange rate, has become higher than the cost of finished products. We have encountered a period when international prices are falling, so our exchange earning capacity is reduced and we have to increase subsidies for our exports. With a large trade deficit, we will have to take on foreign debts, but at a certain level, the money we have to put into debt servicing will offset the inflow of foreign investment. Therefore, we really should seize this opportunity as the world's economies are restructuring and throw some of our coastal manufacturing industries into international circulation. By expanding exports to international consumers, we can earn foreign exchange. This will be powerfully helpful as a complement to our policy of reducing domestic investment and trying to control inflation.

3. Feasibility

Whether or not this is feasible will have to be tested. It will not be determined solely by us, but also by the international market. If the international market will accept labor-intensive products and, if so, in what quantity, are things that have to be determined. 'Labor-intensive' is a relative concept, and it is a concept that changes with time and place. Production that requires more labor at lower cost can be considered labor-intensive production, but this does not necessarily mean hand-made items. In general, any country that is transitioning from agriculture to industry as its base will go through a period of having a tremendous amount of labor-intensive enterprises if that country has a large population and scarce land and capital resources. Japan, South Korea, Singapore, and China's Taiwan have all experienced this period. Some Latin American countries that attempted to leapfrog the process and go directly into a period of capital-intensive industries have found themselves in deep water. In China, we pursued a strategy that favored heavy industries for too long. The result was that development in cities and in rural areas was not coordinated, which is harming the smooth development of our economy. Are labor-intensive products desirable in world markets? Human consumption always operates on multiple levels. Due to differences in income, desires, and periods of time, demand is generally diversified. In high-income developed countries, for example, textiles made of cotton, silk, and linen are in great demand, clothes that used to be mass-produced now emphasize more custom tailoring, and people are preferring ethnic foods and foods that are free of pollution. All of these are labor-intensive products. Even high-tech industries have some labor-intensive links in their production.

Because of changes in the cost structure of their labor inputs, some developed countries have switched to capital-intensive industries and moved the production of labor-intensive products to developing countries that enjoy comparative advantages in human resources. China's share of international markets is out of line with its production capacity. Our total foreign trade accounts for only about 18 percent of GDP, which is a very low percentage. Because of its huge population and vast territory, China's dependence on international markets is also relatively low, so it is impossible for us to drive up our percentage of foreign trade by too large a margin. Nonetheless, the percentage for the coastal regions should be higher, which is to say that there is considerable potential. If the world economy plunges into a recession, both high-tech products and labor-intensive products will suffer, but in relative terms, and the market share of labor-intensive products may somewhat expand. If a recession is limited in scale, and short-term, then there will be more margin for us to enter. Our initial target should be to fill in the market niches that some other countries have recently vacated. As Comrade Deng Xiaoping surmised, it is very likely that a climate of international peace may continue now for some tens of years, and if that is true, the chances of a major world war will constantly diminish.

How are our domestic conditions [in terms of starting such an export program]? First, labor resources are abundant, and the price of labor is low. Although labor quality is low as well, it can be improved. Second, and this is the most important thing, we will need a good economic mechanism, especially a good foreign trade system. The deepening of reforms is meant to create just such operating mechanisms. Third, we already have a certain degree of practical experience, and we have the capital and technology to support the program. In recent years, certain places have already 'strode forth' in this regard, and their results have been good. Capital is unlikely to be a problem if we can liberalize the capital markets and improve the climate for investment.

The aforementioned discusses and confirms the feasibility of this strategy from domestic and international perspectives. But the strategy still has considerable uncertainties. We should be fully prepared for difficulties and problems. For example, when production is directly linked to the international economy, commodity prices and exchange rates will fluctuate, which will be inconsistent with our existing economic pattern. Secondly, artificially carving out areas for preferential policies is bound to cause friction between two types of areas and two types of markets and to distort their mutual economic relations. Major volatility in the international economy and market may occur at any time, and we are not well prepared. Most importantly, raising our levels of technology and management is going to take time. All these are some of the considerations. Meanwhile, we cannot be sure of the ultimate result – we simply have to test, explore, and develop before we can provide clear-cut answers and solutions.

Why should coastal regions be chosen as the entry point for a foreign-oriented strategy? First, they enjoy a geographic advantage. Second, they have practical experience. Third, rural enterprises in the coastal regions are better developed, the farmers are better educated, the cadres know more about business operations, and the enterprises have earned some foreign exchange through exports and have the requisite start-up capital. Fourth, the coastal regions have several major ports that can provide various services and cut trading costs. Shanghai, for example, has been most experienced in trade from the start. It has the traditions, personnel, contact network, and capacity to radiate out into domestic and overseas markets 'on both sides of the swinging door.' We should give priority to developing its potential. Fifth, selecting the coastal regions is also politically important. These places can serve as a model for social modernization so that the income of between 50 and 200 million people approaches the levels in Hong Kong and Taiwan. This can help convince those who are doubtful about China's reunification due to economic disparities.

Why should town-and-village enterprises be selected? It is mainly because they are labor intensive, they are nimble enough to enter markets quickly, and they have sound mechanisms for being truly responsible for their own profits and losses. Town-and-village enterprises have been market driven from the very beginning and have a strong desire to survive through competition. Labor-intensive products are often not long-standing and stable, but town-and-village enterprises are versatile enough to 'turn on a dime' with their quick reactions to market changes. This in no way means that the large State-Owned Enterprises and enterprises in other regions don't have certain qualifications to be foreign oriented. All enterprises suitable for foreign-oriented production should be encouraged.

4. Two policy targets

A host of policy measures will be required to ensure the implementation of the foreign-oriented strategy. As a start, the following two points may help guide the direction of various policy objectives that will need to be made.

1. Grasp reform and promote development

Implementing the foreign-oriented strategy will have to rely on new economic mechanisms. International exchange based on the old systems inevitably leads to huge losses, for without huge losses [to the State] it is not undertaken. Therefore, deeper reforms will be required to ensure that each town-and-village enterprise operates independently, is responsible for its profits and losses, and constantly increases its competitiveness. The development of labor-intensive industries cannot be realized through direct government intervention, by mobilizing large amounts of capital to launch enterprises. In particular, we absolutely cannot 'blindly' expand the size of capital construction. In first place, therefore, we focus on policy.

Labor-intensive industries generally feature small-scale operations, elaborate division of labor, and great market elasticity. They maintain their competitive advantage through continuous minor innovations in products and technologies. They must directly face international markets, be able to bear the pressures of competition, and seek survival and ongoing growth amid competitive risks. Therefore, these enterprises must cultivate the capacity to operate independently, to deal with foreign counterparts, and to make import and export decisions themselves. They must be allowed to transfer the factors of production among themselves rationally so as to improve the efficient use of capital. Reform of town-and-village enterprises must regard this as a primary policy objective.

The reform of the foreign trade system is mainly designed to create an environment in which enterprises can make their own decisions about importing and exporting. A group of enterprises should be guided in the direction of changing from domestic-oriented to foreign-oriented business. They should be encouraged to export more and earn more value-added income, and they should be encouraged to develop external links and organize alliances for supply and marketing services. Intermediary commercial organizations that are diverse in nature as well as in ownership should be developed, and foreign investors should be allowed to register such organizations and operate them according to Chinese law. Foreign trade departments should separate out government administration from corporate management. Foreign trade enterprises should shuck off their monopoly positions. Governmental departments should perform their macro-regulatory functions in a better way.

2. Import in order to export, ensure exports with imports, and expedite the development of foreign-oriented industries

The emphasis of our foreign-oriented strategy is to develop industries that earn foreign exchange. We are aiming at a rolling process of having exports promote imports, which promote further exports. Processing domestic-oriented products with imported raw materials can cause sharp contradictions and must be avoided. We should take bold steps to attract foreign investors to establish processing factories. The policy aims at compensation trade, with supplied materials, designs, and components. To undertake this, we should improve the investment climate.

The transition from a domestic-oriented to a foreign-oriented economy is a very difficult process. The government should work out policies that have both encouraging and restraining effects so that the enterprises can realize that they will derive greater benefits by selling to foreign markets than they would from selling to domestic markets and so that they are willing to make this transition. Special financial institutions will be required to provide working capital. In order to deal with international market fluctuations, local governments and enterprises must jointly accumulate funds for contingencies.

Note

* This is an article originally published by *Reform* magazine in the No. 2 issue in 1988.

11 Economic development in mountainous areas is a major focus for research*

(October 1988)

Mountainous areas account for around two-thirds of China's territory and therefore constitute a vast economic area, while worldwide they account for one-sixth of the globe's land mass. They constitute some one-half or more of the land in Japan, Australia, the Philippines, Afghanistan, Nepal, and Korea. Research on mountainous-area economies is vitally important to China's economic development but also meaningful to the entire world.

Formed as a result of geological movements over hundreds of millions of years, the defining feature of these areas is their elevation. Measurements show that temperature drops 0.8°C for every 100 meters above sea level, which means that places over 2,000 meters high are generally unsuited to growing many members of the grass family. Mountainous areas are characterized by low fertility, steep slopes, and soil erosion and accordingly are most suited to forestry, pastureland, and livestock production, not grain production. Certain policies since the founding of New China emphasized forestry and 'all-round development' of mountainous areas, but these were discontinued for a number of both subjective and objective reasons. There was a period when policies meant for the plains area were also applied to production in mountainous areas. This stymied economic growth and only exacerbated the fact that these are mostly poverty-stricken regions. People only 'woke up' and truly faced the problems after the Third Plenary Session of the 11th Party Central Committee [December 1978]. Faced with indisputable reality, the government began to realize that it should formulate production policies for mountainous regions in accord with local conditions. It should gradually change conditions by improving transportation, cultivating human resources, and taking advantage of local comparative advantages and self-development capacity by employing market forces.

Mountainous areas also constitute one of China's main ecological reserves. 'Production' in mountainous areas therefore absolutely must incorporate the requirements of soil conservation and maintenance of ecological balance. Given their elevation, these places are the fountainhead of many rivers. Their mantle of vegetation is the 'nursemaid' to the waters, meaning both forests and pasturelands. These must be conserved in order to protect soil and water resources and to prevent the effects of scouring erosion. Not protecting forests and pasturelands is leading to soil erosion, silting up of rivers, desertification, and climate deterioration. Research into proper economic use of mountainous areas therefore affects not only economic and social but also ecological efficiencies. As such, it is of major concern not only to our nation but to the whole of mankind. It deserves corresponding attention.

It is true that adequate grain in mountainous areas is a practical issue, but we have more ways to address this now than we did in the past. A scientific approach must be applied to farming on the very limited amounts of arable land, where intensive operations have the ability to increase grain output substantially. In those valleys that are suited to actual farming fields, in areas with slopes less than 25 degrees, small-scale drainage systems can be created to raise grain using terracing and dammed-up water. In the places appropriate for fruit orchards and edible oils, tree crops and woody-plant edible oil crops can be developed. In short, food production should never be abandoned wherever it is truly beneficial and appropriate to use the land for food. Inhabitants of mountainous areas will generally see an increase in income when they diversify their operations, however. With money in their hands, they can put more inputs into the land to boost their own local grain yields, but they can also undertake 'commodity exchange' to acquire grain from elsewhere. We must acquaint local people with the facts of history: our prior policy of 'opening up the wastelands' for farming, by destroying forests and pastureland, was a stupid policy and must not ever be done again. Rampant felling of trees is again occurring in some places. This criminal behavior must be punished resolutely according to law. All citizens must know that once ecological imbalances occur they leave a legacy of problems. It often is impossible to restore what used to be. We should constantly return to and reflect upon the lessons of history in this regard.

Mountainous areas are also a repository of mineral resources in China. Most of the country's more than 150 kinds of minerals are located here, and many of these rank in the forefront of world reserves. Mountainous areas also harbor tremendous supplies of alternative energy sources, including hydropower, wind energy, solar energy, geothermal energy, and other renewable energies. All these advantages present the hope for future economic development of the regions, but they must be approached in a carefully researched, unified manner. Any resource development must be implemented in a planned way. Rampant, 'blind' resource extraction must be prevented.

The investment of human capital into mountainous areas is of particular importance. Employing scientific methods, improving the quality of labor, attracting skilled workers, carrying out work-study programs, and training operational personnel are prerequisites for properly developing mountainous resources and economies. They are fundamental policies that mountainous areas should adhere to on a permanent basis. Right now, people in some mountainous areas are still in an arrested state of slash-and-burn farming. When production is so extremely backward, the first approach of policy must be to address ignorance in order to address poverty. Massive educational efforts must be undertaken. In areas covered by limestone formations (such as karst areas), people essentially live on top of rock outcroppings with no source of water and lack even the most basic means of survival. They should be encouraged to move out of these areas to places with job opportunities. Accordingly, we need to establish labor markets that implement labor mobility objectives. The quality of local populations is an important component of our research into mountain economies.

The book *China's Mountain Economies* (published by the Dadi Publishing House) focuses on a subject of intense concern to all of us: the development of China's mountainous areas. The authors wrote it with a target audience of grass-roots cadres in mind, as well as the general public. The substance and the style are highly individual and make the work a valuable contribution to the field. I recommend it to all. However, it should be noted that this is a newly emerging field of study and will require constant reconsideration and improvement. I hope that the comrades who participated in the volume will enter into wide-ranging cooperation with people nationwide, including experts, scholars, and practitioners. This is a field of tremendous importance, deeper understanding of which will require the efforts of all of us.

Note

* This is a preface written by the author for the book *China's Mountainous Economics*.

12 Reforms in socialist countries must pass the 'test of the market' and the 'test of democracy'*

(May 9, 1989)

As reform deepens, it will inevitably encounter differing understandings of how things should be as we move forward. We are already seeing the manifestation of this with respect to many issues, including the subjects of the 'market' and 'democracy.' Conducting research on the theoretical front is an absolute necessity right now, for a heavy price will have to be paid if our actions are not guided by theory.

Socialist movements have currently entered a 'new stage' worldwide. The bourgeoisie [class 'with capital' as opposed to proletariat, class 'without capital'] in the West are claiming that 'communism is finished' and that reform represents its 'death throes' and a 'retreat to capitalism.' Our understanding is precisely the opposite. Reform represents a new development of socialism, a new development of Marxism, and an advance that stems from serious reflection. Precisely what kind of problems has socialism encountered over the past few decades? One is that we have seen a tremendous gap between socialism as it has actually been practiced and our original ideals. In terms of economic efficiencies and the application of science and technology, socialism still cannot compare to capitalism. Second, in the course of carrying out class struggle, many countries, not just ours, mistakenly mixed together contradictions that belonged in separate categories. Neither of these problems is something inherently unique to socialism. They arise when the economic and political systems of any agrarian nation must be modified as that nation transitions to becoming an industrial nation. Inadequate systems must undergo a process of reform, of self-improvement, so that socialist societies are more democratic, dynamic, orderly, and efficient.

The first problems confronting reform are economic. Among those, the one of greatest import is whether or not socialism and market forces can accommodate one another. There are two schools of thought on the subject. One holds that the State should regulate the market, while market-driven forces should serve to guide enterprises. The other holds that the system can be half market-economy and half planned-economy – that is, have partitioning of different spheres of activity. This second partitioned structure requires two different operational modes, one that relates to money and the other that relates to power. The contradictions are thereby manifold and easily lead to a swapping of one for the other. Free-market economies do not exist in a pure state, even in capitalist countries. These too employy government interventions in markets. Whether or not socialism and market forces can accommodate each other cannot be answered in a simplistic way but rather requires matter-of-fact as well as theoretical substantiation. In this process, in the primary stage of socialism or perhaps even for a longer period, two key problems are going to have to be addressed. One is property rights. An ownership system that takes public ownership as 'primary' but allows the coexistence of nonpublic and diversified ownership is inevitable, but the relationship between private and public assets must be properly handled. Relying on motivation through 'distribution according to work' is not enough. Property rights must be clearly defined. The other key problem is competition. Enterprises must be forced to learn to swim in the seas of a commodity economy and must become exclusively responsible for their own profits and losses. Without a market, there is no competition. At the same time, competition must be regulated and observe certain rules.

Material resources are extremely limited in our country, which is a major constraint on economic development. China will have to work very hard to achieve a per capita GDP of US $2,000. Democracy of all the people constitutes the real superiority of socialism and should be made more manifest in all aspects of life. Passing the test of democracy is going to be even harder than passing the test of market. Not handling it properly may incur political turmoil. Put the other way around, not practicing democracy may incur even greater turmoil. Under the prerequisite that it serve the interests of stability and that it be subject to the constraints of law, implementing democracy is the best choice. We don't want to force people to set their sights only on material interests. We should emphasize social development and have them care more about political, cultural, and mental advancement, things that are more in line with our socialist goals.

Reform is the underlying current of our times, and, as the Communist Party, we should stand at the forefront of that current, guiding its direction and leading the way. The lives of all people in this country should be affected by the benefits of reform and by the benefits of the socialist democratic system and socialist market competition. 'Theory' should be a tool that provides the Party with the means to unite all the people. Once theory is grasped by the great masses of our people, it can become a tremendous material force for change.

Note

* This is an outline of a speech delivered by the author at a meeting on the study of socialism.

13 The objective of reform

Establish a market economy under socialist conditions*

(October 1992)

No matter what system a country adopts, transitioning from an agrarian to an industrial society is the prerequisite for moving from poverty to wealth and from an underdeveloped to a developed economy. China was an agrarian society all the way up until the 1950s, despite its many thousands of years of history. Transitioning now to becoming an industrial society is requiring a whole series of economic restructurings. As the shares of primary, secondary, and tertiary industries change in our economy, our resource utilization has to keep step, moving from labor-intensive to capital-intensive and on to technology-intensive modes of production. We have to reach a number of concrete goals if we are to be a 'moderately prosperous' society by the end of this century. As expressed through economic indicators, these are a way of marking our stages of progress in achieving economic restructuring.

Whether or not that restructuring is successful will depend on how well we do in allocating resources. Every country faces the problem of scarcity of resources. The input-output ratio of resources is a measure of the efficiency of national production and the amount of real national income. Every country similarly has to aim for the economic goal of minimum use of resources for maximum effect; all strive to optimize resource allocation. The two primary means of doing this are a planned economy and a market economy. Naturally, neither of these exists in pure form, in point of fact. The choice is between primary economic systems and which system is used as the main focus.

The traditional way of understanding things is that a socialist country is automatically in favor of a planned economy, since opting for a market economy is tantamount to wanting capitalism. In other words, the feeling is that a market economy and socialism are mutually incompatible. Nearly one-third of the world's people now live under socialist systems, however, so the question of incompatibility has left the bounds of theory and become a very practical issue in how a country makes its decisions. Socialist countries must determine economic policy, and they now have a wealth of contemporary experience that can help guide conclusions and actions. As a socialist country, China chose the route of a planned economy and gained hard-won lessons in the process. As Engels once said, 'One learns faster from the consequences of one's own mistakes than through any other means, and that rule can be applied to a great nation as well as to a great class.'[1] Given this, it may be useful to review our own experience for a moment.

1

We can see at a glance the distortions and rigidities in economic processes that are caused by a planned economy by looking at our own recent past. These distortions impede sustained economic development. The question, then, is whether or not a market economy is the necessary alternative.

Socialist structures in an underdeveloped country like China are necessarily immature, incomplete, and of an initial nature or 'primary stage.' Domestic components of our economy include both public ownership and a large number of individual laborers, private economies [businesses], and cooperative economies [enterprises owned by cooperatives]. The exchange of products between the State and these economic entities, and among these entities themselves, can only be via a commodity-money relationship based on equivalent exchange. None of these parties is voluntarily willing to accept the planned-product allocation used by the public ownership sector. The publicly owned sector itself cannot for long survive a product-allocation system that runs counter to the laws of value. As facts have proven, it too cannot survive under centrally controlled fiscal management of revenues and expenditures. Doing things in a way that puts good and bad performance on an equal level destroys any incentive in people involved in production and results in 'eating from the same big pot.'

All structures in modern economies are increasingly complex due to scientific advances. Those include industrial structure, as well as the structure of capital, technology, and products themselves. Product exchange is in essence an exchange of labor. To 'exchange labor' first requires an exercise in abstraction so that the labor can be given equivalent value. That abstraction translates all different kinds of quantities, qualities, and types of labor into a measure of value that can be exchanged. This is an insurmountable task for a planned economy. It can be handled by a market-economy structure, however, through the natural formation of price 'signals' that are relied upon by all parties to the exchange. The government can and must use what are primarily economic regulatory tools to influence the market, but it cannot replace the market. The government's regulation of the market must be aligned with the inherent laws of the market, for if they violate those laws, they will not be effective.

Markets have the ability to allocate resources fairly well. The unfettered exchange of all products leads all economic organizations to an 'open' state in which all factors of production are transferrable. The need for efficient return on investment can be met by diversified arrangements so that all elements are used properly: people can contribute all their energies, land can contribute all its fertility, and materials can contribute all their uses. Various individual efficiencies become the efficiency of society at large through the mechanism of market forces. The market mobilizes the comparative advantages of diverse parties into an advantage of overall allocation. A planned economy would find it hard to accomplish all of this.

Like everything, market functions are conditional. They face certain constraints, and they too are constantly changing. One can't assume that just because a market economy exists, it will resolve all problems – the 'market' is by no means omnipotent. Certain of society's communal needs, its long-term goals, its rules and procedures, still require governmental intervention or intervention by social organizations. They require communal agreement and compliance. The market is powerless when it comes to moderating the relationship between man and nature, or to resolving such problems as huge disparities in social distribution. Will transition to a market system in China trigger unforeseeable consequences for which we will have to pay a very high price? Will it cause such great turmoil that it threatens State security? Our country launched reforms first in rural areas, nearly 10 years before reform in the urban areas. During these 10 years, the rural areas and the 'open areas' along the coast simultaneously opened out a space in which the market economy was allowed to grow. Not only did family-operated agriculture grow in these areas, in the course of which 170 million households became independent commodity producers, but an effective industrial force appeared, namely town-and-village enterprises. At the same time, individual economies, private enterprises, and foreign-invested enterprises that had disappeared for a time now seized the opportunity and began to grow. All these changes were called forth by 'reform and opening up,' and all emerged against the backdrop of a market economy. In addition to creating soaring opportunities, they should now facilitate the smooth transition in systems and avoid or at least mitigate the mass unemployment and high inflation that often result from systemic changes.

Now is the time to transition to a full-scale market economy. Both urban and rural areas must strive for greater efficiencies. Our former State-Owned Enterprises should be impelled to become market participants and be solely responsible for their profits and losses. Rural areas must disengage from the remaining vestiges of a State-command purchase-and-marketing system and overcome the ills of producing in a way that is divorced from market demand. Town-and-village enterprises must meet the challenge of fierce competition, accelerate their technological transformation, expand their size of operations, and participate in international markets. Public finance must increase revenues and cut spending while implementing new systems. All these will require the cultivation of commodity markets, the establishment of new price-forming mechanisms, and the reinforcement of market regulation. At the same time, factor markets must be improved so that 'operators' have timely access to capital, labor, land, and services in order to participate in the restructuring of the economy. At this point, stubbornly maintaining a two-track system and putting off further reform is inevitably going to slow down the economy and perhaps even reverse it.

Two things must be done simultaneously in the course of systemic change: one is cultivating the market, and the other is transforming governmental functions. Neither of these can be neglected. It will be particularly one-sided and mistaken if the government clings to all its powers on the pretext that the market is 'not yet ready,' or if it takes the other course and relinquishes all powers, including its indispensable role of macro-regulation.

Our near-term objectives in transitioning to a socialist market economy should be as follows.

1. Cultivate a commodity market and change price-forming mechanisms. Consumer goods are currently in surplus, as well as some primary products, which is a sign of insufficient demand. Increasing demand requires an increase of national income. All signs indicate that any increase in personal income will take time. People are more inclined to save than to consume right now, which makes it an opportune time to liberalize prices. The buyers' market can be used to expedite the restructuring of different sectors and to force corporate production to become more efficiency oriented and less quantity oriented. As for rural areas, when grain prices are liberalized, farmers in grain-growing regions can sell their grain at market prices and can still make profits at the current input-output rate per *mu* of land. In addition, they can use their free time to engage in other kinds of business for some extra income.

2. Cultivate factor markets. Bank reform should be expedited, and financial markets should be launched. Accelerated liquidity of capital is a prerequisite for economic growth. To bring inflation under control, we must control the amount of money being loaned. To do this, allowing interest rates to float and enlivening the use of direct financing could be the most effective and practical tools. At the moment, our experiment in starting up stock markets is accomplishing several purposes at the same time. It is meeting the needs of people who want to save, and it is helping 'socialize' property rights. It is accomplishing a diversification of the investing entities as well as a diversification of where investment is placed. It is balancing out the ratio between savings and consumption. Under our current conditions, the stock market cannot be greatly expanded, but we should definitely not consider shutting it down just because we have a few problems. To improve labor productivity, both agriculture and industry in rural areas should increase the size of their operations, with funding coming mainly from the market. For this reason, we should develop cooperative finance and other forms of financing organizations. Shareholding systems are inevitable and are currently underway. We should promote legal-person control shares [shareholding by corporate entities], in particular, as a way to enable horizontal alliances and get beyond the 'walling off' of local economies [that has resulted from our vertical administrative structure]. We must also restructure the overall direction of investments and stop the persistent and wasteful practice of 'redundant' construction projects.

Labor mobility and the flow of technical personnel are beginning, to a degree, but require the assistance of legal regulations that have not yet been enacted. Farmers are now allowed to move among rural areas but not yet into cities. It is still necessary for certain large cities to control the number of their registered residents, but small- and medium-sized cities should gradually ease such controls. Rural people should also be allowed to establish development zones, industrial zones, and small towns with their own financial resources. Allowing mobility of rural people is one means of transforming a closed society into an open society. It is a means of allowing an exchange of resources among regions, as well as allowing some people to get rich first in order to enable all to become more prosperous. In this respect, the benefits outweigh the drawbacks, and mobility should be encouraged rather than obstructed.

As a factor for industrial construction, land is already being exchanged in a preliminary way, but since land ownership is not yet clearly defined, this market is far from being standardized. Arable land in rural areas is owned by the collectives and is contracted out [*cheng-bao*] to farming households for operations. We should extend the length of those contracts so as to confirm that the policy is stable. 'Use-rights' to land should be exchangeable, for compensation, so that we begin to have a market and the formation of market prices. This will ensure that investors receive compensation, and it will spur further division of labor and economies of scale in farming operations.

3. The role of government in a market economy: The government should take the courageous step of giving up all direct involvement in managing enterprises. It should implement a policy of separating out government administration from corporate management and separating out ownership rights from operating rights. It should represent the entire society in its macroeconomic regulatory functions and formulate rules of competition with which all parties have to comply. In the first place, the government should enact a property rights law that protects the rights and interests of all economic players from encroachment. Clearly defining ownership can reduce transaction 'fees.' The government should also ensure that market transactions serve the common and long-term interests of the entire society, and, to that end, an effective tax system and a policy regarding redistribution of national income should be established. Through consultations, the government should encourage and support society in coming up with the best operating systems. It should create the underlying conditions for the formation of a unified national market by undertaking infrastructure projects that benefit all. These include transport systems, communications, irrigation projects, banking initiatives, and so on.

4. Develop tertiary industries and promote urbanization. In economic modernization, the first step is to liberalize control over the flow of the factors of pro duction to the utmost degree. The second is to make available to everyone those services and facilities that can support the growth of improved tertiary industries. Although our tertiary industries are still relatively backward, by the end of the Eighth Five-Year Plan, we should aim for them to constitute around 40 percent of our national income. This is necessary, and I feel it is also possible. Cities are going to have to be the medium by which the benefits of tertiary industries are made available to all different kinds of production. Urbanization will also allow for savings in production costs. The expansion of China's large cities is not a sign of excess urban development – weighing things in the overall balance, our degree of urbanization is too low rather than too high.

5. We should not lose time in striding out into world markets. If we are to move toward a market economy, we must be able to adapt to changes in world markets. The world has undergone tremendous changes since World War II. Economic integration has gained momentum, and a worldwide division of labor has been taking place that is based on the principles of comparative advantage and comparative cost. Countries both depend on and compete with each other. The role of government is quite different in times of peace and times of war. During wars, a country's first priority is national security and winning the war, which necessitates more centralized control over the economy. In peacetime, the role of the market transcends national boundaries and is ever more expansive. Given market forces, whoever has lower costs and greater advantages will be able to play a more crucial role. In the past, economic trends were polarized: the capitalist world developed industry and the third world developed agriculture; one benefited and one suffered; one was civilized and one was backward. Today, the third world can make use of land and labor advantages to develop industry and participate in the global economic division of labor. The emergence of the 'four little dragons' is a reflection of this development. We must open up to the outside world, not only to our own internal markets, and the sooner we do this, the better. The successful economic development in open areas along our coastline proves that this is the correct course of action.

2

The most important aspect of China's experience as it pursues economic reform has been to combine reform with development and take advantage of their integration. In other words, development is being pursued through reform and should be in step with reform.

It is unrealistic to try to complete reform in a short period of time and with a one-off plan, as history has shown us in the past. Any miscalculation can cause economic stagnation and even a state of chaos. Reforms programs in the former Soviet Union and East European countries serve as a prime example. In China, we should focus on an ongoing process of reform, use reform as our constant guide, and not limit ourselves to emphasizing economic development alone. If we apply the same old system to trying to increase efficiencies, accelerate growth, and change our industrial structure, the results will be the same as in the past. Using the old tools for a new job won't work. If China continues to rely on 'extensive production' for economic growth – that is, pursues growth by pumping investment into simply producing more – we will not be able to avoid cyclical volatility, and both the idea behind the approach and the methods used will be unsuccessful.

Our reforms began in rural areas, as noted earlier. We first established new microeconomic entities, then introduced market mechanisms on this initial foundation, which led to the growth not only of agriculture but also industry through the creation of large numbers of town-and-village enterprises. These enterprises took advantage of the 'opening up' opportunity and prospered first along the coastal areas. By the end of 1991, the output of town-and-village enterprises accounted for one-fourth of China's 'national gross social product,' nearly 60 percent of the rural gross social product, and one-third of the national gross industrial product. These enterprises deserve considerable credit for their contributions. First, they provided employment to 22 percent of China's total rural labor force. Second, they helped balance out the two extremes in industrial structure – with heavy industry too heavy, light industry too light, large industries too large, and small industries too small. Third, they incubated the development of new business mechanisms. With these new ways of doing things, enterprises were able to break away from eating from the same big pot, having an iron rice bowl. They relied on themselves for retained earnings, for creating value-added, for growth, for self-restraint, for taking risk. They were highly self-autonomous. They were competitive enough to meet the challenges of survival of the fittest. Quickly becoming more competitive than State-Owned Enterprises, they became an external force that put pressure on those enterprises to reform.

China's old systems created highly entrenched groups of stakeholders through the formation of structures that benefited certain people. These people had preferential treatment in getting an 'iron rice bowl' – that is, having welfare and employment security, among other things. Because of these privileges, some people developed a kind of dependency that was detrimental to economic growth. On the other hand, the system also gave everyone, not just a few, a sense of security, the comfort of thinking that they did not have to worry about making a living, that they would be taken care of from cradle to grave. As we reform these old systems, we will bring about sharp social contradictions if we fail to consider vested interests and simply abolish systems abruptly. That is why reform must be combined with economic development. New mechanisms have to emerge in order to support and nurture new economic strength so that the old economy can be transformed through an incremental increase in assets. The transformation of large- and medium-sized enterprises in cities will inevitably face the problem of having to deal with redundant personnel. By any reasonable estimation, we must abolish the 'one big pot,' but at the same time, all these redundant people will still need to eat. Enterprises are going to have to enhance their corporate efficiency even as they give appropriate pay raises to their workers. When personal income rises, we will have to guarantee an adequate supply of consumer goods for people's needs. If we can develop new economic entities in the course of transforming the old economic systems, and use them to improve people's living standards and increase employment, we should be able to avoid or at least mitigate the risks of sudden mass unemployment and sudden concentrated outbursts of inflation.

Through market exchange, reform can guide our economy in the direction of openness, as opposed to the closed system of the past. Factors of production can begin to move and to recombine in ways previously unknown so that they self-allocate according to market demand. Scarce resources should naturally move toward effective utilization and achieve integrated and balanced efficiencies. A glance back at the entire process of humanity's social and economic development shows that it has moved from closeness to openness. The 'closed' nature of early humans related to their confinement in natural areas and to their familial ties to clan societies. By the time of 'slave society,' slaves became personally dependent on slave owners. In feudal society, laborers became dependent on land that was owned by feudal landlords. The reason capitalism was able to move in the direction of economic development can be attributed to the appearance of an economy that employed labor. Labor became a commodity that could be exchanged for capital. The accelerated flow of capital enlivened all factors of production and brought them into an 'open' state. However, this system of private ownership of capital also brought contradictions to the fore in terms of the 'socialized' nature of production and the private ownership of capital. Public ownership as implemented by socialism is designed to address this contradiction and this 'closed nature' so that economic development can enter an even more 'open' state. At present, however, we have not yet found a reasonable, workable way in which public ownership can be manifested. We are still in a process of practical exploration. In the industrial sector, 'public ownership' in China became State ownership, in which rights, responsibilities, and benefits were not clearly defined and in which the masses were unable to participate. When employees are both 'owners' and also 'employees,' how best can the two different identities be embodied in the structure of a corporation? When enterprises have to be responsible to the owners of assets, yet also have to preserve the power of operating independently, how can they assure that the two things are in accord? These questions have simply not been answered. In addition, our planned economy limited the autonomy or decision-making power of enterprises. To this very day, it has maintained a 'closed' system in which control is maintained in vertical or hierarchical relationships, with few horizontal relationships. Given this setup, efficient utilization of assets doesn't even come into the picture.

In China's rural areas, small-scale agriculture was turned into collective economies that required unified operations – i.e., were monopolized by the State. Specifically, this meant centrally controlled allocation of labor. In this respect, the system was similar to that of industry. Agriculture is quite different from industry, however. Land is spread out, spatially dispersed, while the energy of sunlight is also dispersed. These things cannot be concentrated into factories for the purpose of production. Applying an industrial model to the practice of agriculture was bound to fail. It not only prevented the ability to reach economies of scale in agriculture, but it threw away the great advantage of decentralized decision making by family farms. Moreover, centralized command over labor allocations was inappropriate for a country that has too much in the way of human resources and too little land. Unified labor allocations also threw away the chance to have diversified operations, and this was not something that could be made up for by collectives. We have consistently advocated following the principle of distribution according to work. Since traditional agriculture has a tremendous range of technologies, tools, tasks, and types of work performance, it has been difficult to establish any standards by which to measure 'work,' however. Over the course of 30 years of 'collectivization,' collectives have stuck rigidly to a 'work-point system' that imposed the worst features of egalitarianism on farmers. This naturally deprived farmers of any incentive, and production suffered as a result. One problem, therefore, was that farmers were not paid according to their investment of labor. Another was that their labor was 'closed off' from other external opportunities of employment. This not only took away any chance to earn very considerable amounts of income from diversified operations, but it delayed the division-of-labor process in social [mass] production. From within itself, agriculture was unable to bring forth secondary and tertiary industries that require a social division of labor. As a result, our agriculture simply failed to evolve out of a self-sufficient state, or at least a semi-self-sufficient economy, and move into developed commodity production.

The socialist economy that we aim to establish should have a high degree of 'openness.' It should be a modern market economy that has 'socialized' labor and socialized property rights, and we can only realize such a prospect through 'reform and opening up.' In the course of testing out a form of 'socialism with Chinese characteristics' over the past dozen or so years, we have made sufficient progress that I believe we can now say the vision of where we are headed is already being glimpsed by most people in the country.

Notes

* This is a speech delivered by the author at a symposium (excerpts).
1 *Selected Works of Marx and Engels*, Volume 4, People's Publishing House, 1972, p. 285.

14 Cooperative shareholding systems featuring land-to-shares conversion*

(January 1994)

China has selected four pilot locations for testing large-scale land-use operations. They are Shunyi in Beijing, Nanhai in Guangdong, Pingdu in Shandong, and Wuxi in Jiangsu. Each place is employing a different method, and each has its own merits. We hope these experiments will succeed, but we also allow them to fail, since failure is the mother of success. Any failure has tried out a certain path and found that it leads nowhere, thereby saving others the trouble of taking that roundabout course. Last year, Nanhai reported new results in its attempt to carry out large-scale operations based on cooperative shareholding arrangements. Preliminary results indicate that this path might lead somewhere. Since it touches upon what would be major transformations in how land is operated, as well as ways to protect the rights and interests of farmers, further experiments and work on all aspects must be done. In the following, I just want to point out some theoretical issues and some ways we might go about understanding these things.

1. The primary aims of the shareholding experiment are to define the structure of property rights in a publicly owned economy and to delineate the ownership of interests. For example, the land system must clearly define 'collective ownership' of the land, it must confirm and stabilize the right of a household to contract for use of the land [*cheng-bao*], and it should relax controls over the transfer of land-use rights. When farmers have land-use rights, it is necessary for them also to have the right of legitimate income off the land as well as the right of disposal. In reforming the system of property rights, specific arrangements should be made through multilateral consultations and negotiations among the parties involved and according to mutually acceptable conditions. Without direct participation of the parties, things will not work. When ownership of asset rights and interests is not explicitly defined, it is hard to define economic responsibilities and legal constraints. There are no legal grounds by which the parties involved can resolve the dispute together with the government and the judicial authorities. A shareholding system should not simply be used as a way to raise money. Rather, it is designed to explore how to establish a new system of property rights in a socialist country so as to meet the demands of the operating mechanisms of a socialist market economy.

Shareholding systems are not anything new. Their primary purpose is to optimize resource allocation through a market for property rights. The cooperative shareholding system should set its sights on breaking out of the way that our traditional small-time farming economy constrained free-flowing markets. At the same time, it should be sure to avoid creating new barriers to market circulation.

Everything should be done in accord with local conditions. If conditions are not ripe, a good thing may turn sour and even progress into becoming a disaster. A cooperative shareholding system that converts land into shares cannot be applied just anywhere, used indiscriminately. Whether or not Nanhai has the requisite conditions to carry it out should rely on specific analysis. It should only be done when things are very clear.

2. Nanhai began to introduce a shareholding system into agriculture in 1992, when land as a factor of production demonstrated its multiple functions. Guangdong was the first place to abolish State grain-purchase quotas, and accordingly farmers there had the right to choose by themselves what products they wanted to grow. Land productivity rose as a result, and farmers' incomes along with it. With economic development in the Pearl River Delta, capital inflows increased sharply. Since Nanhai was in a favorable geographic location, its land was soon transformed into industrial assets and used for nonagricultural purposes, while the thriving real estate market further increased differentials in rents. Given these changes, the scarcity of land became starkly apparent, which fanned farmers' expectations for higher returns. At the same time, the scarcity of land sharpened the contradictions in how income was distributed. For more than a decade, most rural laborers had already been finding jobs in nonagricultural sectors. This cut their interest in farming, but it also sharpened their awareness of the value of land. If we want to ensure continued agricultural development, we have to update the way in which we allocate and utilize factors of production, particularly land. All of these became motivating factors for implementing a cooperative shareholding system. The comrades in Nanhai seized the opportunity and introduced cooperative shareholding. This eased the contradictions that had resulted from high and low incomes off land, since people now owned shares of the whole, but in addition it paved the way to large-scale farming operations. It presented one way to avoid a possible decline of agriculture in the course of industrialization. Farmers who had withdrawn from farming and gone 'outside' to find employment were entitled to income off their equity and so were content to stay on working elsewhere. Those farmers who had remained behind were now able to focus on larger-scale operations.

3. The modern shareholding system originated in the corporate structures of capitalist countries. Those included limited liability companies and shareholding limited liability companies. Both economic forms appeared in the advanced stage of capitalism in order to be able to handle the socialization of production [mass production] and socialization of ownership [mass ownership]. In contrast, cooperatives were organized by small producers in order to prevent being exploited by 'capital' and retain their own competitiveness so as to combat the threat of 'larger eats smaller.' Marxism regarded shareholding companies as an internal self-regulating mechanism within the capitalist system. Cooperatives were regarded as an ideal state by utopian socialists, but Marxists saw them as a transitional form used by the proletariat after the proletariat had seized power in countries where numerous small producers had to be organized into a socialist system.

In China, using the shareholding system to transform publicly owned enterprises into modern enterprises, in conformity with a socialist market economy, represents a creative innovation. This is true particularly as the country moves more deeply into reforming its systems. In rural areas, shareholding systems represent a way in which town-and-village enterprises can clearly define their property rights, separate out government administration from corporate management, improve corporate mechanisms, and explore the feasibility of social ownership of collective economies. Individual handicraft trades, family industries, and family sideline occupations can all enter the market and form various kinds of alliances under the rubric of shareholding systems. In this past year, the systems have won general recognition and gained considerable practical experience.

4. Nanhai's innovation was to introduce the shareholding system along with co-operative systems into the agricultural sector. This move was of practical significance in what are now relatively developed regions. The labor force had migrated out of these areas in very large numbers, which precipitated the need to reallocate resources in an efficient way so that fewer people could operate more land by using more capital and more equipment. Some people preferred to stay in their homes but no longer wanted to farm, so community organizations took the initiative in establishing shareholding cooperative agricultural enterprises. They were able to accommodate various interests, those who had quit farming and those who still farmed, those who were represented as individuals and those in collectives. They found a rational way to delineate ownership of collective assets through allocation of shares. This represented a major advance over the previous practice, during the collectivization period [of the 1950s], when private assets were arbitrarily turned into collective assets without compensation.

5. The aims and organizational principles of these two different systems, shareholding and cooperative, are quite different, however. The problem becomes how to integrate and improve them in the course of the experiment. The aim of a company is to make profit, while a cooperative is a not-for-profit service organization. The primary holders of a company are shareholders who are not necessarily the employees of the company. Those shareholders can be both corporate entities and natural persons. The primary holders of a cooperative are its members, who both participate in labor and put in capital and accordingly have a dual role. As to decision-making procedures, a cooperative system uses 'one man one vote,' while a company uses 'one share one vote.' The share capital of a company cannot be withdrawn but can be transferred. The capital inputs of a cooperative can be withdrawn but cannot be transferred. Since a company is an alliance of capital, it is open to society at large. Shareholders of a company that is listed on an exchange are themselves liquid or exchangeable. The largest investor of capital is in a position to control a company, but other shareholders can manifest their own rights and powers by selling out their shares when they feel they are at a disadvantage. In contrast, a cooperative is a labor alliance formed by small proprietors, and so its membership is restricted. In order to prevent a few people from monopolizing the show, business procedures emphasize equality and democracy. Therefore, a cooperative is of a closed nature. We are a socialist country in which the exploiting class has been largely eliminated, but that does not mean that class differences have been completely dispelled. In the primary stage of socialism [in which China finds itself], private economies continue to exist, and foreign capitalists also enter into the picture. For this reason, our national legislation should treat these two, cooperatives and shareholding systems, differently. In setting up cooperative shareholding systems, therefore, we should be selective.

Corporate systems and cooperatives both have strengths and weaknesses. A system that blends the two to create a new form theoretically has the advantage of creating a hybrid that improves on both, but there has been no experience on which to draw in this regard. The Central Committee's No.1 Document in 1985 promoted 'shareholding cooperation.' After that, various places established service organizations that incorporated farming households into companies in order to help them enter the market. When people in Wenzhou [Zhejiang] raised money and set up companies as 'individual [*ge-ti*] companies,' they called them 'shareholding cooperatives.' In February of 1990, the Ministry of Agriculture issued 'Provisional regulations on the farmers' shareholding cooperative enterprises,' after which Zhejiang, Shandong, and Guangdong began to use the same term for their own experiments. Shareholding cooperatives have been implemented in many places by now, but the concept applies primarily to town-and-village enterprises.

Since China's rural areas were fully collectivized in the 1960s, the cooperative system in its original sense ceased to exist. Today, what people are calling a 'transformation' of our property rights system is in fact the process of implementing a shareholding system that restores some aspects of the cooperative system and retains some components of collective ownership. In most cases, the transformation results in ownership forms that are mainly shareholding in nature but that have elements of cooperative systems, or it results in cooperatives that have assimilated some elements of the corporate form. To varying degrees, both retain elements of collective ownership.

6. When establishing shareholding cooperatives under socialist conditions, we must take the best of both and avoid their defects. These entities should embody the following qualities as much as possible.

1. Openness. Members or constituents who put capital or labor into the entities should not be limited to local residents or the employees of the same unit. The enterprises should be able to raise funds from the market and should be economic entities with shares held by the public at large, including individuals, corporations, and investment organizations.

Entities should be market oriented. They should be 'in the market' with respect to property rights, and they should make sure their property rights are liquid.

They can use securities and other forms for over-the-counter transactions or for stock market transactions. They should actively participate in competition and rely on market forces to evaluate their corporate efficiency. Those with better performance will be able to attract shareholders, while poor performers will be ignored. Share issues will be able to draw together financial resources that are dispersed throughout society, and put them to good use for the company, while, at the same time, spreading their operational risk among all shareholders.

Does the fact that some shares will be held by individuals de facto weaken our system of public ownership? We should understand this issue in the way that Marx understood it: 'Assets of this type are no longer the private property of producers who are individuals, separate from one another. Instead, they are assets of producers who are working in union with one another, which is to say that they belong directly to society.'[1] There is nothing even remotely frightening about this.

2. Clear separation of two kinds of rights. Property rights should be delineated as one of two different kinds, namely ownership rights and use rights. The rights corresponding to those two, namely right to allocate capital and right to operate the business, should also be split out and clarified. As Marx said, 'In a shareholding company, [operating] functions have been separated from the right of ownership of capital.'[2] He also said, 'Labor management as a function is increasingly being separated from the rights of equity capital or borrowed capital.'[3] In our country, the shareholding system may be used to great advantage to address our problems of mixed government-business operations – that is, the problem of government administration interfering in corporate management. It should enable enterprises to operate independently. The hiring of senior management can go through an open process of evaluation. Selection of human resources will rely on competitive markets. The system will help us correct such problems as having power concentrated in the hands of too few people and having personnel decisions made on the basis of family ties.

3. Reestablish individual ownership. Marx said that, in a future communist society, 'Individual ownership should be reestablished on the basis of the achievements of the capitalist age, which is to say, on the basis of coordination and the joint possession of means of production that are produced from land and labor.'[4] So far, nobody has been able to interpret this sentence in any clear and precise way. What is quite clear, however, is that 'individual ownership' does not refer to ownership of 'consumption materials,' for the discussion of 'ownership' has never meant simply ownership of consumer goods. In a capitalist society, the working class in capitalist societies all were in possession of consumer goods, and yet Marx still labeled them the 'proletariat,' the 'class without assets.' When individuals possess shares, what they 'possess' is capital assets, but the same single asset is also both possessed by and used by others. This therefore differs from 'private ownership' as it was practiced in the Old Society.

When we talk about having publicly owned enterprises take on sole responsibility for their profits and losses, in the final analysis, we mean that the results of corporate operations must be borne by individuals. If interests are to be jointly shared and risks are to be jointly borne, the prerequisite is that individual economic interests must be clearly defined and made independent. This independence is both a stimulus to individuals and a restraint on public servants. In the past, individual members of our collective farms were wholly reliant on the collectives. Due to various constraints relating to the way our society developed, the collectives could not shuck off that relationship. A cooperative shareholding system allows individuals to own private property, which, to a degree, can be seen as an independent form of material security for the member of the cooperative. It can also be seen as a way to reduce the dependency of a person on the cooperative.

4. Spirit of equality. When implementing cooperative shareholding systems, the 'spirit of equality' that characterized the former system, and the value placed on cooperative members, should be retained and carried forward. Capital has a price, and the right of a given shareholder to income should be ensured. This is a market principle. Capital is created by labor and should be employed by labor and used in the service of labor. It should not become alienated from labor and used as a tool to rule over labor. This is the 'social outlook' of members of the Communist Party. Enterprises are owned by shareholders, but at the same time it should be said that they also belong to cooperative members or employees. The board of directors and the board of supervisors should incorporate legitimate [legally constituted] representatives, elected by the employees, who participate in decision making. The employ of senior management should be subject to collective evaluation. Any matter that concerns the interests of employees should be approved by a general meeting of the collective members. The system of 'one man one vote' and the system of 'one share one vote' should both be used.

7. When cooperative shareholding systems are set up primarily to operate land, the unique nature of land resources should be taken into consideration. Farmers are the creators of what gives land its value. Our Communist Party's 'program' for land reform harked back to the ancient Chinese phrase, 'the one who tills the land shall have his own fields.' In order to acquire the means of a livelihood, farmers waged a very long struggle for ownership of land. In the course of industrializing China, land was 'capitalized' and began to produce differential rents. These should be properly distributed. The implied sense of the household *cheng-bao* system, by which a family contracts for use of specified land, is that the right of land *ownership* belongs to the collective, while the right of land *use* belongs to the farmers. Only when land is actively cultivated by farmers will it produce income. Farmers are asking for corresponding compensation when they transfer their land-use rights, and this is both reasonable and understandable. Land is not portable, and shares are only a representation of income that can be received, a right to income. Allowing their transfer does not affect the common ownership and utilization of land. In short, land has been, is, and will continue to be a very serious issue that should be treated with the utmost caution.

Moving back in the direction of collectively operating land is another major change, following on the adoption of household contracting for land. It moves away from disaggregated, fragmented farming. Some comrades are saying that this is tantamount to taking land from farmers and putting it again in the community sphere and that therefore we should act with prudence. We should not turn a deaf ear to this opinion – if conditions don't indicate we need to change, then we should not arbitrarily change. Agricultural production is different from industrial production. Unifying the rights of ownership and operation in individual households is appropriate to most regions and useful in spurring agricultural development at the current stage. Any change should be based on objective conditions, and if those do not exist, then changing things is dangerous. We should also remember that the 'household economy' is quite different from the former 'small-scale farmer' economy. The latter was bound to break up and change, from small-scale to large-scale production, from self-sufficiency to commodity production, and from diversified family operations to a social division of labor. But this does not mean that family operations cannot produce economies of scale. When our macroeconomic policies change and the structure of employment in China shifts, both of which will be advantageous for concentrating land, different forms of intensified farming with modern methods will be undertaken by households as well.

If shareholding systems are introduced and land begins to be treated as a share right, we should make sure that the farmers' real income is protected, and we should also make sure that the share rights are complete, not partial. It is inappropriate for authorities to use share distribution as a 'administrative tool' that can be wielded to control whether or not farmers undertake family planning, to mete out punishments for crimes, or to try to influence other social behavior. Such things should be treated with extreme caution.

8. Some specific policy proposals:

The very first issue is the structure of property rights. Once the original fixed assets of an enterprise are assessed, and their original sources are identified, they should be treated according to the following principles.

A. The value of fixed assets that derived from the capital inputs of the townships, towns, and villages, as well as their increase in value, should be evenly divided and distributed out in shares among the individuals of the rural area. Withdrawing these shares is not allowed, but in principle people are allowed to transfer and to inherit them. If most people have objections to this principle, restrictive conditions may be imposed. Another portion of shares can be regarded as the public shares owned by the communities of townships, towns, and villages. While the communities of townships and towns may establish shareholding institutions holding control shares, village-level governments can establish welfare fund organizations to manage the income and uses of the equity. Corporate development funds may also be withheld from profits, depending on need.

B. In general, these entities will not have corporate shares. Corporate legal-persons cannot become shareholders in the same enterprises.

The second issue is the distribution of dividends or income from the share equity.

A. In principle, a company distributes profit according to shares and does not guarantee dividends. A cooperative can guarantee dividends, however, but not distribute profit. Dividends can be guaranteed only when shareholders still lack an adequate degree of risk awareness. When profit to be distributed exceeds 20 percent of the value of shares, however, dividend payments should be stopped. When shares have resulted from the conversion of land to shares, then no dividends should be guaranteed.
B. The ratio between distribution according to work and distribution according to ownership of capital should not be something that is a rigid rule. Payment for labor remuneration is included as a cost to the company and is limited to employees of the company. Distribution of profits benefits all shareholders. The two distributions are not the same.
C. If an enterprise is mainly of a cooperative nature, it can draw public reserve funds and welfare funds out of profits so as to manifest the policy of common prosperity.
D. Employee bonuses should be used to regulate the amount of remuneration for labor and should be an appropriate amount. They should not be used to pay out assets of the company, which damages the appeal of any stock offering. Currently, our greater problem is lack of capital, which should be an important factor in decision making.

9. Cooperative shareholding companies should be set up according to administrative districts. All citizens in the district should be cooperative members. Political power should be in line with the size of the corporate organization. Such issues as how to allocate income among industry, commerce, and agriculture and how to effectively separate out government administration from corporate management still require serious study. In principle, economic diversification that has already formed within communities should be maintained. A sound economic structure should gradually evolve. As growth moves in various directions, the economic structure should improve as the market plays its natural role.

Notes

* This is a speech delivered by the author at the conference on land shares in Nanhai City, Guangdong Province.
1 *Selected Works of Marx and Engels*, Volume 25, People's Publishing House, 1974, p. 494.
2 *Selected Works of Marx and Engels*, Volume 25, People's Publishing House, 1974, p. 494.
3 *Selected Works of Marx and Engels*, Volume 25, People's Publishing House, 1974, p. 436.
4 *Selected Works of Marx and Engels*, Volume 23, People's Publishing House, 1972, p. 832.

15 Reform of 'supply-and-marketing' cooperatives*

(November 7, 1995)

1. Stalled-out reform of our supply-and-marketing cooperatives is seriously holding back overall reform of our rural economy, and by now something must be done. Our actions should be considered in light of the country's overall process of reform, however. Problems in reforming supply-and-marketing cooperatives are similar to problems of reforming State-Owned Enterprises, but their status is quite a bit lower than that of State-Owned Enterprises. Reform of State-Owned Enterprises is rightly called an 'attack against heavily fortified positions' since it impinges on the interests of entrenched stakeholders, namely the governmental departments that are the very ones leading the reform. It also touches on a whole range of issues, including property rights, social insurance, investment guarantees, un-repaid bank loans, and triangle debt. In the rural arena, the 'heavily fortified positions' are the supply-and-marketing cooperatives. We must either storm these positions or admit defeat, for we can no longer put off a confrontation. The longer we wait, the more the problems pile up and the harder it is going to be to change. In point of fact, these cooperatives are State-owned commercial entities, not cooperative organizations. Farmers do not regard these cooperatives as their own, and if they are not reformed, farmers will cease to allow them to act on farmers' behalf.

2. Reforming supply-and-marketing cooperatives is an important part of overall rural reform. We should first have a correct understanding of the rural problems. In recent years, agricultural production has been just fine; the problem has been with our mistaken policies. Many people think that grain production has been tight, but, but in fact, China has imported almost no grain and has even exported some. Broadcasting hikes in grain prices stimulates speculation if it is not done properly. The value of mung bean futures currently comes to more than a dozen times actual production. Farmers are quite proactive when it comes to their own food, but they are less enthusiastic about growing 'commodity grain.' The fact that they are not enthusiastic does not mean there is no grain – most households have grain reserves. Farmers will not sell their grain if they don't derive real benefit from it, and right now the pricing system is out of whack and the market is less than perfect. Unreasonable prices and distorted market can be corrected – the problem is how to develop in the future. Nearly all the potential in the existing system has been realized, and it cannot grow to any real degree. If we are to increase our scale of operations, and set new targets, additional investment is going to be required. Rural areas now face huge problems in trying to expand production, including most importantly water resources. If the northern part of China is to increase output substantially, it must build more reservoirs. Yet, right now, dozens of cities in the north have trouble even getting enough drinking water. Another problem: surplus labor in rural areas means that places are densely populated, making it hard to carry out large farming operations. At the same time, anyone more educated and higher leaves for elsewhere – there is a huge migration underway from west to east and from north to south. Only the uneducated surplus labor is left in the rural areas. What areas hold the highest potential for our next rural reform? It seems to me that our efforts should be focused on revamping our system and our organization in innovative ways. In other words, policies still have potential to leverage substantive change. There is still a 'song to sing' in this regard, and I feel we should start with the land system and the market system. Further reform must use intermediary organizations as the 'medium' of the message, as the medium located in between farming households and the market. And the supply-and-marketing cooperatives are precisely the most effective, most fundamental, and most traditional 'medium' of all.

Reform of the supply-and-marketing cooperatives is designed to turn them into service organizations for 'self-service' by farmers, given that they have no means of 'self-protection' in the face of business that is undertaken by government officials and private entities. We are not against business being done by government officials and private entities, but certain unfortunate behavior and certain modes of competition have to be corrected. Falsification by private entities and businesses that are run as monopolies by government officials are improper modes of exchange. They violate the rights of farmers. When farmers have a self-service organization of their own, they will be able to access markets through their own channels. They can help crack the nut of the problem, which is why we should aim for farmers to set up cooperative alliances.

3. What is the rationale behind our introduction of modern modes of operating and selling into rural areas? One, it is designed to counter the inappropriate behavior of government officials and private entities by introducing modern self-service methods. These can help lower transaction costs, widen the radius in which farmers sell produce, balance out supply and demand, and level out volatility. In short, the aim is to enable farmers to raise their expectations. Cooperative organizations can be wide-ranging in substance and application. They can use such financing tools as bonds, futures, and financing of all kinds. All of these should be understood by farmers. Secondly, our aim is to ensure that farmers allocate their resources wisely, that they avoid the pitfalls and take advantage of all benefits. Accordingly, it might be useful to summarize the history of our supply-and-marketing cooperatives. We need to be sure that any such description is complete and does not leave out the defects. It should be explicit about what is correct and incorrect in the cooperatives, what is fact and what is not, what is helpful and what is not.

Supply-and-marketing cooperatives have gone through three distinct stages of development. The first was before 1953, a 'golden age.' The second was after 1954 when 'collectivization,' then the People's Communes, and then the Great Cultural Revolution turned the cooperatives into the 'Second Commercial Department' of the government. They were used as the vehicle through which the State monopolized purchasing and marketing. Cooperatives no longer belonged to farmers. Non-farmer employees became State-employed staff with 'an iron rice bowl.' The third stage was after the beginning of reform.

Our task now is to look at the course of this development and consider what aspects of cooperatives were good and what were not, what went wrong and what was correct. If we can pinpoint key problems, the relationship of these cooperatives with both the State and farmers will be easier to handle. First, we must be fully aware that these cooperatives are in quite a different situation now than what they enjoyed before. Farmers can operate independently, and they own their own resources, now that households are again the unit of production. Only when such independent farmers become their main force will cooperatives truly have 'members.' Secondly, under the new conditions, rural areas have not only ordinary farming operations but also diverse economic components and pluralistic industrial structures. Supply-and-marketing cooperatives can have far greater margin to operate in rural areas now, given the development not only of first but also second and third industries that have much broader operations and greater numbers of products. Third, farmers now have capital, in the form of real cash, and diversified operations. If cooperatives can capitalize on these three advantages, they can accomplish a great deal.

With room into which they can grow, supply-and-marketing cooperatives must now choose their own model for surviving into the future. They can learn from models undertaken in different countries, including Japan and Korea, France and Germany, Australia and New Zealand. We must identify the causes of the success and failure in all these places. One, we must study the relationships between those who are and are not Cooperative members and between for-profit and not-for-profit operations. Cooperatives are not supposed to make a profit from their members or try to maximize profits, but how should they treat nonmembers? If they don't make any profit, they cannot accumulate retained earnings. Second, we must understand how being independent is different from operating as agencies of the government. The State has to keep control over a certain number of commodities, and cooperatives must help it by playing a certain role, but cooperatives must never return to their old road. Three, we must study how specialized or how comprehensive cooperatives should attempt to become. They should be able to expand in the areas of planting and cultivation, particularly where market elasticity is high, such as fruit, non-staples, and tea. They can also pursue industrial diversification, such as agricultural vehicles, processing, housing, finance, specialized, wholesale, and futures markets. All these areas are market 'spaces' into which cooperatives can grow and increase profitability. Four, we must study the relationships between rights and shares. The system of 'one man, one vote' should not necessarily be upheld, and the principle of democracy should not impede the expansion of share ownership. Share placements should be encouraged, and corporate entities can also participate by becoming shareholders. But the question of whether or not there should be a ceiling on share placement deserves consideration. Five, the two rights – that is, the right to operate and the right to 'own' – of the cadres who currently run cooperative organizations should be separated. There should be a 'market' by which to select managers. Should members of cooperatives continue to elect grassroots cadres? Cadre selection by the [Party's] 'organization department' should be combined with or jointly undertaken by cadre selection by the market. The leaders of the specialized cooperatives should be chosen by farming members of these cooperatives. As they grow, supply-and-marketing cooperatives still have to figure out how they are going to finance themselves. They cannot establish banks at the beginning, but they may be able to establish financial investment companies.

In short, all these issues deserve systematic summarization and study. Once correct guiding principles are determined, supply-and-marketing cooperatives can streamline their workforces and decide that they are going to move forward on into a new future.

Note

* This is a speech delivered by the author at a theoretical symposium on the reform of the supply-and-marketing cooperatives.

16 Stabilizing the household contract system*

How to understand the 'two leaps' correctly

(January 1996)

How to handle the issue of land is something that has consistently been of major concern in our rural reform. How to set up and stabilize the system by which households contract for agricultural production is the question. In the decades prior to reform, our country experienced several cycles of debates on this issue. Eventually, farmers took action spontaneously, deciding on their own to replace the system in which 'people's communes' operated under unified command. Some county-level comrades, and also comrades at a higher level, recognized the correctness of this approach and supported it in certain areas during the difficult time of the 1960s. Because of this, these comrades were criticized, 'ousted,' and labeled as 'capitalist roaders.' At the time, just saying a few words in favor of 'contracting production down to the level of the household,' not to mention really advocating the system, involved intense political risk. History plays its own tricks, however, and dramatic changes in the 1980s enabled the change of our entire system as a result of this one breakthrough point, this issue of how to handle production on the land. The change was initiated by farmers themselves, who, in a collective manner that included everyone in the country, were the ultimate expression of 'learning through practice.' Naturally, this did not mean there was a consensus. Some people, for various reasons, were against the policy. Indeed, once the policy had been underway for nearly 10 years, and was proving its effectiveness, opposition developed that was of a very considerable magnitude. People who had originally run with the wind now tacked when the wind changed. They stopped supporting the policy and began to support its opponents. Certain of our comrades went among the people to hear their views directly. They sent back a message to central decision makers: farmers want to keep things as they are. They want a confirmation that this is a stable policy. Together with reactions from other sources, this message drew the attention of our leadership, who then made a correct decision.

Comrade Deng Xiaoping said once that change in the rural areas will involve two leaps: the first was in abolishing the people's communes and introducing the household contract system, a system that should be upheld for a long time. In the future, he said, there will be another leap that involves introducing economies of scale to farming and developing collective economies. He meant that this second 'leap' was very much predicated on the first: we should never misinterpret Deng

Xiaoping to mean that we should return to the mistakes of the past. The reason Comrade Xiaoping emphasized that the household contract system 'should be upheld for a long time' is because he foresaw that the second leap would be a 'very long process' in which farmers would be allowed to make independent decisions, operate independently, and develop commodity production in the context of a market economy. The 'rural household economy' during this period constitutes a rejection of the ruler-ruled relationship that existed in China's old feudal social and economic order. It is formed on the basis of equal commodity exchange. When New China was first established, the country abrogated this 'ruler-ruled' relationship and fulfilled its promise of 'land to the tiller of the land' through the land reform that was carried out under the leadership of the Communist Party of China. Shortly after land reform, however, China established the people's communes and introduced a system by which all purchasing and marketing was monopolized by the State. This occurred within just a few years, when economic conditions were still not ready for it. In the meantime, China also abolished all individual operations of farmers as well as all commodity-exchange markets. This had the effect of suppressing commodity production., The hope that forces of production would 'suddenly grow substantially' simply failed to be realized. A highly developed level of the forces of production turned out to be the prerequisite for establishing and consolidating a socialist system. Therefore, China, in the 1980s, launched reforms designed to improve its socialist economic system. History tells us that social systems never stop evolving. Rural reforms restored family operations, which should be stabilized for a long time, but the economic functions of household operations will change in line with division of labor and specialized production. Allowing households to make their own decisions does not mean advocating isolated operations and sticking to small-time farming as per a primitive economy. Both now and into the future, farming must have both centralized and decentralized aspects, just as property rights must have both 'specialized,' or individualistic, and 'socialized,' or mass, aspects. How these aspects are combined must conform to practical conditions; moreover, they must be explored, created, and chosen by the people themselves. While the Party's guidance is indispensable, it should not act against the objective laws that govern economic development. It cannot act against the wishes of the people. The Party should refrain from acting according to its own subjective preferences.

Note

* This is a preface written by the author for Yu Guoyao's *Collection of Truth Seeking*.

17 Adhere to strategies that allow for sustainable development*

(December 11, 1996)

1. Relations between man and nature

Humanity is and will forever be an organic component of nature, just as humanity is part of the flow of history. Ever since man began to make tools, however, he has changed the equation of human-nature interaction. In primitive times, tools were simple and incapable of causing much damage. As productive means advanced, with revolutionary changes in science and technology, man has increased his ability to govern nature and has begun deplete our precious storehouse of resources in an unmindful manner. Human life and social organization have both progressed remarkably, but at the great cost of disrupting any harmony between man and nature. In this process, nature's 'retaliation' against human destruction is increasingly apparent. The clearest indication is the loss of those natural resources most intimately connected to human life: land, water, and air. In my opinion, environmental degradation is now endangering human survival. At the same time, it is now stimulating people to reexamine their own development goals and search for new paths of development. Sustainable development strategies that began to appear in the 1980s represented a sea change of far-reaching historic significance. They recognized that allowing rampant exploitation of natural resources to go unchecked not only will not solve problems, but will cause further environmental damage and push humanity in the direction of extinction. There have been precedents. The extinction of dinosaurs and many primates ['advanced-intelligence species'] and the disappearance of Mayan and other cultures all had to do with environmental changes. Man is the most 'advanced' of advanced-intelligence species. Endowed with the ability to reflect and endowed with a 'will,' man is not reconciled to becoming extinct, but rather is determined to find ways to sustain and support his own life systems. Man therefore appears to have developed the self-awareness, or consciousness, to pursue sustainable development, which is an extremely fortunate thing.

2. Key factor: adjust the relationships among 'interests'

Having transformed the objective world to a considerable degree, humanity now must decide to improve its subjective world as well. In the past, we did all we could to utilize nature's resources, in the course of which we damaged nature and built up harmful consequences. If we are to mitigate these consequences, we must now summarize our experience and acquire rational understanding so as to improve our own behavior and move forward. In a philosophical sense, however, it is hard to go from being forced to undertake change to recognizing that we have choice in the matter, since freedom is gained only in incremental fashion. Despite progress, we have not yet acquired full understanding. In practicality, a subjective but very real factor exists in our current stage of social development that constrains the progress of human understanding. This factor arises from contradictions between the interests of different social groups. In its perpetual quest for a livelihood, humanity has formulated ways of organizing itself and producing things for itself that contain not only contradictions among classes of people but contradictions among interests of all kinds. One, for example, is that between short-term and long-term interests. Excess cutting of trees and overuse of pasturelands are perpetual examples. A second is that between internal and external interests. Factories dump waste into rivers and pollute downstream water sources that are 'external' to them. Developed countries use oil and timber resources extravagantly for their 'internal' use while acquiring those resources from underdeveloped 'external' countries at low cost. A third contradiction is that between the current and the next generation. The current generation consumes land and mineral resources in a predatory manner for its immediate needs while leaving the problem of depleted resources for those who come later. All these contradictions evolve into a contradiction between man and nature. Society and government must therefore address them in ways that are focused and that build systems or institutions that begin to draw man and nature back into a more harmonious state. Environmental protection is a matter of systems engineering. To establish the necessary scientific foundation for making policy with regard to sustainable development, we must integrate the research of and the measures that are applied by all the various fields of natural sciences, technology, economics, and law. All scientists and practitioners must work together on this.

3. Prevent good things from becoming bad things and stimulate the transformation of bad things into good things

Nature is a highly complex organism in the midst of constant motion and change. Human understanding of nature can only become a 'scientific system' after long and repeated experimentation, testing, and accumulation of practical evidence. The process of change in nature is a process of self-adjustment, some parts of which can be catastrophic to humanity. Not only are earthquakes, floods, plagues, and pests a recurring experience, but the diverse physical, chemical, and biological changes of the Earth affect human life as well.

In addition, due to its limited understanding, humanity often invites greater disasters upon itself when trying to prevent disaster. Examples abound, but a simple cause-and-effect case would be the attempt to kill rats. When we use chemicals to kill rats, we also wipe out the creatures that live on rats. Not only do wild things that eat rats then starve to death, but domestic animals that eat poisoned rats are themselves killed. Any series of deaths disrupts the biological chain. Another example: We increase agricultural production many-fold by using pesticides and chemical fertilizers. One *mu* of good farmland that used to produce only 100 kilograms of grain can now produce over 500 or even 1,000 kilograms. In the process, we harden and alter the composition of the soil, however, and destroy its natural granular structure. Floods are yet another example. We have yet to find a good scientific way to tame rivers. In ancient times, the 'Great Yu' is said to have learned a lesson his father's unsuccessful attempt to stop floods by building dams and diverted the water through alternative channels. This may be a myth, but Yu is still regarded as being successful. Nowadays, however, modern man is attempting to 'turn floods into hydroelectric power' by building massive reservoirs and canals. Not only is this causing a multitude of environmental problems, but it is 'turning water resources into water disasters' and beginning to trigger widespread opposition.

Everything has two sides. We must treat this truism in an analytical way since we can often forego some benefit in certain realms in order to gain more benefit in others. For example, humanity is in no position to stop typhoons in any event, but without typhoons, China would scarcely have developed agriculture. Typhoons bring on the rain necessary for nourishing plants. The appropriate response to typhoons is to strengthen forecasting abilities in order to reduce losses. Floods can similarly be called a disaster, but at the same time they dilute surface pollutants; they help form wetlands that breed aquatic species, nourish organisms, and regulate river water levels. The scarcity of land has lured people into reclaiming farmland from around the perimeters of lakes in order to increase agricultural output. What seemingly is a 'good thing' actually is not: It shrinks lake surfaces and blocks up natural water systems to the extent that some existing lakes, such Lake Dongting, are becoming mere rivers. The Yangtze River is consequently losing a vast flood-relief area as its natural flood-control systems are destroyed. A good thing is being turned into a bad thing. Nature cannot speak in its defense in advance, present all the considerations – instead it simply retaliates against humanity in the end. The disastrous floods that China experienced in 1995 serve as eloquent proof, and the lesson holds true in many other regards as well.

All human efforts in providing for ongoing life are a matter of 'practice,' or practical experience, and a matter of 'learning.' The most effective way to learn is to make mistakes and learn from them, on a regular basis. This kind of learning is what enables humanity to turn 'bad' things into 'good' ones. Some examples: In the 1960s, under the leadership of Comrade Mao Zedong, China formulated a 40-point document on agriculture. This targeted sparrows as one of 'four pests' that should be exterminated. Later, through practical experience, the scientific community learned that sparrows do not in fact eat much grain; indeed, they help preserve grain by eating those insects that damage grain. Preserving the natural enemies of certain insects is a better way to go about things than applying pesticides. Using natural forces to counter natural disasters utilizes the interdependency of the biological chain in service of humanity's production activities. Preserving animal life is often equivalent to protecting humanity itself. Accepting the suggestions of scientists, Comrade Mao Zedong ceased to call for the extermination of sparrows. Another example: Mining can be regarded as a good thing in itself, in order to gain useful materials. If mineral resources are not utilized in an integrated way, however, residual traces can contaminate water sources and harm human health. If they can be used properly and the 'intergrowth metals' can be recycled, a bad thing can become a good thing. Fishing is a good thing, but it can become a bad thing. Catching all sizes of fish in nets destroys the biological chain of marine life: Larger fish that eat smaller fish die out when all fish are caught, and marine resources are quickly depleted. Countries then sign international conventions to restrict excess fishing on the high seas and in coastal waters, turning a bad thing into a good thing. Such examples are beginning to awaken humanity to the issues. For the sake of its own survival and development, humanity must protect ecological balance, must change its established modes of development, and must find new ways for sustainable growth. This indeed has to become our comprehensive approach if we are to move in the direction of transforming the 'bad' into the 'better.'

4. The meaning of sustainable development

The Industrial Revolution began nearly 200 years ago. Since that time, our general process has been to 'reclaim' the environment, post facto, by following the course of 'first damage and pollute, then rehabilitate and reclaim.' That road has exacted a high price, but it has been very hard to take any other. Sustainable development differs from the aforementioned model in making environmental protection a prerequisite for each stage along the road. Each stage of development must lay a sustainable foundation for the next stage, unlike the way in which our current unbridled development destroys the conditions for sustainable development of the next generation. The reason replacing an old mode of development with a new one is so hard is that it not only requires restructuring production but also readjusting the vested interests of all parties. Once a given growth mode is established, it runs along a 'process' the way a train runs along a track. Switching rails can be so 'un-smooth' that it can easily overturn the entire train. The United States uses massive amounts of energy, for example, given its automobiles, farm equipment, plastic products, chemical products, and myriad of energy-needing devices, all of which constantly consume oil resources and, in so doing, also pollute the environment. Yet it is difficult for the United States to reduce energy dependency even a little bit, let alone fundamentally change. Worse yet, Westernization now means modernization. When 'later-to-develop' countries learn advanced technologies from the West, they also introduce a resource-consuming lifestyle into their own countries. Take cars: China does not have space to build more highways and parking lots, and having each person move around in his own car not only eats up space and energy, but also congests traffic. It is clear that China ought to focus on developing high-speed railways and public transport. This now appears extremely hard to do, however, given a multitude of variables. Such variables notwithstanding, China must carry forward in the face of difficulties of which it is only too aware. It must pursue a rational course and prevent the unfavorable side effects, including cultural problems, associated with modernization and industrialization.

Developing countries share a special problem, namely population explosion. By 2030, the world will have 8 billion people. Some 70 percent of these will be in the developing world. With so many people and such scarcity of capital and technology, it is highly likely that developing countries will follow the same old path that industrial countries took in the course of their modernization. They will try to harness the environment first and then reclaim it later, rather than addressing problems in sustainable fashion as they go along. China must break away from this approach. Prevention of environmental damage must come first. We must blaze a new trail for sustainable development and create our own innovations, and we must start it now, within the final years of the twentieth century.

There is only one globe, and environmental protection is a global issue. Damage to the environment by any one country affects the environmental quality of all neighboring countries. On this issue, all countries are bound by a common cause and must weather the problems together.

While developed countries will have to bear more of the costs of protecting the world's environment, developing countries must carve out new paths and explore new modes of economic growth. They should pursue growth by relying more on science and technology and human capital. They must conserve the two major factors of land and capital; they must squeeze out all available money for scientific research and for education. They should impose fines or other legal sanctions on environmental polluters in order to ensure harmony between economic growth and social development. No government can solve the problems unilaterally by formulating an ideal plan. Systemic factors should be introduced to turn technological advances into inherent and automatic mechanisms for appropriate growth. Governments and institutions should put environmental protection on a 'track' that is driven by nonhuman systemic factors.

First of all, we must clearly define property rights so that all resources have their 'owners' and their legally responsible agents and management institutions. Nobody should be allowed to eat for free from the same big pot. Everybody should have an awareness of his role and should participate in market competition, work hard to innovate in different directions, increase technological inputs to develop production to boost income, and thereby use resources in a manner that is rational and effective.

The world economy is just entering into global integration, which means that larger markets can enhance economies of scale, with resources being used on the most efficient basis. Comparative advantages can be exchanged; factors can be mobile. Developing countries should make use of international capital to develop their national economies and should make use of their advantage in human resources to participate in an international division of labor. They can balance out their disadvantages with advantages, avoid excess consumption, and thereby reduce environmental damage.

The 'market' uses price signals to reflect the scarcity of resources. Compensation for use of resources stimulates improved utilization. Fresh water used to be used like air in the past, for example, no money required. From now on, it must be recognized as something that is incredibly precious, and we must adhere to policies that require compensation for its use. Oil prices will continue to rise in the future, which will stimulate efforts to find substitutes through science and technology, and this too is an inevitable trend. There are areas beyond the reach of market mechanisms, however, for which government intervention is required. That is why individual countries enact their own laws and the world community enacts common laws – to protect the environment and harmonize local interests with those of the greater good.

5. The fresh water and land crises

Through the Rio Declaration on Environment and Development and the Twenty-First Century Agenda, China pledged its commitment to the world: protect the environment and ensure sound social development. This is a great challenge to China, with its huge population and limited resources. When averaged out over the population, all resources are scarce, but this is particularly true with respect to land, water, and oil. Land is nonrenewable. Solutions to the scarcity of land can only be found by improving and increasing inputs. For example, instead of expanding the acreage of arable land, biotechnology and genetic engineering must be used to create new varieties that are more resistant to draught, cold, and salinized and alkaline soils. Microbial enzyme technology can be used to substitute organic for chemical fertilizers, turn stalks into feed, prevent land degradation, and reduce the energy consumption required for grain production. China's amount of arable land has declined dramatically due to population growth and the construction activity associated with industrialization and urbanization. We must conserve our remaining arable land, and we need special legislation and strict enforcement of the laws in this regard. Other resources have greater alternatives. Oil can be partially replaced with wind power, solar energy, tidal energy, and other renewable energies. Clean nuclear fusion energy is also a promising source. The more difficult problem is water. Agriculture must have water. China has 600 million *mu* of irrigated farmland, which consumes 80 percent of all our water resources. Energy development also needs water. One ton of water must be pumped out for each ton of coal that is extracted. Water consumption by factories, humans, and animals is also on the rise. China's north and west regions are currently facing a crisis in water supply. Off-the-cuff calculations indicate that about 20 percent of the extractable groundwater has already been extracted. In some parts of the northwest region, no water is found when a well is dug down as far as 1,000 meters, and around 70 million people are currently drinking contaminated water. Excess forest felling has greatly reduced spring and stream flows and dried up certain rivers. In 1995, the Yellow River stopped flowing for 133 days. According to calculations, we will need to 'replenish' 60 billion cubic meters of water by the end of 2000 just to meet minimum demand. The south-to-north water diversion project involves monumental engineering efforts, yet it is still unclear whether or not we will achieve the desired results. We should step up our efforts to develop inexpensive seawater desalination projects. In the meantime, we should strictly enforce rules on paying for water. We should make the industrial use of recycled water much more widespread, as well as techniques that conserve irrigation water.

Water-control methods should be improved, and the Yellow River is the prime example: By the time it reaches the areas between Shaanxi and Shanxi Provinces, the Yellow River is already carrying 1.6 billion tons of silt. When yet more reservoirs and power stations are built upstream, the riverbed will be even more elevated, and flood control will become even more difficult. In some reservoirs, silt is accumulating at such a pace that runoff water has to be used for power generation. The Sanmenxia [Three Gorges] dam is a case in point. The reclamation of the Yellow River is a mega issue. In some places in Gansu and Shaanxi Provinces in recent years, farmers have been building cisterns by themselves to collect water in the fall for use in the spring. These cisterns can both irrigate crops and trees and help reduce mud and sand siltation into the Yellow River. This appears to be working but is by no means a fundamental solution. Restoring vegetation coverage is another important measure. Our country has many areas with limestone formations that are dotted with underground caves. Any precipitation flows on down into the caves, while most surface areas are covered by bare rock, and any soil covering comes to three centimeters at most. The scarcity of water contributes to scarce soil and scarce foliage. When we talk about reducing poverty by relocating local residents, we are referring to places like this that are now totally unsuited to human habitation.

The extent of forest coverage in our country is only 13 percent, while desert encroachment in the northwest region is ongoing. Desertification has been spreading at an annual rate of 2,460 square kilometers in recent years, bringing the total area to 1.689 million square kilometers. We must therefore undertake major development of forestry since with forests come improved water resources. Forests also help prevent wind and flood erosion and contain desert encroachment. In protecting the environment, one of the first things we must do is to plant trees and create forests.

6. Bright prospects

Since the early years of the twentieth century, ecologists have been warning that if humanity continues with the lifestyle and production modes that were adopted after the start of the industrial society, humanity will inevitably face a shortage of resources and intensified ecological degradation. We must take these warnings seriously. A minority of scholars believe that the best option is to restrict consumption and simply live a kind of primitive utopian life. This of course is unrealistic.

Humanity cannot but depend on nature for its survival. This is simply an unchangeable law. While respecting the laws of the objective world, however, humanity can transform the realm of nature and improve the quality of life. In the course of doing this, it can transform its own understanding and improve the material measures it uses to control natural processes. This too is something we can predict. A path of sustainable development must be found for social production, and I believe it is a path that will be found.

We have seen birthrates dropping in some developed countries and the start of protecting the ecological environment. The minds of government leaders in all countries are coming to grips with the fact that there is only one globe. They are beginning to take joint action in protecting the environment and coordinating economic growth and social development in their own countries. We have also seen that the scientific community has made and will continue to make breakthroughs in biotechnology, genetic engineering, and the research and development of new energy sources. We are convinced that the global development of the market economy will help various countries to complement each other in resources and advantages and correct the waste of resources to a degree. Market economies, if backed by national legislation and international agreements, can help correct the lopsided and selfish focus of humans on immediate concerns at the expense of future interests, the emphasis on immediate demand at the expense of the needs of future generations. Market economies, if backed by national legislation and international agreements, can spur humanity to become both more self-encouraging and more self-disciplined.

Will a focus on 'sustainable development' prevent developing countries from catching up with those that are already more advanced? History indicates that any country that emphasizes improvement of its social systems and the development of science and technology can catch up from behind. Britain took 360 years to double its economy, while the United States, Germany, and Japan took a much shorter time to reach that goal. The later the starting point, the faster the process. The Four Asian Tigers accomplished the task in 20 to 30 years, while doubling economic output took China only 18 years after the start of 'reform and opening up.' This has been called the 'China miracle,' but it only proves that a scientific revolution can bring about a 'leap-forward' effect. Lines of demarcation – boundaries – among different countries still exist, and China must definitely become richer and stronger instead of remaining poor and weak. The prerequisite for this is that it uphold a socialist agenda that adheres to Chinese circumstances. If China is to pursue sustainable economic development, it must take advantage of knowledge that already exists, even as it further develops science and technology. In social development, we must consider all-around development of the human being. We must focus not just on economic growth and on overtaking other economies, but on the mentality or 'thinking aspect' of our human resources. We must 'catch up from behind' not only with regard to economic growth, but also with regard to social progress and the protection of nature. The Chinese people are quite capable, and I believe that the prospects look pretty good.

Note

* This is a lecture notes delivered by the author at the LEAD International Training Course.

18 Contracted family operations should be kept stable for a long time*

(October 27, 1998)

Rural issues are eternal issues. They involve so many factors that 'ultimate truth' is not something one can ever hope to find. Instead, we learn through constant practice.

Not long ago, a foreign friend asked me how our productivity can be so high when a family farms only six or seven *mu* of land [1 *mu* = 0.1647 acres, so 7 *mu* = 1.15 acres]. He said, 'The whole world is pursuing economies of scale in agriculture, while China is advocating super-small family farms. We all thought China would be importing food, yet by the trade figures, China is still exporting some.' I responded that we too had been advocating economies of scale and believed that family operations were too small. At the end of the day, though, we still rely on them. Looked at purely intuitively, we see that family operations operated throughout history and still exist today and that although the scale is smaller now than it was in the past, productivity is higher. People's communes were larger in scale but lower in productivity, and as a result, everyone decided to get rid of them. Family operations now are smaller but more productive, so everyone has enough to eat. The main consideration is that farmers now have the right to operate independently, something they never had before. When we began reform and opening up, we also implemented a market-economy system that allowed farmers to make decisions on their own. They were no longer subject to outside constraints and allocations; they became their own masters. In brief, first, market competition and equal exchange stimulated the enthusiasm of the producers, investors, and laborers. Second, farmers now have long-term land-use rights, so they are motivated to work hard and build up a surplus. With a surplus, they have the ability to create yet more surplus and to expand their personal wealth. All of a sudden, rural areas are bubbling with able people and entrepreneurs. All of this is due to the power of the market.

During the stage [of socialism that we call the] 'New Democratic Revolution,' China must establish socialist public ownership. 'Establishing public ownership' implies that private ownership still exists, but as we establish 'public ownership as primary,' we still intend to retain small-time farming operations for a long time to come. Our current stage of 'collectivization' is also a form that retains small-time private ownership. The reason China must undergo this period is due to the very long time that our country existed under a feudal system. Ours was a feudal society quite unlike the independent city-states of ancient Greece or the feudal lord system or manor system in Europe. Ours was a society under the unified control of an imperial structure, a society in which 'the entire realm belongs to the emperor.' Family operations existed, but farmers did not have stable land ownership. The emperor of each dynasty introduced a different form of managing the 'fields,' but, at the end of the day, each emperor could arbitrarily take over those fields. He certainly did not exist to help protect farmers' property rights. The first emperor of the Qin Dynasty introduced the *shoutian* system, in Wei it was *tuntian*, in Western Jin it was *zhantian* system, in Northern, Sui, and Tang it was *jingtian*, in Northern Song it was *guantian*, and in Ming and Qing it was the *jietian* system. In all these systems, China's form of feudalism never included any rules or decrees for protecting private property. This was quite different from the way in which feudalism operated in Europe, where Roman Law and later the Napoleonic Code were part of a long tradition of protecting the rights of individuals. In China, farmers were always dependent upon others, emperors and landlords, or 'patriarchs' if landlords were not available. (In Guanzhong, for example, 'where landlords did not exist,' as the saying went, there was feudalism nonetheless under the rule of patriarchs.) This very long tradition of dependency persisted even after we were successful in confiscating the land of landlords, unseating local despots and gentry, and setting up our own new form of government. We eradicated the old power structure, but we were not successful in eradicating the old traditional consciousness of Chinese farmers. The profound legacy of feudalism was too hard to root out in any short period of time. Dependency as a cultural trait continued: The relations between monarch and subject, between father and son, the 'three cardinal rules and the five constant virtues,' continued to fix people in specified positions relative to one another. This tradition made them continue to be ideologically conservative and consequently insensitive to the stimulus of a commodity economy. Chairman Mao Zedong was right when he said that the business of a small-time farmer was unable to jump more than three feet high.

In the [earlier] Democratic Revolution, we realized the principle that 'the one who tills the land shall have his own fields.' We were unable to realize the emancipation of the minds of those who tilled the fields, however. That process takes longer and involves two elements. One is reliance on the market economy and 'equal exchange' to motivate the creativity of farmers and erode their conservatism. The second involves reliance on democratic politics to ensure mass participation and collective decision making and to instill in farmers the realization that they are masters of their own affairs.

China's 'people's commune system' [established in the 1960s] abolished both private ownership and any vestiges of a market economy. The system was first and foremost all-inclusive: everyone who reached the age of 18 could join, but at the same time it was a closed system in the sense that, once you were in it, you had no freedom to get out. Second, having abolished the free market, the system took away all rights of farmers to choose what they wanted to do with what they produced.

We have now restored 'family economies' and the market economy. At the same time, [in the bigger picture] we are still situated at the 'primary stage of socialism' and still need to learn the hard lessons of the Democratic Revolution. How is China to develop socialism given that it is both a backward country and an 'Eastern' country in terms of its cultural heritage? The answer is: not from textbooks. We must rely on practice and learn the lessons of what we have experienced, positive and negative, over the past 20 or so years of reform. In 1980, an old comrade told me that we should not even dream of using this crazy system of 'contracting output quotas to individual households' in order to solve the problem of food. He said that even Chairman Mao Zedong failed with the grain issue, despite mobilizing every single person in the country. In fact, we can solve the problem, and it involves changing the traditional mentality of our farmers. It involves relying on the market economy, on organizing things differently, on having farmers make decisions by themselves. We can turn traditional farmers into modern farmers and traditional agriculture into modern agriculture. People generally talk about 'taking advantage of public for the benefit of private.' What we are talking about here is 'taking advantage of private for the benefit of public.' This means exploiting the market economy and the private economy in the interests of socialism, within acceptable policy limits. As to how far we are going to allow the market economy and private economy to develop, that is a debate that needs to be deferred until the appropriate time in the future. The reason is that socialism requires the realization of 'all-around human development,' and all-around human development requires economic progress, mental progress, and political progress. All of those things are our initial task.

The fact that 'super-small' household operations can be highly efficient is not because the 'small' is superior but because the fact of systemic change contains its own impetus. The size of operations should not be small forever, and we are definitely not saying, 'the smaller the better.' Size can be a matter of both large and small at the same time, depending on circumstances.

Beyond the issue of size of operations, the more basic problem with China's agriculture is the disparity between a massive population and a tiny amount of land. This is a problem that will be with us for many years to come, and it will affect farmers' income for years to come. Our first priority in addressing the problem of income is to proceed from practical conditions and alleviate the weight on farmers by protecting price levels, increasing investment and capital construction, and replacing what are now known as 'fees' with what rightly should be 'taxes.' A key element in this will be confirming the 'negotiating status' of farmers, their right to their own voice in the process. It may be that having people who 'eat State-supplied grain' [i.e., cadres who are State employees] can indeed speak in the interests of farmers, but as a system it would be better to set up such things as farmers' associations so that farmers begin to manage themselves. Our second priority is to develop rural enterprises and to accelerate the process of urbanization. The long-term solution to raising the income of rural people is to enable a shift of people toward urban areas for employment. Small cities and towns should be the main medium for this process, and small- and medium-sized enterprises should be the focus, not large enterprises. Smaller enterprises have tremendous vitality. They account for 98 percent of the total number of enterprises in the United States and 91 percent in Japan. If we fail to develop small- and medium-sized enterprises and small cities and towns soon, urban–rural contradictions will only build up and haunt us in the future. In Longgang, in Zhejiang Province, farmers are doing remarkably well by constructing whole cities with their own capital. Concentrating people in such cities is conserving land while it helps develop tertiary industries. It enables farmers to enjoy the benefits of industrial society – including, most importantly, an education.

One final point. I fully commend and support the decision of the Party's Central Committee to keep land contracting as a system unchanged for the next 30 years. I do not think that the possession of equal amounts of land will or should be maintained forever. The 'equal amounts' that households are contracting to farm right now is merely designed to seek equity at the starting line in the competition of a market economy. Inequities that will definitely arise from ongoing competition cannot be solved by having government authorities 'adjust' land allocations. That will severely affect the long-term expectations of farmers. If they think that their land will be adjusted once every three to five years, their property rights will be destabilized to such an extent that they will be unwilling to make investments in the land. Real adjustments must rely on the marketplace, including the market for land. Giving the farmer a share of land means giving him a share of land rents, which is both the means of making a living and a form of employment security. Preventing him from seeking employment outside his native place, or taking back his land once he leaves his native place for employment, is not a way to solve the problem. If a person wants to work elsewhere, and make a bit of money from an 'outside' job as well as his contracted land, that is fine. We should maintain our commitment to his contract for 30 years. The amount of China's overall land is not going to change, whereas our population continues to grow – from 1.25 billion right now, it is expected to reach 1.6 billion in the future. Trying to achieve absolute equity with respect to the amount of land per farmer is therefore impossible. We can only assure that the starting line is fairly equal. In the future, we must use other tools to achieve equity, including social security systems, transfer payments, and taxation. In the future, some people will suffer and others will gain; some people will become richer and others will become poorer. Other solutions will be found for this kind of polarization, for land reallocations alone will not work. Development is of paramount importance. We must have development policies that are reliable – that is, stable – and we must seek to resolve the problems we are bound to encounter through expanded growth.

Note

* This is a speech delivered by the author at a theoretical symposium marking the 20th anniversary of China's rural reform held by the Ministry of Agriculture.

19   Farmers should be 'free men'*

(December 15, 1998)

1. Since the 1940s, the world economy has itself been undergoing reform and adjustment. China's rural reform is both a continuation of our internal social changes over the past decades and a whole new systemic innovation that grew up to meet the trends of this world development. This second development has had the effect of further 'liberating' our farmers by correcting certain distortions arising from past changes and by releasing the entire rural economy from its previous isolation.

We must be very clear about one thing. The direction in which China's reform is moving includes changing the operating system by which we functioned, changing the ways and methods of socialist construction, changing specific structures, and pursuing innovations in both our systems and organization, but it does not include changing the ultimate goal of socialism itself. Those who think we are abandoning socialism and replacing it with capitalism are wrong, but those who think we are making only minor adjustments and not systemic changes are also wrong. We are not going to change the fundamental system, for that fundamental system is socialism. Socialism aims to liberate the forces of production, and we will not give up the goal of common prosperity.

2. Why must we carry out reform of rural areas? Our past practices ran counter to the wishes of the people themselves, the farmers, and to the fundamental requirement that socialism improve the forces of production. The Central Committee of the Party first promoted 'taking the path of collectivization,' and the farmers acquiesced. After a few years, farmers found that they had neither freedom nor enough to eat. They asked if output quotas could be contracted down to the level of individual households, all the while maintaining the collective system. The answer was no, that such a practice would be tantamount to 'taking the capitalist road' and going against socialism. Farmers later asked again, the answer was again no, and this process then continued for over a decade. Quite a few cadres [in administrative positions in rural areas] went ahead and contracted output quotas to individual households anyway, and quite a few were singled out and punished as being 'rightists' or 'rightist opportunists.' Back then, not only did we refuse to listen to farmers, but we proceeded against their proper interests. Ignoring the principle of 'distribution according to work,' we set up people's communes that mandated 'large' and 'public.' Egalitarianism was triumphant. For example, due to material scarcity, we had to earmark 50 percent of harvested grain for distribution according to the number of people or people would have starved to death. At the same time, there was no incentive to work, and production kept on going down – we entered a vicious cycle of extreme egalitarianism leading to declining agricultural production leading to ever more intense egalitarianism. In the end, we simply had no alternative but to accede to the people's wish to have individual households contract directly for agricultural production quotas.

At the end of 1978, after the Third Plenary Session of the 11th Central Committee of the Party, our [Communist Party] thinking began to liberalize on many issues, but with respect to this issue of contracting farm output to households, we refused to budge. We felt that output quotas could be contracted to groups, but not to households – going it alone was still strictly prohibited. At the time, we were able to resolve many issues, including rehabilitating people who had been 'unjustly,' 'falsely,' or 'wrongly' sentenced in the past. The process was called opposing the 'two whatevers,' and we managed most of the 'whatevers' properly, but we still failed to address this problem of rural agricultural production. Real reform in rural areas did not in fact begin until after the Central Committee of the Party issued Document No. 75 in 1980. This Document permitted poverty-stricken regions with a total population of 200 million people to experiment with 'family-contract responsibility systems.' These were essentially various ways of dealing with production that farmers themselves had come up with as a result of handling their tiny 'private plots.' Yields from the private plots were multiples of what they were in collective fields, which inspired farmers to apply the same techniques to larger areas of land once they were allowed to do so. The process evolved – it did not happen all at once, for it went from 'contracting labor,' to 'contracting output,' to 'all-inclusive contracting.'

3. China's rural reform, which has been going on for 20 years now, has focused on two fundamental aspects. One has been reform of the ownership system, and the other has been reform of the planned-economy system. Ownership reform modified the ownership relationships of what were formerly 'people's communes.' Basically, we devised a way of operating land that was still publicly owned: Land was still 'owned by' the collectives, but it could now be 'operated' by individual households, under contract. Simply put, 'ownership' belonged to the collectives, while 'use rights' belonged to the farmers. At the same time, we replaced the planned-economy system with a market economy. Before reforms, the State purchased all surplus farm products and then redistributed them among everyone in the country in a State monopoly system. Farm products were sourced according to quotas placed on producers and supplied to consumers by the State according to plans; farmers had no right to decide on how their own production would be used. We are currently gradually liberalizing trade and opening up the market for agricultural products to allow farmers the freedom to deal with their own products as they wish. This 'goal' as set by the Central Committee of the Party has not yet been fully realized. At present, we are following a two-track system, with planned purchases and market trading going on in parallel. Except for grain and cotton, the prices of other farm products are set by the market. Even though [grain and cotton] are not yet liberalized, our ultimate goal of marketizing farm products remains unchanged.

4. Our rural reforms have made astonishing progress, but there is a great deal of potential still to be realized. We must work further to bring farmers out from under the shadow of both feudal society and a 'natural economy.' During the long period of feudalism in China, farmers were fully dependent on the powers of emperors, landlords, and patriarchal societies and developed no capacity of their own for independent action. The family operations that we are now advocating are designed to turn farmers into independent commodity producers who can trade with society as they wish, who are solely responsible for their profits and losses, and who seek their own growth. Subject to market forces, they can form alliances as they wish to carry out business. In the past, farmers' groups based on collective farms were indeed 'alliances,' but they had little or no autonomy, which should now be changed. Farmers must have the ability to join up and work with each other, not only in 'alliances' but with full 'autonomy,' in order to participate effectively in market competition and to support one another in case of problems. They should not have to fight single-handedly or fall prey to the strong. The process will be, first, to allow farmers to have independence and become 'free men,' then for them to form 'alliances of free men.'

With respect to the current situation, farmers still do not have full opportunity for independent development. They lack full freedom to participate in markets, and they lack the right to move where they want in order to take jobs. Their autonomy with respect to how they operate is highly fragmentary. We are deepening reforms step by step, but it is highly desirable to move out from under this transitional period as soon as possible.

Once farmers have full autonomy over how they operate land, plus the freedom to engage in market operations, the next step is democratic rights: we must ensure that they fully enjoy the political democratic rights to which they are entitled. This should be manifested first in expanding the right of farmers to self-governance. Township and village cadres should be chosen through direct democratic elections. Secondly, farmers should have their own organizations. If local governments impose arbitrary fees on people, or infringe upon their interests, farmers should have the ability to negotiate on their own behalf, to protect themselves. They should have their own representatives or agents who work on their behalf. Right now, the Central Committee of the Party is highly aware of the need to reduce the burdens imposed on farmers, and the media is also speaking out on behalf of farmers, but farmers themselves do not have their own representatives for direct dialogue with the government. For a long time, our 'household registration system' has prevented farmers from moving from one place to another, but in fact it is impossible to prevent the mobility of people. Right now, a 'surplus labor force' of over 200 million people needs to flow from the countryside into cities to get jobs. This is to be supported: On the one hand, when farmers work in cities, they settle down and become urban residents, which is good. On the other, their migration into cities reduces the pressure of too many people working the land, and farming is thereby enabled to turn to economies of scale. Households can begin to operate tens or even hundreds of *mu* of land [0.1647 acres per *mu*, so 500 *mu* would be 82 acres, for example]. Increased labor productivity and improved use of technology will gradually take hold. Efforts are underway to revise the household registration system, and we hope that this problem will be resolved in an appropriate manner quite soon.

In sum, once farmers have the right to economic autonomy or economic decision making, they should have the corresponding political right to democratic decision making. All forms of discrimination against farmers should be abolished so that they become people who enjoy the full rights of citizenship. It is quite insufficient to think of farmers merely as suppliers of farm products; we cannot focus our attention only on how much grain, vegetables, and meat they provide. As Karl Marx himself said, the communist society of the future must be an alliance of 'free men.' He also said that communism refers to all-around human development, not only in an economic but also in a political and cultural sense. Every farmer must receive an education. While elementary education should be universal, vocational education should also be developed, and more farmers' children should become graduates of high school and college. The society of the future will be a knowledge economy, and agricultural development is going to rely on science and technology. That means training personnel, which in turn means improving education. Farmers should become laborers who at the same time are knowledgeable and cultured, able to compete, people who start the race on an equal footing. We are just in the process of moving toward that goal.

5. Maintaining stability in the system of contracting out operating rights to land is not the same as saying that land cannot be transferred. Farmers should be allowed to transfer their operating rights to land – that is, their land-use rights – and they should be able to do it for compensation. Some farmers who have gone to work in cities are willing to hand their land over to other people for operating, but they are not willing to pass it over to the local [Party] 'committees.' They fear that if they lose their city job, they may have to come back and find they are now without land. Allowing farmers to transfer land with compensation can give those working in urban areas a sense of security. The rents derived from their 'compensated transfer of land-use rights' is something equivalent to an insurance policy.

In 1999, the Central Committee of the Party decided that land contracting would remain unchanged for 30 years, the land ownership would be clearly defined, the land contracting rights would be kept stable, and land-use rights would be liberalized. This is a good system and should continue to be implemented for a long time under a 'legalized' structure – that is, one that operates under legal guarantees. Under market-economy conditions, we are against the practice of constantly using administrative measures to adjust the land operated by farmers. It is also not good practice to adjust land in such an egalitarian way that a share of land is given to a newborn child and a share of land is cancelled when a person dies. The original purpose of egalitarian distribution was to ensure a fair starting point. From then on, differences in development and economic income are natural phenomena that cannot be corrected by administrative means. Only when farmers are allowed to operate land independently will they maintain a sense of responsibility toward it. Knowing that they can receive income from the land allows them a form of ownership that is measured in a discrete period of time. As to what will happen in 30 years, Comrade Jiang Zemin has said that when the 30-year deadline arrives, the system can be extended if everybody wishes to do so. This is designed to make the property rights system a long-term one, and it should be recognized that it does not stand in opposition to our socialist system. In order to strengthen their economic status, farmers may still form cooperatives or other entities that reflect their own interests. This great conceptual change [of extending the validity of the contracting system] does not reflect the understanding of just a few individuals but is embodied in a Decision of the Central Committee of the Party. It will greatly stabilize the entire countryside as well as help ensure sustainable economic development.

History develops, and so does Marxism. Not recognizing that fact will eventually lead to divergence from the will of the people. If people try to predetermine solutions for such major issues as full-scale social reorganization by basing their opinions on works of Marx and Engels that addressed specific conditions of over 100 years ago, they will fail. Even more problematic is if they base their judgments on their own personal preferences. If they try to force solutions in a mandatory way simply because they hold power in their hands today, they will in the future be doomed to failure. One of the great contributions Marx made to mankind was to shift the theory of socialist development from a Utopian to a scientific approach. Marx and Engels consistently refused to describe specific models for socialist societies. Engels once said something to the effect that 'we are believers in constant discovery, and we do not intend to impose ultimate rules on humanity. You will not find even the trace of any details or predictions about the future in our writings.' In China's agricultural system, family operations are bound to change. As to how they will change, we can only say: things separate, they decentralize, and then they come together again. Beyond that, we leave the rest to future generations to figure out.

Note

* This is a speech made by the author in an interview with *Beijing Observer* reporter Wu Shiyi.

20 Sustainable utilization of water resources*

(March 11, 1999)

1. Water resources pose a massive problem for China – one that is also going to be hard to resolve. The difficulties lie first in understanding the problems, before even getting to the point of trying to solve them. It is therefore good that we are holding this meeting, gradually coming to a common understanding as we discuss things.

2. China is a water-scarce country. Total resources are estimated at something over 2.8 trillion cubic meters, which comes down to 2,340 cubic meters per capita. Data from the Ministry of Water Resources puts China sixth or seventh in the world in terms of total resources but behind 100th place in terms of per capita water possession. The lack of water is felt more strongly in the north than it is in the south. Water is indispensable for industry, agriculture, and daily life, and it is necessary for humans and animals. Therefore, the demand is enormous. By some calculations, the per capita need for water in China will be 6,000 cubic meters by the year 2000, so the discrepancy between what we need and what we have is huge.

As we discuss water today, we should recognize that water is not only a 'general-resource' issue but also a major economic issue. If not properly handled, it may evolve into a political issue. Disputes over water have been going on since ancient times, but the battles are getting fiercer by the day. Not only is China seeing a rise in disputes over water, but foreign countries are as well, and the disputes are even leading to war.

3. The following reasons are behind the very serious problem of water in China.

First, water is unevenly distributed. Southern China, which accounts for over 30 percent of the country's territorial area, has 80 percent of its water resources. The northwestern and northern parts of China, which account for 64 percent of our territorial area, have less than 20 percent of water resources. The provinces of Shaanxi, Gansu, and Ningxia in the northwest region and the Huaihai region in the north have arid regions that cover 3 million square kilometers. Some of these places are not only arid but also extremely cold, and the availability of water in some ethnic areas determines the question of human survival.

The second factor is environmental degradation. Recently several comrades made an inspection tour of the sources of the Yellow River and visited nearly 20 counties and cities as part of the research. Some areas are suited only to grasslands. Since local authorities encouraged the inhabitants to raise more sheep, an overabundance of sheep have now decimated the grasslands, causing soil erosion. In the middle reaches of the Yellow River, far too much water has been diverted, exceeding the capacity of the Yellow River to replenish it. In the 1950s, a total of over 10 billion cubic meters of water was being diverted from the Yellow River on an annual basis. That figure has now risen to 30 billion cubic meters. The water diversion project in Shanxi Province is just one example. Mining of coal in the past caused groundwater depletion, which has severely affected the availability of drinking water in the city of Taiyuan. By now, it is not even possible not to divert water to the area. Meanwhile, in southern China, land reclamation of areas around lakes has dried up 540 lakes from the original 2,500.

The third factor is pollution. In these instances, water that is available is either totally unusable due to pollution or is too low quality to be used for most purposes. Out of 600 cities that use neighboring rivers as their water source, more than 90 percent are using water that is polluted to different degrees. About 58 billion tons of pollutants are discharged into waters each day, making many rivers uninhabitable to aquatic life. Today, drinking water has become a problem not only to human beings but to domestic animals.

The fourth factor is policy. In the northern areas and especially the arid regions where total water supply is insufficient, environmental degradation is resulting from the lack of unified water distribution mechanisms and the lack of scientific methods for water management and water use. For example, groundwater gets depleted when surface water is used up, upon which people unscrupulously begin to draw water from deeper levels. This ultimately causes an irreparable water deficit. In the Hexi Corridor [Gansu Province], water diversion projects have created many man-made oases but in the process have destroyed more natural ones. In order to prevent water seepage, people line ditches with plastic material or cement, which damages the riparian ecosystem along the banks as well as prevents replenishment of groundwater.

For a long time, we advocated the construction of reservoirs. In 1953, when I was transferred from the Central-South Bureau to the Rural Work Department of the Central Committee of the Party, Deng Zihui was chairman of the department. Everyone was tremendously excited about having Soviet experts plan the construction of the Sanmenxia Reservoir. The Rural Work Department prepared a speech for Deng Zihui to deliver at the National People's Congress. Chen Boda read it and commented that it was not descriptive enough, however, so he added a poetic sentence to the effect that the Yellow River would soon be flowing clear as a bell. The Great Hall of the People erupted in tumultuous applause. And what has happened since then? The reservoir has been declared useless due to the siltation problem. When a reservoir dams up water, it also dams up silt. When a river is allowed to flow naturally, it carries that silt away. To this day, we have not resolved this fundamental problem of our reservoirs. Without reservoirs, however, and with only 50–400 millimeters rainfall, one *mu* of farmland can at most produce 100 kilograms of grain. But if irrigated with diverted water, the output of the same farmland can be as high as 500 kilograms of grain. The dilemma is that reservoirs increase yields, but they also increase silt accumulation. Some people are now opposed to building reservoirs, but sheer opposition alone will not solve the problem. The key is to research and arrive at better solutions.

4. What is our way out of this dilemma? It seems to me we have two choices: either find new supplies, or reduce consumption. Water conservation remains essential, but we must make sure that conservation efforts cover the entire river basin, from upstream to downstream. We must give proper consideration to the water needs of daily life, industry, and agriculture, but we should place equal importance on the needs of the ecosystem. In the past, this major consideration was neglected, and it should now receive more attention. In some places, animal husbandry should be stopped and pasturelands should be restored. Farming should be stopped and the land should be planted to trees. Planting trees and encouraging forests is an effective way to conserve water. Different arrangements should be made for areas that have different amounts of rainfall, whether 50–100, 100–200, or 300–400 millimeters. These arrangements should take into account the number of people in the area, the number of livestock, and the most suitable crops. Any slope of over 25 degrees is unsuitable for growing grain. Grain was in short supply in the past, but that is not the case now. When Comrade Zhu Rongji visited the northwest region, he said that grain growing should be stopped on steep slopes, local residents with insufficient food should be relocated, and forest felling in the upper reaches of rivers should be banned. I approve of these observations. We should firmly implement Zhu Rongji's ideas and, in the meantime, we should make proper arrangements for the life of farmers and forestry workers.

In arid regions, local people are now using a method of storing up water in the fall, when it is available, for use in springtime. Meanwhile, a foreigner recently told me that he was willing to establish a factory in China to produce pedal pumps for use in small rivers and small wells.

Just now, we heard Buhe [vice president of the National People's Congress] say that the price of water is of key importance. Public water sources, such as the water of the Yellow River, should be distributed in a planned and supervised way by the Yellow River Committee. Any water that is used must be paid for. Water used for industrial and agricultural uses must be treated, using new pollution-cleaning technologies, and then recycled, and the price of water should incorporate those costs. Only when water prices are raised to appropriate levels will water-saving technologies be used.

Diverting water from the south to the north is inevitable, and sooner or later we will have to take this route. If we aren't looking out into the future, we will have problems in the short run. There is a clear danger of having rivers in the north dry up, and when that happens, it would be well to have alternatives in the works. Water can be diverted from the south along both the central and western lines.

Some comrades propose that nuclear explosions be used to attract water vapor to the Qinghai-Tibet Plateau. This is a bold idea that would require huge investment and carry unknown risks. Therefore, water and ecological experts should be organized to carry out earnest studies and then come up with proposals. I believe that once we have a clear understanding, we shall have a solution. Meanwhile, our comrades at the Ministry of Water Resources are saying engineering-based water conservancy should evolve toward resource-based water conservancy. This represents a major advance in understanding, which I thoroughly support.

Note

* This is a speech delivered by the author at a meeting on water resources.

21 Use the economy to motivate people, and use democratic politics to unite people*

(October 1999)

1

Deflation is a monetary phenomenon. Does sluggish domestic demand originate solely from monetary tightening? If so, it should be resolvable simply by issuing more money. Having done this, and not resolved the problem, shows that it derives from other causes and that we should analyze it from a more systemic perspective. Even a proactive fiscal policy, coupled with monetary policy, cannot expect to produce immediate effects, 'to see the shadow of the pole the minute the pole is set up.' Our GDP used to grow at 8, 9, 10 percent a year and has now dropped to 6, 7, 8 percent, but this is still not so bad. It's acceptable.

Changes of historic proportion are beyond the ability of any one individual to modify. On the one hand, man himself creates history, but, on the other, man's behavior is subject to history's constraints. We have to abide by that rule: in going for 'more, faster, better, and cheaper' with respect to building the economy, if we go only for 'more and faster' at the expense of 'better and cheaper,' we will find ourselves just correcting all the mistakes in the end. We eliminated private ownership, and we now have to restore it. In a specific stage of history, private ownership is a necessary element of the social structure, not something that any one person created and not something that 'man's will' can eliminate. When it still accommodates development of the forces of production, there is a reason for it to exist. Until certain other elements are sufficient to supplant it, it will not exit from the stage of history, and if it is prematurely dismissed, it will simply return. Our experience over these years has taught us that the ownership system cannot be 'all one color'; it has to be 'variegated' at the primary stage of socialism. It has to utilize public ownership as the dominant mode but still retain private ownership. Realizing this is simply a matter of accepting the facts. We should treat the issue of development and growth in a similar fashion.

2

Our outstanding macroeconomic problem right now is sluggish demand. The government has therefore adopted all kinds of measures to stimulate domestic demand, and I believe that in time demand will pick up under the impact of these correct policies. The process of letting go of the command economy and moving toward a market system is bound to take time in such a huge country. People's expectations have to change, along with other adaptations. How we encourage this change is what we now need to focus on in our research and our policy. Since the issues lie mainly at the level of systems, we need to prepare ourselves to address two great challenges: one is the test of adopting a market system, and the other is the test of adopting democracy. If we are to pass these two tests, we must use the market system to motivate people, and we must use the democratic system to unite people.

When we talk about using the market system to motivate people, we mean that economic growth must be pursued through increasing production, and this requires a freely competitive environment. A market economy is a competitive economy. Market exchange is a spontaneous economic phenomenon that is intrinsic to human society. The market functions to evaluate product scarcity and give out price signals according to conditions of supply and demand. It guides resources in the direction of rational allocation of goods and thereby serves as a stimulus to producers to create income.

Market competition brings with it disparities in growth. These are inevitable but must be kept from going to extremes. This can only be accomplished through continual growth, a constant increase in the forces of production so that the majority of people benefit, the middle class becomes a majority, and overall social equity is maintained. As this occurs, a few people will continue to live in poverty, and it is imperative that we carry out our work of poverty alleviation properly by establishing an effective social security system. In the meantime, we must also uphold an ownership structure in which public ownership is primary, while diverse economic components develop in tandem, so as to pursue all-around social and economic development.

3

In parallel with the market economy, we must use democratic politics to unite the people. People's needs are not entirely economic. They need to be able have free choice, to participate in their own governance, to become more cultivated human beings. Our country is a democratic republic with 'laborers' as the primary component. People themselves should be the main force in determining the direction of major State policy. People are 'natural,' but they are also 'social' beings, and personal development relies upon the development of society at large while, at the same time, the 'free development' of mankind is predicated on the 'free development' of individuals. A democratic country must create a free and democratic environment for its people and encourage its people to seek their own emancipation. In the meantime, it should draw together views of all kinds in forming a unified will, a system of law and order, and the commonly recognized 'rules of the game.' Therefore, if we are to build 'socialism with Chinese characteristics,' we must reform not only our economic but also our political system. It is true that we already have a realistic form of democratic political process as expressed in our people's congress, but this is not good enough. In addition to democratic elections, it is very important to have mechanisms that provide checks on power, for they can prevent the current regime from ruling in an autocratic fashion, making dictatorial decisions that abuse power. The economic, cultural, and political traditions of all countries are necessarily different. Their democratic political systems also differ as a result, and the world cannot mandate uniformity. Nonetheless, democratic generalities exist in the midst of particularities, and these should be expressed in all countries, no matter what kind. Democratic systems are a tremendous globalizing current of our times. During the transitional period to communism, a 'people's democratic republic' and local autonomy are necessary choices. During wartime, we found that contradictions between ourselves and the enemy were paramount, and therefore we were required to limit the scope of democracy. We are now in a period of peace, however, with internal contradictions being paramount, and it is consequently imperative to expand the scope of democracy. We must mitigate contradictions among the people and unite the majority. China is a socialist country, and the Communist Party of China is the ruling party. The ruling party can consolidate its leading position only when it wins the broadest support from the people. Only when both the market and democracy are put on a sound basis will we be able to hope for 'stability under heaven.'

4

Since the Third Plenary Session of the 11th Central Committee of the Party [December 1978], now almost 20 years ago, China has maintained a two-track system that incorporates both a planned and a market economy. In reform's initial stages, we first addressed rural land issues and aimed at stabilizing the major problem of farmers' livelihood, which was the correct approach to take at the start. In terms of urban reforms, we focused on the 'contracting system' for enterprises, and, since we lacked a nationwide market, market information was sketchy, and competition was unequal, we concentrated on growing the non-State-owned sector. People all said that this was 'incremental reform.' The non-State-owned sector included rural enterprises, foreign-invested enterprises, the 'individual-economy' sector [ge-ti], and the 'private-economy' sector. By the time this force had grown to account for over 40 percent of the country's GDP, it was being called 'a new army making a sudden appearance,' also referred to as 'the deferred release of the suppressed forces of production.' People now began to say that this was 'gradual-advance reform,' although this term was woefully inadequate in describing the implications of the kind of growth we were seeing.

The negative side effect of emphasizing this concept of 'gradual advance' was that it prolonged the existence of the two-track system. The two-track system contains both monopolistic and competitive elements. As a result, it has triggered certain problems. First, it has distorted prices and thus impeded the rational allocation of resources. Second, it has led to rent seeking and hence to corruption. Third, it has impeded free circulation of product inputs, which has destabilized the monetizing and marketizing of the economy and negatively affected the growth of a commodity economy. Distorting factors have become 'causes' for 'results,' which has brought on a vicious cycle. The way to resolve the problem is, in brief, to accelerate and deepen reform.

Reform inevitably involves a readjustment in special interests. It is rare that everyone is satisfied with the results. Reform allows for 'trial and error' and should be bold, for it incorporates a learning process. Strategically, we should not be afraid to tackle problems, but tactically we should take them seriously. We should dare to explore and dare to move forward.

5

By now, it has become necessary for us to do a number of things.

First, we must provide ways for non-State-owned enterprises to receive financing. We must rally our forces in reorganizing our various forms of financial institutions, including non-State-owned – non-banking, local, and 'private.' We currently have four major State-owned banks. Given the huge number of non-State-owned enterprises, it is hard for those State-owned banks to finance both non-State-owned and State-Owned Enterprises. Essentially, State-owned banks are now unwilling to grant loans. I specifically asked a loan officer of the China Construction Bank about this. He said he loaned out RMB 100 million last year and was very afraid it would not be paid back and that he would be held responsible for his entire life. I asked him how much he was accustomed to loaning in the past. He said RMB 800 million a year. He was unconcerned in the past to loan out 800 million, while today he worries about loaning out 100 million.

In the past, the non-State-owned financial institutions serviced or were the counterparts of the non-State-owned enterprises. We had over 400 'trust investment companies,' in addition to 'cooperative funds,' 'credit cooperatives,' and 'investment companies.' Then came the 'real estate fever,' and money was in short supply. All these institutions attracted investors by offering super-high interest rates, then loaned it out for even higher interest. Some loaned massive amounts to people who simply made off with the money, which led to a run on the institutions by depositors. A financial debacle was the result, which led to stringent financial controls. Strict financial discipline is absolutely necessary, but, at the same time, non-banking financial organizations must be allowed to develop. Restrictions create a market for going around them: we must realize that illegal, high-interest-charging loan sharks fill the space when legal organizations are not allowed to exist. Qualified institutions should be permitted, if they operate under the strict and effective supervision of the People's Bank of China. New institutions should also be allowed to develop under controlled conditions.

Second, it has become imperative that we reform the way we handle our grain operations. Long experience has now proven that we are incurring a loss in the range of hundreds of billions of RMB through State monopolization of the grain trade. As the restructuring of rural production proceeds, we should make the grain trade subject to market forces. The greater the liquidity of a commodity, the higher the efficiency with which it circulates. When there is only one buyer, only one entity serving as 'operator,' circulation is inadequate and information is scarce. This can amplify cyclical fluctuations in production and make problems of buying and selling even harder to manage. Moreover, the State has to cover the costs of the four and one-half million people currently on the payroll for operating our grain trade, which pushes up operational costs. This [grain-trade] department also keeps its own interests in mind, which affects its behavior. Now the State Council has decided that low-quality grains such as early rice spring wheat will cease to enjoy 'protective prices.' This represents an advance from the policy of 'unlimited purchase,' and I hope that the reform will go even further. The Central Committee of the Party has explicitly said that agriculture has arrived at a 'new stage of development,' that farmers' needs have shifted from 'getting enough to eat' to 'earning more income,' and the Committee would like to see farmers producing higher value-added products as opposed to low-quality grain.

One day, an old comrade said to me, 'Food is everything [heaven and earth] to the people. With grain in hand, people's minds are set at ease. And indeed, why not? The more grain people have, the better.' This comrade was unaware of the fact that that old saying, 'food is heaven and earth to the people,' does not hold true for all eternity. Things were not easy to handle when grain was scarce, but after 1984, when we had so much grain we couldn't sell it, things did not get much better. Farmers are hurt if grain sells at low prices. In the final analysis, agricultural products should rely on prices that are determined by market forces as the best way to guide production. It is going to be necessary for the State to use its 'risk funds' to build up grain reserves and use those to level out market fluctuations. It would be even better if grain quotas could remain at fixed levels for several years.

The third thing we must address is urbanization. People have been calling for 'urbanization' for years, and finally we are seeing some results, for the Planning Department is beginning to consider the issue. Still, there are debates about whether emphasis should be placed on developing big cities or small ones. My view is to let nature take its course. China is so vast, and only 30 percent of its population is currently living in urban areas. Our level of urbanization lags far behind the changes in our industrial structure, to the extent that cities of all sizes are underdeveloped. From the perspective of land conservation, large- and medium-size cities are more efficient, but it is no good to build only large cities. Rural people want to have an economic and cultural center within a certain radius. Cities of all sizes should form networks, rather than substitute for one another, and the process should be organic. The Ministry of Construction may have its own internal standards for guiding the process, and it is fine for economists to put forth proposals, but all of this should leave plenty of room for discussion.

Fourth, with regard to China's accession to the World Trade Organization, this is the trend of the future. The globalization of trade will bring ever more benefits to already-developed countries, while less-developed countries will be at a disadvantage. This is unavoidable, but at the same time trade is a two-way process, not necessarily a zero-sum game. Just because you win does not mean that I lose. We can take advantage of our strengths – for example, due to high labor costs, developed countries may stop producing certain products, and, with cheap and abundant labor, we can then enter. Once our technologies develop, we can enter into new competition with developed countries. Developed countries must find markets for their surplus capital, and China is precisely the market for which they are looking. As they 'come in,' we can 'go out.' In the area of agriculture, we can exchange food for food – exchange our high-value-added vegetables, fruit, aquatic products, and meat for their grain.

Note

* This article was originally published by the *Financial Magazine* in Volume 10, 1999, and was revised when being included into this book.

22 Historical status of small- and medium-sized enterprises*

(October 24, 1999)

1. I am in favor of the call to develop small- and medium-sized enterprises.

2. In the 1950s and 1960s, China sought 'large and public' and rejected 'small and private.' When this pursuit was linked with the great ideal of socialism, it became an entrenched form of ideology.

3. Economics too has its theory about 'economies of scale' and tends to believe that larger is better. When modern industries arose in the nineteenth century, mechanized large-scale factories appeared, and in more recent years, multinational companies have been madly merging and acquiring in the fields of banking, automobiles, aviation, oil, chemical engineering, and others. To a certain degree, size is undeniably one of the factors influencing production: there is a certain truth to the idea that bigger is better.

4. We have to admit that only when material wealth is concentrated does it have real effect. 'Concentration' can be done in levels, however, and should indeed be differentiated. Unlimited concentration and absolute equality of distribution can also have the counterproductive effect of destroying vitality.

5. The world's economy must necessarily be diversified, with variation in quantity and also variation in 'nature,' including public, private, and various forms of mixed ownership.

6. The term 'private economy' means that the capital is privately owned, but in order to maximize returns off that capital, production is necessary, and production has the effect of expanding social wealth. Making use of the private economy is beneficial and indeed necessary to the nation and the people of an economically backward country. This is a truth that Chairman Mao expounded upon in his work *On New Democracy*. Trying to jump beyond this stage of development prematurely does not work. History also proves that pursuing a form of all-embracing public ownership is not any better for the people in the end, is not any more efficient or conducive to eventual democracy than a pluralist economy with mixed public and private ownership.

7. Public ownership that is 'all of one suit,' as they say in mahjong, is an artificial 'ideal' construct made according to an overall design by political organizations. Any other form of ownership must be eliminated in order to carry out this design. This is so, even if those forms could also contribute to growing the forces of production. The greatest economic drawbacks of a singular socioeconomic structure are that such a structure eliminates competition and weakens personal participation, initiative, and creativity. It also impedes technological advance and the accumulation of capital that results from human activity, which is indispensable to social progress. A review of the development of human history indicates that past societies with different economic structures, from slave to capitalist, all employed private ownership as the dominant form while incorporating certain forms of public ownership. They did not employ a singular form of ownership. For the same reasons, socialist countries may rely mainly on public ownership, but at the same time they should retain the proper amount of private ownership. Since our Party initiated reforms at the Third Plenary Session of the 11th Central Committee of the Party, China's basic ownership structure in this 'primary stage of socialism' has taken public ownership as primary while diverse economic components develop in tandem. This structure will remain unchanged for a long time. It represents a systemic evolution that conforms to the laws of history. It also expresses the scientific nature of our Party's economic decisions.

8. Once private ownership has been affirmed, there is no reason to favor the big and discriminate against the small. Under China's existing conditions, most of the privately owned capital is small in quantity, and capitalization of the individual-economy sector [*ge-ti*] is even smaller. Small-scale economies can grow to become large-scale economies, however. Right now, small- and medium-sized enterprises account for about 60 percent of China's total social production and 96 percent of the number of enterprises. In rural areas, small farms and small enterprises account for an even larger share. Shanghai's statistics indicate that six times as many jobs are created for every 10,000-yuan investment made by a small enterprise than the same amount made by a large one. Small- and medium-sized enterprises have other irreplaceable advantages: In keeping with demand, they increase diversification of products; they mobilize disaggregated funds, scattered throughout society, and turn them into investment and social wealth, helping to create a middle class; they provide intermediate products to large specialized enterprises, thereby refining the degree of division of labor in society; they broaden the tax base, increase tax revenues, and stimulate the growth of a more prosperous society. Furthermore, they constitute an innovative force for change, which is something arising from the new-technologies revolution. Small- and medium-sized enterprises can use their human capital to overcome their small size, and they are able to shine in particular in the information industry.

9. These points should not be used as arguments for regarding large, publicly owned enterprises as an unnecessary economic form. In a socialist country, the existence of the State-owned economy is not only of economic but of very great social significance. The State must prevent individuals from monopolizing resources and creating polarization. The development of some natural resources and the production of certain public goods involve huge investments and require a long time to recoup those investments. Such large projects are in the fields of water conservancy, transportation, mining, and energy, among others, as well as large financial undertakings and large trade transactions. None of these would be possible without State investment. Nonetheless, the State's financial resources are limited. The government percentage of total savings in the country dropped from 38.5 percent in 1978 to 1.7 percent in 1995. In that same period, personal savings rose from 11.6 percent to 56.3 percent. Therefore, the government cannot assume too much responsibility. When we say the public economy plays the leading role, rather than merely talking numbers, we are talking about the ability to regulate and exercise control. Right now, we should be able to merge together or auction off 300,000 of our State-Owned Enterprises. Some can become solely owned operations, others can adopt a shareholding system. The State can invest and hold control shares, or it can swap capital for shares and use that capital in a more flexible way – use less money to do more things. In addition, lots of products and services and lots of competitive industries can be left to social collectives, private sectors, and individuals to operate. Fair competition featuring the principle of the 'survival of the fittest' should be introduced to give incentives to those more competitive enterprises to establish modern governance structures.

10. In solving development problems, discrimination against small- and medium-sized enterprises simply because they are small and private will only lead to worse problems and is absolutely inacceptable. Our past advocacy of both public and private ownership, and large, medium, and small enterprises, should be reintroduced and should prove effective again today.

11. We should adopt proactive policies that support small- and medium-sized enterprises. At present, these enterprises are facing two main difficulties: financing and technological support. Due to the impact of the Asian financial crisis, money is tight, but this should prove to be a temporary factor. We should be able to solve it in a timely manner with energetic fiscal and monetary policies. In the long run, however, a better systemic environment should be created for smaller companies.

First, the government should establish a special institution to provide these companies with integrated services and to unify the policies and regulations that extend protection, support, and guidance.

Second, a financial support system should be launched. The 'rectification' of the rural financial order and the closing down of those financial cooperatives that have committed illegal acts have created a doubly difficult situation for town-and-village enterprises. Not only have they lost the funds they invested, but they now have no channels through which to borrow more money to recoup those losses. Our priority must be to launch a new rural financial market.

A large number of these smaller enterprises have had to shut down after State-owned commercial banks tightened their lending policies. Faced with an extreme shortage of working capital, they have had to lay off workers and suspend operations, to the detriment of everyone. As per common international practice, China should establish a credit guarantee system exclusively for small- and medium-sized enterprises. To tighten up on credit risk, collateral policies and repayment conditions should become far more stringent. Membership-based organizations that pool funds to serve as guarantee for loans should be established, mainly with corporate funds but supplemented with inputs from public finance. These should be responsible for assessing the assets of a company, its operating conditions, its credit rating – in short, for providing the background information on which commercial banks grant loans. Experiments should be conducted before these become widespread; we should avoid springing out of the gate without adequate preparation.

To encourage investments, tax and loan incentives should be offered to small- and medium-sized enterprises.

Third, a 'technical services system' should be established. Personnel should be recruited to collect sample products, applicable patents, and market information for small- and medium-sized enterprises and to provide them then with publicly available technologies, tests, financial audits, and technological innovations so that they can undertake targeted projects.

Fourth, the process of urbanization should be accelerated. Small- and medium-sized industrial enterprises must rely on proximity to one another to save on transaction costs. They must rely on nearby intermediary service organizations, such as accounting, legal, technical, and others, to realize their technical and managerial innovations, develop their markets, and sell their products.

Fifth, we must set up a system of legal guarantees for smaller companies. From the large numbers of legal disputes that are being brought forth, it is clear to see that legal guarantees are lacking. A beneficial legal environment provides the necessary conditions for social development. It ensures rational utilization of resources and orderly commodity exchange. It increases overall economic efficiencies and greatly cuts trade costs. The importance of a functioning legal system for commerce should never be underestimated.

Sixth, education and training should be intensified to improve the quality of corporate personnel.

12. In terms of numbers, town-and-village enterprises constitute two-thirds of all China's small- and medium-sized enterprises and provide 130 million jobs to the rural population. In 1997, these enterprises accounted for 27.7 percent of the country's GDP and one-third of its total exports. They have become an indispensable part of the country's economy. In recent times, however, these enterprises have seen their local advantages gradually being eroded, and they are finding it hard to maintain their original growth rates. The reasons are due to changes in the world around them as we accelerate the process of moving from a planned-economy to a market structure and as the sellers' market has now given way to a buyers' market.

What does the future hold for these town-and-village enterprises? People are raising concerns and wondering if they will survive. I believe that rural enterprises will continue to develop because they are deeply rooted in China's rural areas, and our rural areas have always depended on diversified operations to support growing populations and to make up for shortfalls in farming income. Diversified operations are a prerequisite for the future well-being of farmers. In addition, the State also relies on their ongoing development to ensure that hundreds of millions of rural people earn at least a certain portion of nonagricultural income. This is necessary to alleviate some of the negative consequences that have arisen from the reform process, the transitioning of economic systems, and the lag time in realizing urbanization.

It is quite true that town-and-village enterprises will inevitably have to change and will diversify in the process. Their form of ownership, currently 'all the people on a small scale' – i.e., ownership by collectives or local governments – will evolve into shareholding companies and cooperative organizations. To team up on using services and cut costs, some enterprises will come together and form towns and small cities or will move into cities. When these enterprises break out of the restrictions placed on 'local' and 'regional' trade, they will have to give up some of the preferential treatment they currently receive [from 'local' governments]. If they can 'take care of' and accommodate community interests, however, they will find they still can enjoy cheap rents and cheap labor. Because of the mutually beneficial relations between 'community organizations' and 'enterprises,' problems of compensation to corporate leaders who are at the same time agents of the 'publicly owned economy' must be resolved, including problems of 'privately owned enterprises wearing red hats.' These involve the difficulties associated with 'special systems' and many technical measures with regard to handling those systems. These problems must be solved by forming a standardized legal structure that is arrived at through discussions, negotiations, and mutual compromise. It must be a system that is in accord with principles of fairness and equity. The various levels of our [Party] leaders did not address these problems soon enough, and the situation has got ahead of them. This is causing some problems that ought to have been avoided. Nonetheless, it is a case of better late than never. Mending the sheep pen after the sheep have gone doesn't mean that it is forever too late to start the process.

Note

* This is a speech delivered by the author at a theoretical symposium on the development of small- and medium-sized enterprises.

23 Agricultural industrialization and 'dragon-headed' [leading] enterprises*

(November 10, 1999)

1

The Chinese view the dragon as an auspicious animal. In point of fact, the animal kingdom does not include any such beast, and it was the Chinese people themselves who invented the concept. Be that as it may, applying the term here suggests that 'rural areas are set to take off.'

One must have a dragon head in order to 'take off.' The number of 'dragon head enterprises' in rural areas is small, but the ones there are have tremendous vitality. They may be facing difficulties right now, but I believe that these are temporary. The problems were precipitated by the Southeast Asian financial crisis, but they have also arisen in the midst of overall economic change. Right now, China is in a period of economic contraction. The Chinese economy has enjoyed two-digit growth for nearly 10 years, and, once an economy has grown that fast, it is only natural for it to have a correction. The way this is being reflected in monetary terms is deflation. As a result, most Chinese enterprises, not just dragon heads, are feeling the difficulties.

Contraction began to change, however, in the fourth quarter of 1999. With State investment of funds, exports began to pick up, and corporate losses began to narrow. The slide in the growth rate has become less dramatic. The growth rate for the fourth quarter is expected to reach 7 percent or even higher, and the rate for next year is unlikely to be lower than this figure. Even if it is, it won't be by much. Of course, if the rate does drop by a lot, things will not look good since people's daily lives will be affected. For example, if the growth rate is 5 percent, everyone will see their income dropping, which is hard to take. If it is 6 percent, that one extra percentage point can be used to improve people's lives. Our days will be better off yet if the growth rate is about 7 percent.

Given this situation, dragon-head enterprises will be facing problems, but they will not be problems that are insurmountable. Agriculture will see new growth, and therefore its dragon heads will also enjoy growth. Looking on into the future, the prospects look quite good.

2

Why is it that the dragon-head enterprises have appeared just in recent years, no sooner and no later? It is because rural reform has begun to show its effect in recent years. Distorting factors of the past have gradually been ironed out, and the forces of production have gradually been liberated. As a result, China's agriculture has entered a new stage.

The chief characteristic of this new stage is that people have enough to eat and to wear. Cereal (grain) supply is sufficient in an average year and is in surplus in a good year. When both urban and rural residents shifted to wanting to eat well, as opposed to wanting just to get enough to eat, this stimulated changes not only in what farmers were planting but also in the whole structure of the rural economy. Quantity, and especially the quantity of grain and cotton, was the previous focus, while now the emphasis is on quality, output, and efficiency. Farmers are diversifying their operations as well as the crops they plant. Their orientation is toward increasing their income – income has become the main goal. And if income levels are to increase, structure must be optimized.

In this situation, the government's guiding principle with respect to agriculture emphasizes agricultural industrialization. Agriculture is an industry. The very concept of its 'industrialization' means its mode of growth must be transformed from extensive operations to highly efficient operations. Nearly all developed countries have experienced this change in the mode of agricultural development. For example, China's Taiwan province called it a transition from traditional agriculture to 'meticulous' agriculture, and Japan called it 'efficient' agriculture. Another part of the change involves the interaction between the primary, secondary, and tertiary industries and the 'lengthening' of agriculture's industrial chain. Realizing the integration of trade, industry, and agriculture, increasing the value-added component of products, adding such new factors as labor, capital, and knowledge to products to amplify their supplementary value, even by several fold . . . all of these are part of the change. If a kilogram of wheat is ground to flour, the flour can be sold for more money. If the flour is turned into cakes, the cakes can be sold for even more money. Therefore, we are beginning to see a change in the interaction among the primary, secondary, and tertiary industries.

The result of this is that agriculture is beginning to be able to accumulate capital. In addition, agriculture is developing socialized services, forming economies of scale, setting up necessary support systems, providing guarantees for sustainable growth and for increases in farmers' incomes. These are the general trends in both developing economies of scale and in modernizing China's agriculture.

As the world constantly advances, not only should we arm agriculture with high technology and focus on tangibles such as financial capital, but we should arm it with the intangible asset of knowledge, of human capital. America and Europe, but particularly America, have been introducing information technologies to agriculture including microelectronic, computer, space industry, and genetic engineering technologies (such as cloning). [In 1995], the American Lester Brown wrote a book that asked the question: *Who Will Feed China?* He looked at China's agriculture from the perspectives of water, fertilizer, land, capital, and existing technologies and concluded that, after some few dozen years, China's agricultural development would not keep pace with its population growth.

He left out new technologies, however, and others responded to his book with the belief that through new scientific developments, agriculture will enjoy a whole new future.

In this respect, China's dragon-head leading enterprises will play a certain role.

3

Dragon-head enterprises constitute a systemic innovation in rural areas. The innovation was able to build on the foundation that our policy affirmation of 'family operations' had laid.

Agriculture produces biological organisms. It is a form of production that 'produces' living matter. Crops, domestic animals, poultry are all living things. Unlike ordinary factory production, agricultural production is a 'factory' for living things. Families 'reap what they sow' – the relationship of benefits received is very direct. Given the familiarity of farmers to their land, they have a unique form of efficiency that cannot be replaced by other factors, which is why family operations have persisted for so long in China and throughout the world. The problem with this is that the scale of family operations is not cost-effective, so alliances and economies of scale are called for. When the former Soviet Union instituted its collectives, it erased the effectiveness of the family and later had to reform by privatizing and restoring family operations. Family operations are not immutable. They too must restructure along with changes in the forces of production, and they too must eventually find proper forms of allying with others – this is an inevitable trend. We have consistently advocated diverse forms of two-level operations. Supply-and-marketing cooperatives are one such form, and village-based community organizations are another. 'Companies plus rural households,' namely dragon-head leading enterprises, are also a good embodiment of this principle. They represent a systemic innovation that has arisen during the transition from a planned to a market economy. Diverse forms of cooperation also exist in the United States. One farmer there can be a member of as many as five or six cooperative organizations, in addition to which there are many associations (such as the soybean association, the strawberry association, and so on). These help address problems that individual families on their own cannot handle.

In the future, dragon-head enterprises will be able to accommodate integrated large-scale agriculture by pursuing diversification and specialization. In Simao Prefecture of Yunnan Province, research institutions and governments have jointly invested in tea companies and experimental small-grain coffee, which has greatly increased farmers' income.

4

Dragon-head enterprises should now focus on the following issues.

First, make sure to maintain a very close relationship with farming households, for they provide the primary products for you to process. Keep in mind that they represent not only your small workshops and small production units, but also your investors. You can spread your risk by using decentralized methods, by assigning production tasks to millions of farming households. Since agriculture is a risky industry, it is hard to run large operations that require high fixed costs. Family farms have the advantage in this respect.

In the age of Industrial Revolution, bigger was better, but today, in the information age, 'small is beautiful.' In agriculture, we should not 'hate the big and love the small,' however, or vice versa, for large State farms and small family farms both have their advantages.

Dragon-head enterprises should form entities with farmers that share mutual interests, for the relationship between farmers and enterprises is less that of 'buying and selling' than it is of profit sharing and risk sharing. Purely commercial operations should of course be allowed to exist and should not be eliminated.

In forming alliances for mutual interest, two key issues must be resolved, the first of which is pricing. Prices must be at reasonable levels that allow smooth relations between both producers and sellers and among the 'three parties' – namely farmers, companies, and consumers. There are several methods of setting reasonable price levels. The first is to establish a contract price and then return profits. Milk companies in Western countries use this method with the farmers who raise their dairy cattle. They return back a certain amount of profit to dairy farmers depending on the amount of milk that has been supplied.

The second method is to set a 'protected price,' which is also called a floor price, in addition to a ceiling price, which is the market price. If the protected price is too low as compared to the ceiling price, it should be raised appropriately so that the farmers will not suffer. When the market price drops, the farmers' income can remain unchanged. The third method is to set a fixed price that already incorporates a degree of profit. The fourth method is agency marketing, which specifies the amount of fees for intermediaries. The two sides share in risk whether selling prices are high or low. Intermediary companies must provide inexpensive and high-quality services, the most important of which is technical (such as improved varieties), followed by marketing and information services.

Second, dragon-head enterprises should diversify the forms under which they operate. The modern economy exists in a diversified state. China went through a period in its recent history of overemphasizing 'large and public.' Privately held enterprises, most of which were small in scale, were totally wiped out, and as a result we brought on an 'economy of scarcity' that suffered the syndrome of being starved for investment. We are now advocating a system of diverse forms of ownership, still taking public ownership as primary but incorporating the concurrent development of private ownership, collective ownership, shareholding ownership, and ownership through partnerships. Rural forms of cooperation are based on family operations, which means 'companies plus rural households.' Nonetheless, we also cannot do without public ownership since large irrigation projects, transportation projects, power grids, and other public facilities produce products for the public at large and must be publicly owned.

A shareholding form of ownership can help raise funds from society and thereby overcome the problems of funding that neither government nor individuals can handle. Both capitalism and socialism can employ this method of financing; it does not belong to one or the other. Shareholding companies must be strictly regulated, however, and must have sound systemic constraints. Their governance structures should include the general meeting of shareholders, a board of directors, and a board of supervisors as well as the management team.

Private ownership is a form that integrates the owner and operator in one person or one entity. The incentive to perform well is a function of whether or not one makes money: losing money is a negative incentive, whereas making money stimulates even better performance. Individually operated enterprises therefore also have their advantages.

To give a brief example: One company, a husband and wife team, started up a company with RMB 20, making *bao-zi* [steamed buns]. They realized they were not making much money doing this and so went around looking at how other people operated, first in China and then in Singapore. They applied what they had learned to their company when they came back and soon found they were doing business in the range of RMB 20,000. The point of this story is that one should not look down on small beginnings.

The third and most important thing that dragon-head enterprises should focus on is the quality of products. The health of their business lies in this key element. With good products that are inexpensive yet high in quality, any enterprise will enjoy a certain market share. Without good products, the enterprise will have no market share at all. Our hybridized rice is piling up in warehouses, but quality rice can't even meet the demand. A good product can create its own market and develop its own demand. McDonald's and Burger King have created their own large market shares in China. We may be able to create an overseas market if we can only modernize soya milk and *you-tiao* [a kind of elongated donut cooked on the spot].

5

Finally, I want to touch briefly on the relationship between dragon-head enterprises and their local communities. The enterprise is inseparable from the community, and it is also inseparable from the rural population. The dragon-head enterprise requires a 'space' in which to grow, and that is provided by the community, which supplies the land. The enterprise requires a certain environment that includes electricity, roads, telephone service, irrigation systems, and so on, and all of these are provided by the community. Without them, infrastructure costs would all have to be borne by the enterprise, at prohibitive expense. This relationship is therefore not something abstract but has very real material value and mutual benefit. Development of the community is in the interests of the enterprise. Put the other way around, enterprises should contribute to the healthy growth of the community in order to make use of the benefits itself. It should help with establishing schools, paving roads, and laying in phone lines, and it should help in building up both the mental [spiritual] and the material culture of the community.

Note

* This is a speech delivered by the author at a meeting on the experience of China's leading enterprises held by the China Council for the Promotion of Rural Development.

24 Thoughts on the Wenzhou economic model*

(May 25, 2000)

The mayor has delivered a thorough and substantive account of Wenzhou's experience as it went through the development process. Inspired by his remarks, I want to share my personal thoughts on the issue.

1. Spontaneous order

Wenzhou's economy is a spontaneous economy in that it came about on its own and is owned, operated, and shared by the people of Wenzhou themselves. It is also an economic order [structure] that is stable and sustainable.

In the past, there were two main views with regard to 'society,' advocates for two different schools of thought. One held that it was possible to design a master blueprint for social transformation. That blueprint should contain detailed descriptions of how the future would work, including how it should be organized, how distribution should take place, what kind of culture, politics, and lifestyle people should have, what people should study, and so on. In general, designs of this nature were created by great scholars. The other held that it was possible to design a general orientation and a basic law for social development but that a detailed blueprint was not a good idea. Instead, people should look after and fight for their own interests themselves, increase their own social welfare. This second school felt that an expanding order would thereby form spontaneously through self-generation. History has now proven that the more detailed a social blueprint tries to be, the harder it is to conform to reality and the easier it is to fall into the trap of Utopian dreams. As the key example, Utopian socialism did not succeed and therefore was replaced by the Marxist materialist view of history. This turned 'socialism' from the Utopian path in the direction of science, but, even so, socialism was limited by inadequate information as it undertook 'practice' or experimentation. As a result, we made mistakes. We introduced a singular form of public ownership and distribution only according to work. We forbade the concurrent practice of other forms of ownership and distribution. After 20 years of trying out this master design, we were forced to undertake reform. The 'design' did not conform to the realities of the 'primary stage' of China's socialism.

History indicates that in the course of 'spontaneous' or self-generating order, a pioneer strikes out first, to set an example. That induces others to follow, creating a chain reaction that self-replicates and forms a new structure and a new system. The process constitutes a kind of general rule.

Wenzhou's economy is concrete evidence of that rule. In the 1950s, farmers in Yongjia County spontaneously began to have individual households contract for producing the grain quotas that had to be delivered to the government. On their own, they began a special land management system that was supported by the county's Party Committee, and that soon became the model for the over 1,000 villages in Wenzhou Prefecture. Later on, this movement was 'beaten down' – that is, it was suppressed, and the county leaders were all punished. People in Wenzhou refused to give in, however, and continued down the road blazed by Yongjia County. Periodically, they kept contracting output quotas to individual households, and they went further in introducing this spontaneous mechanism to cities.

Zhejiang Province has long had too little land for too many people, so starting in the Ming and Qing dynasties, its people began emigrating to other places to work. They went throughout China, and they also went abroad. After Liberation [1949], overseas travel was forbidden, so people had to find nonagricultural employment right there at home, and as a result they began to produce such small commodities as clothing, shoes, hats, low-voltage electrical appliances, eyeglasses, and business signboards. Since these small commodities had large markets, they attracted more and more investors. Once China began reform and opening up policies, the new market orientation further catalyzed family operations into operating on a larger scale. Individual economies [*ge-ti*] developed that clustered enterprises into much larger groupings. This spontaneous or self-generating expansive economic order then began to spread from Yongjia County throughout Wenzhou Prefecture. From Wenzhou, it spread to Taizhou and to all parts of Zhejiang Province, making Zhejiang, with its minimal natural resources, into a major economic force. Right now, Zhejiang and Guangdong Provinces are vying neck and neck in terms of provincial output. Each contributes more than more than RMB 70 billion to China's GDP.

It is worth noting that, in this process, local governments in Wenzhou have simplified their functions and do not directly intervene in the daily micromanagement of business operations. Instead, they focus on improving the macro environment, on planning for infrastructure development. They provide regulatory functions as according to law, they carry out public works, they set the 'rules of the game,' and they provide public services, improve taxation systems, improve financial stability, and invest in capital construction. The destitute, dirty mess that the area of Wenzhou used to be has been transformed. Roads are now wide, markets are clean, traffic runs smoothly, and the power supply and communications systems are secure. The area has truly realized the hopes of the Central Committee of the Party when it asked local governments to strengthen their control over their economies. The Party Committee of Zhejiang Province explicitly declared what it called the three 'letting go's.' This meant giving free rein to the development of the market economy, giving free rein to the development of diversified forms of ownership, and giving free rein to the development of comparative advantages. From the higher level of macroeconomic governmental policy, this served to confirm the self-generating order that was already underway. It enabled all of Zhejiang Province to embrace the same economic orientation. We are already beginning to see a new order that allows individual economic gain to be aligned with overall social and economic development in a coordinated and balanced way.

2. The effect of concentrating people: The results of urbanization

Commodity production involves costs, one of which is known as 'transaction costs.' Theoretically, such costs are zero in a free market economy. No such thing as a true free market economy exists in the world, however, and, in reality, markets face all kinds of uncoordinated obstructions that cause friction. In order to avoid unfair competition in the conduct of commodity exchange, people require 'rules of the game,' the setting up of which requires discussions, meetings, and disputes and negotiation, all of which involve time and attendant costs. Since transaction costs must be paid, the desire is to make them as cost-effective as possible. To do this, Wenzhou people first united all kinds of 'individual economies' or small companies into various larger entities, using many different forms of ownership systems. Some were shareholding companies, some cooperatives, some joint-venture operations. The appearance of these alliances enabled production to develop into 'mass' or 'social' production. At the same time, the alliances allowed transaction costs to be internalized and hence lowered. Trading centers or markets were established in order to increase the volume of exchange. These were called small-commodity specialized markets. By 1999, Wenzhou alone had 4,347 such markets, with turnover of more than RMB 360 billion, the highest amount of turnover for one prefecture in China.

In the olden days, China had a common practice of 'piling into' a specialized market for a specific commodity. The term in Chinese was '*zhadui'er*,' essentially meaning to get together in a pile. Vendors found a suitable place to congregate so that all those engaged in the same trade could facilitate the purchases of customers [who were generally wholesale customers, buying for resale at retail markets elsewhere]. Wenzhou resurrected this practice. Its button market has become famous both inside and outside China as a prime example of how the system works. The markets support production in both villages and townships: each village specializes in one product, and each township specializes in a particular industry. Linked together, they form a whole manufacturing process. Some towns have even been built expressly for developing a product, which has taken the expansive process one step further. The town of Longgang is a typical example. The number of administered towns in Wenzhou has gone from an original 18 to the current 144. The urban population of Wenzhou accounts for 40 percent of the total, which is 10 percentage points higher than the national level of 30 percent. Province-wide, the number of administered towns has risen from 200 in 1978 to 1,000 in 1998.

Small towns are important not only because they are small but also because they are connecting points, or 'nodes,' for urban networks. Networked together, cities have the capacity to develop new forms of relationships among people. Those 'in the network' can get hold of product inputs that they need more easily, and they can master operations, production, and service far more readily than if they were on their own. Secondary industries that are located in towns have access to all kinds of services that reduce their internal costs. In areas where businesses are dispersed, companies find it much harder to grow quickly since they lack all the accounting firms, law firms, and transport and communications facilities that urban centers provide. Growing such things in-house, trying to be all-inclusive, only increases costs. Not only does concentrating business in towns help to facilitate the buying of services, but it aids in gathering information. Companies can arrange their production and allocate their labor depending on what they learn. They can use the Internet to send out information on themselves as well, to gain social recognition for their efforts, and to benefit from social coordination and cooperation.

An economy cannot develop fully if it relies only on division of labor among families and does not take advantage of division of labor among society at large. Towns can promote the socialization of production, which in turn can promote the socialization of the relations of production. Urbanization, industrialization, and socialization represent three different sides of the same phenomenon. They are the practical conditions on which society relies in order to make progress.

When people concentrate in towns, they also begin to produce a 'concentration effect.' The growth of the commodity economy radiates an influence into peripheral areas, stimulating their economies as well and creating urban–rural integration. Wenzhou people 'pile in together' wherever they go, both inside and outside China. They have created a 'Zhejiang Village' in Beijing, and there are a number of such villages in Italy. Over one million Wenzhou people are scattered around China today, and over 300,000 are currently living in various countries around the world. This has created a mega network within which Wenzhou people can learn from one other, support each other, coordinate their external relations, and expand their business operations outside their own native homeland. When a person leaves the network, he finds that he loses all of the benefits and opportunities that went with it, so for that very reason, the network itself is a very strong factor in ensuring ongoing cohesion.

3. Structure and functions of a mixed economy

Small- and medium-sized enterprises constitute the main force of the Wenzhou economy. The ownership of these enterprises is mixed: some are owned by townships, some by towns, some by individuals, and some by partnerships. Taken altogether, they constitute the largest share of Wenzhou's GDP. In the age of the Industrial Revolution, a 'big' enterprise was regarded as a 'good' enterprise. Today, in the age of the 'Information Revolution,' a 'small' enterprise may be just as good. A small enterprise combines the decision making and the physical labor in one and the same person, which is highly beneficial to more intelligent and conscious application of innovations. Innovative mechanisms are also closer to the unit of production, which in turn is beneficial to raising the speed of technological revamping, allowing for more tangible efficiencies, the ability to win market opportunities, and the ability to absorb better personnel and more capital from society. In Wenzhou, a small enterprise can be established with a RMB 500,000 investment. Since there are so many small enterprises and each is like a small school training entrepreneurs, small enterprises also boost economic growth and help realize full employment.

Large enterprises are also needed for their economies of scale, so Wenzhou has been developing a number of them. These are exploring ways to become modern enterprises and are trying to avoid the pitfalls of other large Chinese companies – overly rigid behavior with countless rules and procedures, layers of bureaucracy leading to slow decision making, and reliance on established ways of doing things.

In other parts of Zhejiang Province, rural enterprises were showing the negative side to being owned by local governments. Reforms were instituted in recent years, including the introduction of shareholding systems to allow employees to own shares. Members [of the cooperatives] were allowed to own shares, but cadres were given the right to own a relatively larger proportion. Investigations show that the reforms have brought about tangible economic results. Even at a time when the national economy is in the doldrums, rural enterprises in Zhejiang Province continue to show steady growth.

As for the large State-Owned Enterprises in Zhejiang Province, assets continue to grow, and these continue to play the leading role in the economy of the province. These companies are capital intensive and require less labor, and right now they are cutting staff to increase efficiency. Small- and medium-sized enterprises have the ability to take in the laid-off employees, which reduces the pressure on the government. This is helpful in providing a window of time in which it would be very beneficial for the government to expedite the establishment of the social security system. The development of Zhejiang's non-State-owned economies therefore provides an external environment in which State-Owned Enterprises can proceed with their own reforms.

4. Innovation adds new impetus to economic growth

Wenzhou's economy is a people's economy. It is an economy in which ordinary people are relying on themselves for their own survival and development. 'More work, less talk,' or even 'all work, no talk,' is the rule in Wenzhou. With a level-headed approach, people simply put their heads down and get things done. Regrettably, the hard work of Wenzhou people was disrupted by the debate in our recent history about 'do you call it socialism or do you call it capitalism?' and 'do you call it private ownership or public ownership?' As a result, Wenzhou's economic development has been through a certain kind of brinksmanship. In the early 1980s, a few people complained to the Central Committee of the Party in Beijing to the point that one of our Central leaders said that the government had lost political control over the place. [Restrictions were then put in place.] In the face of these, people in Wenzhou simply continued to work as they had always done, behaving according to what they recognized as objective laws that had to be obeyed. They were able to use the facts of reality to turn around their critics. That was a good tradition to follow, and Wenzhou should never forget it, but at the same time Wenzhou should never be content with its past accomplishments. The successes of the past have just created a new starting point for the future. The day that self-complacency sets in is the day that one begins to fall behind. This applies to a nation and a local region as much as it does to an individual.

Recent newspaper reports are saying that several enterprises have pulled out of Wenzhou. People are asking, 'Why did they quit if Wenzhou is so good?' One enterprise noted that it had asked the government to solve a problem it was having with land but that no action had been taken for over five months. Another enterprise said that the corporate burden was not so heavy in the past but had become exorbitant now with the increase in various government-allocated expenses. These were newspaper reports, and I have not done any independent checking. I just pass the information along, 'in its original wrapping,' for your reference.

Despite its great achievements, Wenzhou must be oriented toward the future and toward the world. It must successfully participate not only in our domestic competition but in international market competition, and China's accession to the World Trade Organization presents a new challenge in this regard. It is also, however, a new opportunity. The challenge comes because we have to reduce our tariff rates [overall] from 31.5 to 14.5 percent. For general industrial goods, the rate will go from 24.6 to 9.4 percent, clearly from a high to a low percentage, from a two-digit to a single-digit percentage. On information-technology products, the rate will be dropping to zero. In the future, we will be allowing more foreign goods to enter China. Accession to the WTO is also an opportunity, however, since China will be enjoying the same preferential terms in its exports to over 100 WTO members. From now on, we will be moving into ever fiercer international market competition.

Wenzhou used to be very competitive in domestic markets. From now on, it will have to stand the test of international markets, and it must prepare for and actively accept this test. If Wenzhou can export more products, it will be able to provide more foreign-exchange earnings to the State, which will improve our balance of international trade. This will allow us to keep from losing too much in the process of 'opening our doors to the outside,' or even not losing at all.

WTO accession is neither a hidden trap nor a free lunch. It is simply an unavoidable reality, and, in face of this reality, Wenzhou must work harder. The general goal is technological and systems innovation, with regard to which I have the following proposals.

First, improve product quality. Among the two major commercial innovations that Wenzhou has made, one was to correct the practice of producing inferior counterfeit goods and improving overall product quality. This has won Wenzhou considerable credit and should be recognized. Today, its technologies need further improvement so as to improve quality, reduce costs, create brands, and enter the international market. To this end, Wenzhou should establish a technical service center, compile a product catalogue, and renovate its plant equipment. It is time for Wenzhou to 'go up another level,' as the Tang poem says of climbing the pagoda, to see out further over the horizon.

Second, dare to innovate. Institute a full awareness of innovation, bring in and cultivate human capital, and renovate your production technologies. The competition of today is a competition of science and technology, which in turn is a competition of human resources. Wenzhou's industries originated from individual economies and mainly from family operations, which have their strengths but also their drawbacks. Their key weakness is that they are bound by blood relations, which creates a barrier to allowing in new and different kinds of people. Attracting the best talent requires being open to all kinds of people. Our economy is evolving in the direction of a knowledge economy, but that does not mean that it eliminates materials. A knowledge economy increases the knowledge content of products and thereby improves the ratios of production inputs; human capital becomes the prime factor of production. Wenzhou must therefore place a strong emphasis on education. While the government should run schools, the private sector should too, and the efforts of the Zhengtai Group and the Dongfang Group are visionary in this regard.

Third, a knowledge economy requires venture capital and the development of cutting-edge technologies. We should make widespread use of computers a priority, including the use of computers in design. It is imperative that we make extensive use of the Internet in collecting, transmitting, and broadcasting information and to discover and create business opportunities.

Silicon Valley represents the 'new economy' in the United States. Enterprises there are small-scale but highly innovative. Most of the corporate personnel have above-college-level degrees. People are free to discuss and exchange ideas in informal venues, create new-technology ideas, and swiftly turn them into reality. Silicon Valley also has venture capital organizations that exclusively support high-tech projects that are still in the process of research and development. Some are successful and some are failures, but the successes outnumber the failures, and the earnings outpace the costs. Venture capital already exceeds USD 10 billion and is still growing.

Both the Wenzhou municipal government and the business community should consider setting up venture capital investment funds, to support projects that are currently at the research stage, so as to greet the advent of the new age of the knowledge economy. I am very fond of the fable of the tortoise and the hare. The tortoise moves along slowly, but he never stops, and, at the end of the day, he wins. In addition to keeping themselves from being too self-complacent, the people of Wenzhou should strengthen their awareness or mental approach toward innovation and keep in mind that the complacent hare lost the race in the end. Innovation is indispensable both for consolidating the achievements already made and for building the future.

Note

* This is a speech delivered by the author in Wenzhou City, Zhejiang Province.

25 Brief remarks on innovation*

(July 18, 2000)

1. 'Innovation' is necessary for countries, or societies, to move forward. Applied to theory, systems, and technology, it is an inherent condition within societies that keeps them from being left behind as the world moves on. Innovation allows people to grasp existing knowledge, create new knowledge, and apply both to economic and cultural endeavors and the transformation of society. The central element in the process of innovation is people. The primary consideration, therefore, is enabling people to be creative. This includes enabling them to study, to understand things, to increase their own human initiative, to constantly open out, advance, transform themselves as they also transform the objective world around them and become a vital force for building socialism. As the people of a country or a nation become more innovative, they become a material force in social transformation. This solidifies into both spiritual and material civilization and expedites social progress.

2. Innovation of systems is of primary importance among all the various kinds of innovation. Innovation requires stimulation from a systemic environment that is conducive to change. History is witness to the fact that societies that advocate democracy, respect freedom, and clearly define property rights and protect them with legislation have the dynamics for continuous innovation and become leaders in technological change and the evolution of systems.

Britain, the Netherlands, and other Western European countries have been the cradles of contemporary capitalist economies, while the United States is now the most economically developed country in the world. Marxism was born in Europe, and many Nobel Prize winners are from the United States, all of which is not unrelated to the advocacy of civil rights, freedom, and a clear delineation of property rights in both Europe and America.

3. Democracy is simply when the primary power of a nation rests with the people. Democracy is inseparable from freedom and is only possible when there is freedom. The existence and ongoing process of democracy and freedom requires a long period of cultural growth – that is, the sifting out and accreting of culture that occurs in the movement of history. China has long been influenced by a system of autocratic feudal rule and, as such, is a country that lacks the traditions of democracy and freedom. If it is ever to destroy the 'feudal order,' it must advocate democracy and respect freedom. The Communist Party of China was able to destroy feudal rule, but that did not mean it was able to obliterate all vestiges of feudal order in our country. After long, hard struggle, a revolutionary war, and land reform, the Party enabled people to 'turn their lives around.' It enabled them to establish a people's democratic form of government, which was truly an earth-shaking change. When the democratic revolution shifted in the direction of a socialist revolution, however, the 'cutting edge' of the struggle was aimed at capitalism, and at that point it was hard to avoid providing 'nooks and crannies' for the old patriarchal ideology to lodge itself. That ideology is still influencing people today. It is keeping them from protecting themselves through the exercise of democracy and freedom. Chairman Mao Zedong once said: 'If the broom doesn't find the dust, that dust will stay right where it is. It won't voluntarily make itself go away. Without changing the old, there is no new. Breaking [the old] means making [the new], and that means innovation.' Today, as we go further in our economic restructuring, we absolutely must incorporate innovation into our political system.

4. Innovations in theory are manifested in the constant improvement in a nation's capacity to 'think,' to reflect upon things. Without theoretical innovation, a nation's way of thinking rigidifies. The Communist Party has paid a tremendous price and spent dozens of years in trying to lead the people toward a socialist future. It has made creative successes and also creative mistakes, both of which provide valuable material for our understanding of theory. In this regard, one critical change is worth paying attention to: as people experience the actual practice of socialism, their traditional way of understanding socialism is constantly being transformed.

5. Socialism will inevitably replace capitalism – as a historical process, this is something about which we should not have the slightest doubt. However, in the process of history, it is also inevitable that different countries will choose methods for that replacement that are in keeping with their own national conditions.

A century ago, someone asked Engels about the specifics of his blueprint for socialism. He essentially responded with the comment that there is no blueprint for socialism. There can be no detailed preconception of the system and organization of a future society, and no preconceived model should be imposed on society. Socialism is in the midst of ongoing development.

6. The doctrine of socialism was born in the West. Through revolutionary practice [implementation], it was transformed into a State social system that appeared not in advanced capitalist countries of the West, however, but rather in underdeveloped countries on the margins of capitalism that were Eastern, such as Russia, China, Vietnam, Laos, and Korea.

Without exception, all of these countries instituted a socialist model that featured a high degree of public ownership of the means of production and a planned economy of fully centralized power. In China, once the victory of the democratic revolution was completed, the first thing the working class did after seizing political power was to change the system of ownership. It then organized people's communes along the principle of 'large and public.' The working class pursued 'continuous revolution under the precondition of the dictatorship of the proletariat,' it took 'class struggle as the guiding principle,' and it determined that a singular form [mono-form] of public ownership was the goal to pursue. In the course of this, the working class ignored the Marxist principle that 'the relations of production must conform to the development of the forces of production,' and it set aside and disregarded the ultimate goal of socialism as being 'the pursuit of free and comprehensive human development.'

The resulting closed market, high degree of centralized power, and singular form of ownership blocked the development of the forces of production and stymied economic growth. Not only did these features lack mechanisms to stimulate producers to produce, but they led to serious problems that should have been avoidable. These included the necessity to 'eat from the same big pot,' the 'taking of free rides,' and power dealing, or, in other words, the exchange of power for money.

7. After several decades of actual practice, people began to have doubts about the goals of our system as described earlier. The Third Plenary Session of the 11th Central Committee of the Party was the fulcrum that leveraged change in the early 1980s. It enabled structural change in our economic system, a shift to a focus on 'modernization' and the development of production, and the implementation of ownership systems that 'took public ownership as primary but allowed diverse forms of ownership to develop in tandem.' It began to restore private economies in both urban and rural areas. In the 1990s, we moved further in restoring a market-economy system.

Once the former Soviet Union disintegrated, in the early 1990s, Russia and the countries of Eastern Europe began their own economic transition. This was an expression of the fact that previously socialist countries were now undergoing systemic evolution. Specifically, in terms of ownership systems, they were restoring private ownership while retaining certain elements of public ownership. How should we interpret this change? It appears to be the case that if an economically backward country eliminates private ownership too early, when its system of private ownership can still enable growth in the forces of production, then getting rid of that system in too hasty a manner sacrifices production that must still be utilized. It is an effort that attempts to transcend reality. This therefore can be interpreted as a 'partial flaw' but not a rejection of the entire process given the tremendous accomplishment of setting up socialist countries in the first place.

8. From a long-term perspective, until we reach the stage when resources flow out in unlimited quantity to meet the constantly increasing demands of humanity,

people's concept of 'property' is not going to disappear. For this reason, at different developmental stages of history, ownership of the factors of production will be manifested in various structures. Distinctions between public and private ownership will continue to exist. Such economic aspects as commodities, markets, and capital will be maintained. Their existence will not change the underlying socialist nature of our country. Our understanding should reflect the fact that maintaining these things is conducive to maintaining social stability and conducive to accumulating resources for industrialization. Under our current historical conditions, allowing people to possess some personal property and have an initial form of property-rights allocation is beneficial.

Socialism can only be built on the basis of forces of production that are more advanced than those of capitalism. For this reason, at a specific stage in development, it is necessary to utilize elements of private ownership to prepare the forces of production for socialism. Of necessity, in order to eliminate exploitation and polarization of society, and to realize common prosperity, an economically backward country must go through an extended period of transition. Demanding quick results is counterproductive. Mao Zedong said that, in its transition to socialism, China would have to go through a period of 'new democracy-ism.' That was, theoretically, an innovation, but unfortunately in practice the 'transitional period' was so truncated that what ensued brought on economic distortions. The demands of historical development and of reality cannot be leapt over. Our current reaffirmation of the fact that China is in the primary stage of socialism, and our current systemic arrangements whereby public ownership is primary but diverse forms of ownership develop in tandem, are measures taken in full accord with the Marxist outlook on historical development. They are also choices made in accord with the theory of Deng Xiaoping. In the foreseeable future and after several development stages, once wealth has been accumulated to a certain degree, once people's material and cultural needs are more fully met and overall human development and human freedom is more fully expressed, people's concepts of 'property' will change. All of this will require a long process. Therefore, the statement that 'socialism is in the midst of ongoing development' is still quite valid today.

9. In the early 1980s, China entered into an age of reform and economic transition that involved comprehensive systemic innovation. The results have attracted worldwide attention. Establishing a market-economy system, as the core of the policy changes, has introduced international practices and has garnered a certain degree of success. Certain other systemic issues are still in urgent need of similar innovations.

10. Standardize treatment of urban and rural areas. One unique feature of China's resource endowment is a huge population sitting on a limited amount of land. Surplus labor in rural areas now totals around 130 million people. On the one hand, we need to create job opportunities by extending the 'industrial chain' and integrating agriculture, trade, and industry. On the other, we need to start shifting population in a manageable and planned way. That means opening up the labor market between urban and rural areas, developing small- and medium-sized enterprises in cities, and, before the end of this century and in a staged way, absorbing 100 million farmers into employment in cities. These measures will release 150 million *mu* of farmland from the burden of too many people, allowing for economies of scale in agriculture and increasing the income of farming households. At the same time, through expanded capacity of municipalities, they will spur the development of infrastructure and increase the consumption of urban residents. From a number of different angles, they will 'pull forth' production and start us on the road to more sustainable development.

11. Reform education. July is a very hot month, and, in taking college exams [*gao-kao*], students find that they are also being baked [*gao-kao*]. Some are fainting right there on the test site. Some are cheating by various means in advance due to the pressure. Each year, parents spend a great deal of time and money on the process, ever hoping their children will make it safely across the narrow 'log across the river' and have the chance to go further in their education. There are far too many candidates for the number of positions in China's senior high schools, let alone universities, and this has long been recognized as a serious problem. Countries with well-developed education systems make it easier to get into universities but harder to graduate, while in our country the opposite is true. Meanwhile, the Central Committee of the Party has advocated quality-oriented education. The people who administer the schools find that hard to achieve. Under the pressure of a system that mandates a once-a-year, standardized nationwide exam, they are almost forced to carry on with exam-oriented education. They have to 'fit into the groove' and find it very hard to change. Actions speak louder than words when it comes to making innovations in school education systems and advocating quality-oriented education. Rather than simply announcing a desire for quality, a series of policy measures should be taken to radically increase the number of enrolled students. These include allowing a diversity of investing entities to run colleges and universities. The unified examination system should be changed, but, in addition, individual universities should be allowed to enroll their own students under their own conditions. The time of examinations should also be changed to an earlier or later date. All of these should not be difficult things to achieve.

12. Establish a social security system. This is a policy to ensure long-term peace and stability. It must be taken to help stabilize the labor force and address the security needs of both the employed and the unemployed. It should be put into practice as soon as possible by raising funds through taxation and through realization of the State-owned economy.

One of the hardest problems facing reform of State-Owned Enterprises is how to deal with losses incurred through State-policy-required spending and how to differentiate between such losses and those incurred in the normal course of business. Policy-related losses include expenses incurred by institutions that have had to pay for all social security and medical costs of their employees, including both those who are still working and those who are now retired. By rights, these social security expenses ought to have been borne by the State, but instead they were all imposed upon State enterprises. In order for State-Owned Enterprises to begin to operate as functioning businesses, these deficits now need to be stripped off their balance sheets and covered by public finance that is dedicated solely to that purpose. The aim is to lessen the weight of debt on State-Owned Enterprises and complete reform as early as possible so as to bring them in line with the requirements of a modern corporate system.

13. Renovate the political system. Economic reform must rely on reform of the political structure in order to support and sustain human beings. As the supreme organ of power, the People's Congress must fully manifest the essential requirement that our people are masters of their own house. It must provide legal and material safeguards that protect people's basic rights, including the right to social equality and the right to life [existence] and development [growth]. In addition, it must seek for mechanisms that provide checks and balances over all levels of governmental organization and that restrain overly autocratic or centralized power. When government leaders at all levels of government make policy decisions, this will help prevent mistakes prior to the fact and will reduce ex post facto losses.

The leadership of the Party must be upheld. While the Party leads reform, however, it must also reform itself. Eradicating corruption has the full support of the people. As the ruling Party, in order to effect a radical cure, the very first step is for the Party to distance itself from 'examination and approval' procedures relating to all kinds of economic activity [i.e., opportunities for corruption]. The Party must focus its energy on the formulation of major policies. It should give priority to political leadership and political supervision.

Since a longstanding and deep-rooted feudal tradition holds back the vitality of our national growth as a whole, it is even more important that we promote democracy and the rule of law, that we be human oriented, protect human rights, and make every effort to contain any behavior that infringes upon those rights, from any direction. The government should maintain transparency in all its dealings, attract as many people as possible to participate in governance, promote local autonomy, and increase the ability of rural residents and ethnic minorities to participate in governance and hold opinions on governmental affairs.

One principle barometer for distinguishing a modern democratic country from an ancient feudal empire is the degree to which a country respects the people's right to choose. Marx once said, 'The essence of "man" is not some kind of abstraction that is inherent in each single individual. In its real manifestation, the essence of man is the sum of all of man's social relations.'[1] Man is a social man, not a natural creature living in an isolated state. As a social being, man has diverse needs: material, spiritual, the need to exchange, to undertake productive labor, to enjoy things. These demands are met by individual persons through their social relations, relations that are formed under specific environmental conditions; they are met through their transformation of the objective world; and they are met through the continuous realization of innovations. The development of an individual person and his efforts to satisfy these needs should always be respected by others. Likewise, he too should respect the needs and the efforts of others to meet those needs. For this reason, the suppression and exploitation of different classes of people must be abolished. This is wherein lies the significance of 'communism.' This is also why [we] members of the Communist Party must continue to fight for the realization of communism.

14. Advocate freedom of speech. 'Freedom of speech' is a constitutional right of the people in China. In 1961, at the '7,000-person conference,' Chairman Mao Zedong vigorously espoused 'let the people speak!' While the primary voice should be advocated, divergent views can and should be voiced and debated. This is the necessary price for establishing 'democratic supervision,' and it is also a necessary means by which human beings can raise their level of understanding. Lively thinking is a good thing that should be welcomed instead of smothered. Practice is the sole criterion for testing truth – this major conclusion was clarified and decided upon after heated debate at the Third Plenary Session of the 11th Central Committee of the Party. Supporting the primary voice of Marxism is not in conflict with advocating democracy and freedom – the two complement the development of one another. Which is better, 'letting everybody have his say,' or 'what I say goes'? Chairman Mao Zedong advocated the former. Marxists are not afraid of debate.

One school of thought has it that the primary need of the Chinese people is 'development,' in the sense of enough to eat and enough to wear, and not democracy. This represents a narrow interpretation of the 'right to development' of our people. It also underestimates the need of our modern population for other basic rights, outside the scope of a minimal subsistence. This school of thought represents a mode of thinking that separates out economic growth from social progress.

In addition to these, there are many other systems that are in urgent need of innovative approaches, including setting up capital markets, improving how we use resources, environmental protection, and so on. I cannot elaborate on these here due to limited space, but they are also very important.

15. Technology is a determining force in social progress. The current revolution in information technologies, for example, has reduced differences in time and space and accelerated the process of globalization. All countries around the world are abandoning closed-door policies and implementing proactive measures that both 'open up' to the outside and advocate democracy on the inside in order to accommodate the innovative requirements of global competition. Opening up to the outside world enables a country to utilize two markets and two sources of resources, among which are technology and capital. Advocating democracy on the inside enables a country to take advantage of its comparative edge in human resources, to realize innovations in systems and technology, and to work as a team pulling together for national modernization. Currently, international capital, led by that of the United States, has had 'first-to-market' advantage in using its capital to obtain economic benefit by plundering resources from weaker countries. This had exacerbated the polarization between rich and poor countries of the world and represents the negative side of globalization.

To deal with this new economic hegemony of international capital, third-world countries must strengthen their own competitive standing. They must not only become strong in themselves and self-reliant, but also must support one another. They must adopt new technologies so as to change the situation in which technological revolution has long been monopolized by a few major countries. China should utilize the information technologies provided by the Internet to develop new technologies, transform our traditional economies, broaden our process of 'opening up,' and actively participate in market competition. Competition spells opportunity. It stimulates progress, helps cultivate talent, and helps boost our national strength.

16. China's accession to the World Trade Organization is fast approaching. By joining this organization, China will gain a voice in the establishment of the 'rules of the game' of world trade. At the same time, China must observe the principles of trade liberalization and further open its markets to accommodate more foreign commodities. China must increase its international competitiveness through various means that include both economic and noneconomic factors. Market competition is a test of both commodities and human resources. For this reason, we must go further in deepening our reform by improving the environment for democracy and the rule of law. We must regard the development of our education a 'top priority among priorities' and deploy our forces accordingly.

Notes

* This is a speech delivered by the author at a meeting on innovation convened by the China Society of Economic Reform.
1 *Selected Works of Marx and Engels*, Volume 1, People's Publishing House, 1995, p. 60.

26 Prospects for and vitality of a 'mixed economy'

(May 13, 2001)

1. Right now, what is being described as the 'primary stage of socialism' features a socioeconomic form that 'takes public ownership as primary, with diverse other forms of ownership developing in tandem.' This looks familiar. We saw it in the 'liberated areas' before the founding of New China, as well as in the early years of New China, so it is something like seeing the old familiar swallows return. Back then, the percentage of public ownership was quite small, but there were no major differences in other regards. After a century of hard work, China evolved from being a semi-colonial and semi-feudal economy to a 'new democracy-ism' economy, and then on to the primary stage of socialism, which has been a very long road indeed.

2. On New Democracy-ism was a whole new innovation in theory by Mao Zedong. It contained three main propositions. First, the Chinese revolution would move ahead in two steps. Second, new democracy-ism contained two stages, old and new. Third, 'new democracy-ism' has components that relate to the economy, to politics, and to culture. Viewed today, the five types of 'mixed economy' as described in the third proposition are still relevant. Those included the coexistence of a State-owned economy with national capitalism, state capitalism, a cooperative economy, and an individual economy. The question we need to study is whether or not this social form of organization will be a long-term, or instead a short-term, form of economic transition.

3. The proposition that the Chinese revolution would move ahead in two steps indicated that in order for communists to 'struggle to realize' socialism, they must first complete the democratic revolution against imperialism and feudalism. After that, they could move on to the socialist revolution. Mao Zedong did not elaborate a great deal on this in his writings. He emphasized, however, that China's democratic revolution was part of the world socialist revolution, the future course of which was socialism. He said that the 'democratic revolution' must and could only be completed under the leadership of the working class and its political party. This qualifier was the reason it was called '*new* democracy-ism.'

4. Comrade Xiaoping once said, 'As for what socialism might be, or Marxism, we weren't really all that clear on the subject.'[1] The prescribed definition of these things in the past was 'comprehensive public ownership, a planned economy, and distribution according to work.' This was the model of the former Soviet Union. Actual practice in both China and the Soviet Union has proven that this model neglects the forces of production and, as a result, not only causes economic rigidity but causes the inequities that arise from a hierarchically based distribution system. The model was inappropriate even as a transitional stage and therefore had to be reformed.

5. History has proven that Mao's proposition that the Chinese revolution should move ahead in two steps was correct. It would have been impossible to accomplish the whole task in one fell swoop. In the early days after Liberation in China, our 'modernized' economy accounted for about 10 percent, while the ancient way of doing things accounted for about 90 percent. After seizing political power, it was inappropriate for the working class to rush the transition to socialism, and a staged process should have been set up for building a new democratic society. Indeed, the Joint Program adopted in 1949 by the Chinese People's Political Consultative Conference did not mention socialism at all, for good reason. A mere four years later, however, the 'general line' put forward in 1953 for the transitional period most unexpectedly launched a 'socialist transformation.' This not only rejected the proposition that the Chinese revolution should move ahead in two steps, but it abandoned new democracy-ism and the legal documentation to support it that had been adopted as the 'Joint Program' by the Chinese People's Political Consultative Conference. This was very similar to the way in which the former Soviet Union put a stop to Lenin's New Economic Policy. The difference was that, in China, it was Mao Zedong who negated Mao Zedong. The result was that both countries established a type of socialism that was not backed by the forces of production. Deng Xiaoping's term for this was 'unqualified socialism.' The consequence of this 'unqualified socialism' has been that both countries are now facing the task of reform.

6. 'No social order ever dies away before all the productive forces that it can accommodate have served their purpose. New, higher relations of production never appear before the material conditions for their coming into being have matured within the womb of the old society itself.'[2] China eliminated private ownership in the 1950s, yet private ownership was reborn in the 1980s. Capitalist economic factors are growing faster than ever before, while that 'unqualified socialist model' is already washed up. There could not be better proof of the views expressed by Marx and Engels more than a century ago.

7. The 13th Party Congress [October 25–November 1, 1987] defined China's 'social order' as being the 'primary stage of socialism' and clarified and confirmed that this definition would remain unchanged for 100 years. This 'primary stage of socialism' is a new concept. It carries on and further develops the concept of 'new democracy-ism.' It incorporates many implications. One is that when China builds socialism, it cannot copy the models of other countries but instead must proceed from its own national conditions and take its own path. A second is that 'we are building socialism,' we cannot return to 'capitalism.' In 1982, our new Constitution was adopted. In light of the changes in the country's political, economic, and cultural life since the founding of New China, it provided that the People's Republic of China is a 'socialist republic' of the 'people's democratic dictatorship' under the 'leadership of the working class' and based on a 'worker-peasant alliance.' A third implication is that we explicitly defined our social order as the primary stage of socialism. One decisive factor in that choice of words is that the level of our forces of production is quite far from 'overtaking' the level of advanced capitalist economies, or even from reaching the level required for a socialist society. China can only proceed in deliberate and prudent fashion, trying not to be too anxious for quick or for pure results. China must allow for diverse forms of ownership, with public ownership as primary, while other forms of ownership develop in tandem, and it must allow this practice to continue for a long time. Likewise, it must also allow for diverse principles of distribution, with 'distribution according to work' playing the leading role, but as only one among many roles. China must work hard to develop a socialist commodity economy and to promote the formation and growth of a socialist unified market. In the meantime, reform of the political system and the building of socialist democratic politics must be carried out in a gradual and orderly manner under the leadership of the Communist Party. In light of all these things, Deng Xiaoping clarified that, from a theoretical point of view, a socialist society could only be built with the hard work of generations of people, or even dozens of generations. Some people questioned this term 'dozens of generations.' In fact, not a single word of his proposition needs to be changed.

8. Starting in the 1990s, our country returned to a market economy. Market-driven forces are guided by competition, which means that both public and private sectors must meet the test. Under competitive circumstances, enterprises must accelerate the frequency with which they restructure capital and upgrade products. In this process, both the State-owned and private economies will at times advance but at times face setbacks. Despite this, the overall structure of a mixed-ownership form of economy will not vanish because its existence is tied to the present state of development of China's forces of production. This kind of economic structure has quite a considerable vitality since it can accommodate diverse economic players, mobilize social capital when it needs to, transform reserves into investments in effective production, increase market supply as necessary, and satisfy social demand. Property rights exchange can substitute for product exchange, which increases the efficiency of capital by making it that much more liquid.

9. The nature of a market is to allow competition, which is only right and proper. It is inappropriate to use a formulaic approach to the competition of human societies, however, for example by quoting Darwinian survival of the fittest: 'Living things compete, nature selects, and the fittest survive.' Man is not only the consummation of society, but an economic being and also a social being. Market competition proceeds according to commonly agreed upon rules of the game; the results of competition are not necessarily life and death but rather can incorporate win-win situations. Society has 'class struggle' but also 'class compromise,' which means that different classes play against each other but also safeguard each other's common interests. For this reason, at a certain period in history they can reach consensus, form a systemic order, maintain social stability, and seek common development.

This is one reason capitalist societies can recover and even flourish after periods of facing total ruin. Of course, the inherent contradictions between the socialization of production and the private ownership of the means of production in capitalist societies cannot be resolved through compromise. That socialism will supersede capitalism is inevitable in the end.

10. In the year 2000, China's GDP ranked seventh in the world while its per capita GDP ranked 140th. Employment is an outstanding problem in a country with such a huge population and so little land. As an indispensable part of market economies, the private sector within China's 'mixed economy' has the ability to concentrate funds that are scattered throughout society and put them to productive use so as to make up for the deficiency of public funds. The private sector can also provide more job opportunities and increase tax revenues for the development of public undertakings. Private enterprises have long-accumulated experience and expertise in advanced management, all of which can be put to use for society.

11. As the ruling political party, the Communist Party is in charge of guiding economic work, and in doing this it must be sure to take all factors into consideration. While it ensures constant economic growth, it must also promote constant social development. It must attach equal importance to material and spiritual civilizations and strike a balance between efficiency and equity. Social welfare should be the shared benefit of all, and society should be fair and equal. The Party should ensure that our people avoid social polarization and are able to pursue common prosperity. These are all socialist ideals, and they are ideals that the market is incapable of addressing. The government must therefore enter into the economic arena and make necessary interventions. The Party must never for a moment forget to support the efforts that poverty-stricken classes of people are taking to improve their own lives. The State must provide the necessary financial assistance to assure that these people enjoy equal opportunity to share in prosperity. That includes measures to increase employment, to assure universal education, and to enable people to improve their general humanity. In implementing macroeconomic regulatory controls, the government should not have an eye just on the economy but should also be focused on social equality and concern for human affairs.

12. Before the founding of New China, Mao Zedong made the comment that there was too little capitalism in China rather than too much. He said that China still needed to utilize capitalism because China's capitalism was more advanced than feudalism. He once severely criticized a faction within the Party that held 'purist' ideas. Later, in his book *On New Democracy-ism*, he advocated controls over capital, but he excluded controls on any capital that was conducive to the national economy and the people's livelihood. At this point, his use of the term 'control over capital' did not mean the total elimination of capital. Shortly afterward, however, as leader of the Party, he proposed conducting a grand experiment over the course of the next 10 years. In 1953, he launched the 'socialist transformation'; in 1956, the goal was to realize full and comprehensive public ownership. Mao believed in what he thought was a universal law: since the seizure of political power had brought about a certain growth in the forces of production, changing the structure of ownership should bring about an even greater result. He thought that, if socialism failed to occupy the 'battleground' of the rural areas, capitalism would inevitably move in. In the anti-rightist campaign of 1957, he called for 'raising up the "class without capital" and obliterating the class with capital.' Following that came the setting up of the people's communes and a policy of 'large and public,' in the implementation of which Mao vowed to 'exterminate private ownership from the face of the earth.' These 'leftist' policies, which attempted to supersede reality, exacerbated the 'Disastrous Three Years' that began in 1959. The moment he discovered that things were not as he had hoped, Mao made timely adjustments. At the Zhengzhou conference, he presented the decision to oppose communal-property tendencies, indiscriminate resource transfers, and intentional exaggeration of figures. Following on that policy determination, he issued a 60-point document on rural work, which brought the economy back from a state of chaos and turned it in the direction of stability and new growth. Up until that time, the mistakes committed by Comrade Mao Zedong could still be classified as the price society had to pay for exploring the path of 'Sinifying' the Marxist model. They could be seen as a mistaken form of innovation. Most unfortunately, at the Tenth Plenary Session of the 8th Central Committee of the Party, Mao took the step of changing the Party line as formulated by the 'Eighth' [in session from 1956 to 1969] with regard to the primary contradictions in Chinese society. He declared that the contradiction between the proletariat ['class without capital'] and the bourgeoisie ['class with capital'] was the main contradiction in Chinese society. Based on this judgment, he launched a full-scale class struggle that continued for over 10 years. It started with the 'Four Clean-ups Movement' in 1964 and continued with the 'Great Cultural Revolution' in 1966. This plunged China into an ultra-leftist chasm, bringing tremendous damage upon the country and creating a cataclysm of historic proportions.

13. The resolution adopted at the Third Plenary Session of the 11th Central Committee of the Party [December 18–22, 1978] led the entire Party and the entire country out of its 'mistaken understanding.' It determined that China would build 'socialism with Chinese characteristics,' and it formulated 'Deng Xiaoping theory.' Since the end of the 1970s, reforms have been launched that include the restoration of a mixed economy. Our national income has been increasing, and things are going well.

In recent years, reform has entered the stage of addressing the issue of property rights. We are currently using shareholding systems to transform State-Owned Enterprises, collective enterprises, and also individual [*ge-ti*] and private enterprises. A shareholding system means that share rights as interest-bearing capital are owned by individual persons, while use of the capital is determined through certain democratic procedures. Under the present historical conditions, shareholding can be regarded as a form of socialized capital. Karl Marx called it a kind of 'internal self-denial within capitalism.' Shareholding systems can be used by both capitalism and socialism. Half of all families in the United States participate in shareholding, which is an indication of the degree of 'socialization' of the ownership of capital. Whether or not this has the potential to evolve into a new society is something that deserves further study.

China has now had 10 years of experience in promoting shareholding procedures and developing capital markets. The achievements are impressive, but the situation is far from being as 'regularized' as it ought to be. Our stock market is of a highly speculative nature, which leads to such negative consequences as the exploitation of minority shareholders by private majority shareholders. The rules of the game must be constantly improved so as to protect the interests of all investors.

14. The advanced nature of socialism should be made manifest when its labor productivity outperforms that of capitalist labor, but any rise in productivity is a process of comprehensive economic, political, and cultural development. It cannot be accomplished overnight and requires a period of quantitative change. We used to talk about the theory of continuous revolution. If we are referring to constant improvement in the superstructure to meet the needs of improving productivity, in different stages of 'revolution' of a different nature, then that is correct. In achieving constant improvement in the superstructure, however, policies must be relatively stable since frequent change is not helpful to economic growth. The theory of continuous revolution is undesirable if we take it to mean that the Chinese revolution tries to accomplish two steps simultaneously that ought to be accomplished in one. The 13th Party Congress introduced the theory of the primary stage of socialism, affirmed the necessity of a period of quantitative change in our economy, and stabilized all effective policies. These moves helped promote the overall development of the national economy and therefore were a correct choice.

15. Some people are asking: If we now have a 'primary stage of socialism,' what is the 'advanced stage' going to be like? Since socialism is in the midst of ongoing development, details are hard to describe, but, in addition, we should not design out any specific plan according to our own subjective ideas. What can be confirmed is that our experience over the next 100 years will create the conditions for guiding China in the direction of the liberation of the forces of production and the realization of a common prosperity. Our past experience is full evidence of the fact that China should not pursue a singular or mono-form of public ownership when it looks at development models. Both public ownership and private ownership are predicated on the existence of the other. In different periods, the one that is more dominant will change, and each will also have different forms of expression. In our current period of socialism, public ownership is mainly expressed in terms of socialized ownership while private ownership is mainly expressed in individual shareholding, partnerships, and so on. In the distant future, the concept of property rights will disappear along with ownership once there is an abundance of material wealth. Forms of ownership will constantly change along with changes in the forces of production. Mandatory measures may produce some temporary results but will not substantially affect the efficiency of production. Economic diversification is a 'natural order' in the development of history; progress is possible only when there are differences, contradictions, competition. As prior differences and contradictions vanish, new ones appear. Were this not the case, a state of quietude would descend on the world.

Notes

1 *Selected Works of Deng Xiaoping*, Volume 3, People's Publishing House, 1993, p. 137.
2 *Selected Works of Marx and Engels*, Volume 2, People's Publishing House, 1995, p. 33.

27 Give farmers national citizenship*

(June 1, 2001)

Rural periodicals are meant to publicize the Party's principles and policies. At the same time, they should also be the voice of farmers, reflecting their needs and their hopes and wishes. Not only publishers of periodicals but our governmental departments should take this issue seriously.

Some comrades note that our Central Committee of the Party is already taking the issue of agriculture very seriously by raising the status of rural people, consolidating the worker-peasant alliance, and so on, since farmers account for 70 percent of China's population. They say that this has been the policy all along. When compared to 'urbanites,' however, not only have people living in rural areas not been accorded the same rights of citizenship but they have been subjected to certain discrimination. We have been voicing an appeal on this issue for years, and we must continue to do so until it is properly addressed.

Many phenomena serve as evidence of farmers' failing to receive 'national treatment,' or citizenship.

1. For dozens of years, people living in rural areas have not had the right to move about freely. It is extremely difficult for them to leave the countryside and change their fixed 'status.' This situation is hardly to be found anywhere else in the world. [Note: '*shen-fen*' refers to more than the Western sense of 'status' since it legally defines a person in terms of his social benefits and civic rights.]

2. The right to education: All citizens should be equal in this respect, yet children of farming families, who account for 70 percent of our population, claim only 30 percent of university enrollments. Children of urban residents, who account for 30 percent of the population, claim 70 percent.

3. No social security system has been established in rural areas. People without jobs in rural areas are not officially described as being 'unemployed,' and they are thereby denied any unemployment relief. Yet it was our farmers who bore the brunt of paying for China's industrialization. For years, China practiced a system of State purchase and sale of all farm products, which were 'purchased' at super-low prices in order to subsidize State investment in industry. At a rough estimate, the contribution that our farmers made in this regard comes to between RMB 600 and 800 billion [over US $100 billion at current exchange rates].

4. The tax burden on farmers is extremely heavy right now. The Central Committee of the Party regards this as a problem of the utmost seriousness, but high taxation by local governments continues despite Central prohibitions. The staff of township administrations has gone from a dozen people or so to some 100 to 200 people. Farmers cannot cover this burden of excess staff, particularly when the authorization to undertake rural construction has been released down to local levels and expenses are locally controlled through diverse channels employing these staff.

5. Rural public health and hygiene services are inadequate. There is just one 'health worker' for every one thousand people. Even the 'cooperative medical service' that we used to have has disappeared.

6. Lack of employment opportunities for farmers. Urban–rural disparities have only been widening in recent years. Investigations indicate that farming income is so low that it can only sustain a farmer with minimal food and clothing. Right now, around 80 million rural people are transient, shifting between urban and rural areas in order to find employment. Professions are not open to them in urban areas – all they are allowed to do are menial and exhausting jobs. Recruiting units of urban enterprises make it clear in writing that an 'urban household registration' is required to get a job. Wages paid to farmers for nonagricultural work remain exactly what they were 10 years ago. Not much is left after living expenses are paid for, so more than a dozen people normally cram into one room to live. Given the pressure of high costs and low wages, we have 80 million people who are increasingly mentally unbalanced. The State has no systemic arrangements for dealing with what is a very destabilizing factor. A few people have taken the risk of setting out on a life of crime. This is a problem that should not be neglected.

7. The land system: When the Party transformed the collective economy by implementing a system of contracting production to families, farmers were pleased because these moves were in their interests. Now, however, some localities are making modifications in land allocations all the time, minor adjustments every year, major adjustments every three years. Without any sense of security, farmers are not inclined to put investments into their land. The official policy that states that land contracting 'will remain unchanged for 30 years' in fact lacks any set of legally binding enforcement procedures to guarantee that it happens. It also lacks the support of any legal aid organizations.

8. Most of China's poverty-stricken people live in rural areas. Although China has alleviated poverty for some 250 million people, 30 million still live in poverty, and many are returning to poverty. China should not overestimate its success in this regard.

9. Unlike urban inhabitants, farmers need funds to cover the costs of their farming operations, and yet it is extremely hard for them to get loans. By State regulations, land cannot be used as collateral. By bank regulations, loans cannot be extended without collateral to back the loans, and all that farmers normally have for collateral is land.

10. In [our current] age of socialism, farmers have 'turned their lives around,' and feudal suppression has been abolished. Yet at the same time, the establishment of democratic systems is incomplete to the extent that sharp contradictions are beginning to arise between the cadres [Party officials] and the masses. 'Local autonomy' of village residents is a concept that still lacks any regularized application, while the autonomy of townships has not even been put on the agenda.

Farmers still lack political organizations to protect their own rights. At one point, certain old comrades wrote to the Central Committee of the Party, appealing for the establishment of 'farmers' associations.' Xiaoping responded that this would be fine in principle but to give it three years and then look at the issue again; if associations were still necessary, the Party would set them up. For various reasons, we were unable to take action later on, and so the issue remains. Farmers have their own groups and associations absolutely everywhere else in the world, but not in China.

The aforementioned 10 examples are just a rough sketch of the situation. All of these show that the 'citizenship' of rural people in China is different from the citizenship that urban residents enjoy. Moreover, these problems have not just sprung up recently but have been festering for several decades. They still have not been corrected. In economic terms, we have what is called 'systemic inertia,' which reinforces dependency on a certain course of action. Nobody dares to change it, and nobody even dares to challenge it. Even if people do dare to respond to the issues, the issues will remain unresolved for quite a while since they are now entrenched. Carrying on without any action at all, however, is going to lead to social problems. I sincerely hope the problems will be at least addressed during the 10th Five-Year Plan period [2001–2005].

Where do most of the difficulties reside? The chief problem is that China has too many farmers. State finance cannot bear the cost of taking care of them, while shifting the population to the industrial sector is too slow. As a result, 70 percent of the population is engaged in food production for consumption by 30 percent of the population. Meanwhile, overstocked grain inventories are forcing down prices, making it even harder to raise the income of farmers. Recently, we have seen a ray of hope: the Central Committee of the Party has decided to abolish the household registration system. Once this happens, intermediary institutions should be set up in rural areas to assist the transient population of farmers in finding jobs under a proper and regularized system.

Finally, considerable effort is going to have to go into building towns in order to shift one hundred to two 100 to 200 million farmers into urban centers. Only by reducing the number of people engaged in agriculture are we going to be able to raise farmers' income. Some people are questioning the small size of family operations and wondering if we should not return to the system of collectives. This would not resolve anything. It would not reduce the number of people on the land or boost labor productivity, let alone create economies of scale. We have to put our efforts into increasing the level of urbanization, fostering small- and medium-sized enterprises, and helping our cities prosper. We must also set up legal systems and established procedures: the contract law and a law on taxes and fees should be given priority in our legislation.

Note

* This is a speech delivered by the author at the 45th anniversary of the launch of the Newsletters on Rural Work and the meeting on rural economic development during 10th Five-Year Plan period.

28 Industry must repay agriculture*

(December 5, 2001)

1. Agriculture has long been the main source of funds for State investment in industry. Now that industry accounts for over 50 percent of the country's GDP, it is time to switch directions and have it start repaying agriculture. For a variety of reasons that keep industry from showing a profit, however, inputs of the industrial sector into the 'green box' of agriculture are anemic and inadequate. As a result, industry continues to draw its funding from agriculture, and the 'dual urban–rural structure' as described by development economics remains entrenched.

2. Due to resource constraints, we have a very tense situation with respect to the amount of arable land per capita, particularly given the highly uneven distribution of water. Raising the level of urbanization is of ultimate importance to our economic growth, and we must accelerate urbanization, but at the same time cities themselves consume land. Right now, they are eating up around 1 million *mu* per year. And if a full half of our rural population was shifted into urban areas, the per capita arable land of those farmers who remained would only increase by around 10 *mu* per household. That amount of land still constitutes a super-small-scale agricultural economy.

China's agriculture is a vulnerable industry. Without intensive land resources, international comparative advantages in the sector are impossible. Insisting upon nationally self-sufficient operations involves very high costs that impinge upon trying to improve people's lives. The advantage of cheap physical labor is undeniable, but if farmers can become better educated, they themselves will turn into human capital. In international markets, we are going to have to trade off our inability to produce land-intensive products for products that are labor intensive and knowledge intensive.

Joining the World Trade Organization will enable China to pursue mutually beneficial trade and equal exchange according to the principle of 'national treatment.' China has established quotas on the tariffs it can impose on imports. The import of 20 million tons of wheat requires a corresponding expenditure of foreign exchange (it is estimated that 40 million tons of soybeans are not yet entered into the calculations). This foreign exchange expenditure requires earnings from exports, and what we are in fact earning money from is the export of labor. It is clear that we must implement an import substitution policy with regard to our agricultural products. We must utilize both domestic and foreign markets to turn our agriculture into an export-oriented sector while importing certain products at the same time. Our problems regarding farmers, rural areas, and agriculture in general cannot be solved internally, either within the agricultural sector itself or within China. We must 'jump out' of our own borders to resolve them internationally.

3. Agriculture itself must self-correct and self-adjust to handle an evolving situation. Adjustments should be guided by market forces and should include cultivating markets for capital, land, and labor. We must also redeploy our forces in dealing with the market for the primary agricultural product, namely grain.

Note

* This is a speech delivered by the author at a meeting on the basic conditions of countryside, agriculture, and peasants.

29 Raise the degree to which farmers are represented through organizations*

(December 6, 2001)

The task of reforming our policies on food security, including reserves and imports, must be approached in an overall way as we put forth reform proposals. Right now, our Foreign Trade, Planning, and Grain departments all set forth once-a-year plans on an annual basis. This approach is tantamount to 'hugging the Buddha's feet at the last minute to get his help.' It is too arbitrary and does not allow for long-term strategic planning. As a result, we have been wasting quantities of money, throwing it into what appears to be a bottomless pit. If these funds had been given to farmers, they would have been 'moderately prosperous' long ago. The very reason that China decided in 1986 to resume negotiating for accession to the World Trade Organization was to promote reform. Reform is by now an irreversible process, but in undertaking reform we must consider broader issues than just commodity purchasing and agrarian employment. We should take advantage of the opportunities presented by entry into WTO to evaluate the overall issues that need attention most. We should, in particular, redefine the rules and systems that govern our approach to food security.

While we are in a transitional period from traditional agriculture to modern agriculture, most farmers in China are still at the stage of traditional operations. Once we join WTO, they are going to have to align with the modern international market and will then be facing a host of new problems. As farmers, operators, and commodity producers, how can farmers best organize themselves to deal with WTO accession? How can we help increase their organizational capacity? These are matters of urgent and practical necessity.

One question is whether or not the way small households contract for production will change and, if so, how. Right now, when a given household sells some few dozens of kilograms of grain, the cadres of the locality have to chase after the grain on the one hand, and they then have to chase after the payment on the other – i.e., the transaction goes through them. If large-scale operations and big-time contractor systems are introduced, local cadres will be relieved of this duty. Central and west regions of China are still operating on a small scale, as are farmers in the east, so the question then becomes how to organize them to undertake larger operations. Considerations include the economics of different aspects of agricultural production: what laws govern their operation. We want to make sure to take advantage of China's comparative advantage in labor.

One solution might be for our farmers to grow more vegetables, flowers, and fruit and to develop the breeding industry and the more refined value-added processing. It is not realistic to have hundreds of millions of farmers all adopting the same model, but nonetheless, the general problem is one that will be upon us very soon. Other problems are approaching us fast and furious. Our only approach can be comprehensive 'openness' and reform that is going to test unprecedented limits in scope and depth. WTO accession requires that we adapt ourselves to international rules, which alone will bring its own challenges. 'Government failure to respond' is a highly practical problem that will in the future be forcing a real transformation in our governmental institutions and that will also be propelling reform of our political system.

We cannot change the policy of contracting production to households, which will remain unchanged for 30 years, and we certainly cannot abolish the way families operate farms, which is widespread practice around the world. Larger-scale operations will be the result of moving farmers off the land – they are not the cause of that migration. The question remains how to increase our scale of operations prior to being able to move large numbers of people elsewhere. One option might be 'counter-contracting,' although some are opposed. If we are not in favor of having large companies contract for land, how then are we going to increase size of operations? All of these issues must be explored.

European countries as well as America place strict controls on having nonagricultural companies purchase farmland. The soybean and wheat associations in the United States are intermediary organizations of a cooperative nature – farmers expand the size of their operations by joining them. Could we develop something similar? It may be that some comrades are not in favor of rural cooperative organizations dedicated to farmers, but it remains a fact that farmers really do need organizations of their own to handle matters that they themselves are not equipped to deal with, including how to interact with fiercely competitive foreign as well as domestic markets. The role of such organizations is quite different from government and also different from enterprises that join up companies with farming households, since companies and enterprises exist to maximize their own self-interest. Could we perhaps learn from the way the U.S. Department of Agriculture handles its relations with farmers? Sell five-month futures contracts, for example, so for a period the government is directly subsidizing farmers? The real question underlying all of this is who is going to represent the farmers in signing the contracts. U.S. farmers sell 60–70 percent of their grain through cooperatives. In Jiashan, Zhejiang Province, the State-owned grain distribution center established a company to import rice-husking equipment. That company then signed contracts with farmers to grow high-quality rice. The contracts were signed on the basis of receipts for seeds that farmers had borrowed money to buy. A group leader was in charge of inspection and coordination for every 15 to 20 farming households. After the high-quality rice was purchased from farmers, it was processed with the newly imported equipment and sold quite well. More companies and enterprises could cooperate with farmers on this kind of 'order-based agriculture.'

We simply must start to set up organizations (farmers' associations) that represent the political and economic interests of farmers. In the mid-1980s, I met with Deng Xiaoping, and he asked me, 'What problems are farmers facing?' I responded, 'They need organizations to represent their own interests. Would it be possible to set up farmers' associations?' Deng Xiaoping said, 'The Party represents the interests of the farmers.' I said, 'The Party represents the interests of the whole people at large, and it represents the interests of the government. Farmers still have their own special interests.' Deng responded that the matter could be considered and that we could set them up if there continued to be the need. He said we would not decide right away but should wait three years to see how things developed. As things developed, the 'June 4 tempest' intervened, and the matter was dropped from the agenda. In the 1990s, some old comrades once again proposed that farmers' associations be established. A leading comrade of the Central Committee of the Party said: 'This issue has been on my desk for a long time and I have authorized the Central Office on Policy Research to look into it.' In the end, though, it was still, 'Let's wait and see.' Now China has joined the WTO and is constantly dealing with nongovernmental organizations from around the world. We should revisit the question of having our own such organizations. China must now very seriously look into raising the level of farmers' organizational capacity by setting up farmers' associations and various other specialized technical bodies.

Note

* This is a speech delivered by the author at a national forum on agricultural cooperative economic organizations.

30 A recommendation to exempt farmers from taxation*

(November 9, 2002)

Taxes and fees paid by farmers come to between RMB 250 and 300 billion every year [roughly US $35 to $40 billion dollars].

On the occasion of the 16th Party Congress, I put forward the following proposal to the Central Committee: explicitly exempt farmers from taxation for five years, and after this five-year period, implement the same personal income tax system in rural areas that is implemented elsewhere. My reasons are as follows.

1. During the War of Liberation, our farmers sacrificed hundreds of thousands of lives on behalf of the founding of New China. After Liberation, they worked hard to produce the grain that subsidized the building of the country. Each year, they provided between 40 and 50 billion kilograms of grain to the State-monopoly purchase-and-marketing cooperatives for consumption by the nonagricultural population and for the development of our country's industrialization. That grain was 'sold' at low prices. After putting in these contributions as their own investment, farmers are now entitled to a share in the earnings from that industrialization. In the past, agriculture subsidized industry. Today, industry should subsidize agriculture.

It is clear that completing this change is going to take some more time. Nonetheless, the current situation of farmers is really precarious. They are urgently in need of consideration by the Party and the government.

2. Our country is endowed with resources that include a huge population on very little arable land. Nearly 800 million farmers operate less than 2 billion *mu* of land (130 million hectares). That comes to 2.2 *mu* per capita, with each household operating a little over 10 *mu*, or less than one hectare. Agriculture is a vulnerable industry, exposed to risks from both nature and the market, so it is often in a state of uncertainty. In the meantime, the productivity of land cannot grow indefinitely. With a little over 2 *mu* of land, a farmer can survive but not reach our national goal of a 'moderately prosperous' life. Seeking a living outside agriculture is essential, whether by working in local enterprises or working as a laborer outside the farming sector. Eventually, the 'farming problem' has to be resolved outside the sphere of agriculture by moving people off the land and thereby enabling the remaining farmers to become more prosperous. Turning so many farmers into urban residents is going to require sweeping changes in various systems, all of which are limited by economic realities and will require a long period of time.

3. Looking now at the relationship between farmers and the government: in addition to the implicit tax in the low State prices for 'unified grain purchase and marketing,' and the scissor-price differentials at which farmers have to exchange [low-priced] farm products for [high-priced] industrial inputs, farmers still need to pay direct taxes. These include a 'land-use tax,' a 'special agricultural and livestock tax,' a 'slaughter tax,' the so-called 'three deductions and five charges' tax, as well as other fees apportioned among farmers by local governments. In aggregate, farmers pay between RMB 250 and 300 billion in taxes each year. The per capita annual income of a farmer is RMB 2,366. He has to pay RMB 314–377 in taxes and fees each year, which takes up between 13 and 16 percent of his income. After deducting the amount he will need for crop inputs the next year, the average farmer is left with RMB 1,500 for daily living for a whole year.

4. The average annual income of an urban resident is RMB 6,859. Nominally, the ratio of an urban income to a rural income is 2.9 to 1, but in real terms the ratio can be as high as 5 to 1, and the discrepancy is widening. A World Bank analysis of 30 countries indicates that average discrepancy in incomes between urban and rural areas worldwide is generally below 1.5 to 1; it is rarely above 2 to 1. We must adopt measures and put real effort into moving in the direction of narrowing this urban–rural discrepancy in China.

5. The urban–rural discrepancy as indicated here deserves the concerted attention of the Party and the government. It is going to be necessary to 'take care of' a whole category of low-income farmers who are in an extremely low-income bracket.

I recommend that we exempt farmers from taxation for a period of five years. In doing so, we deliver the following message: 'In addition to leading nationwide economic development and improving people's lives in general, the Central Committee of the Party wants to bestow greater concern on low-income farmers, the costs of which will come out of the redistribution of national income.' Burden reduction is a more practical measure than direct subsidies.

A survey of practices around the world shows that most countries do not collect [what is known in Chinese as a] 'vocational tax' from farmers but, on the contrary, extend agricultural subsidies to them. Our country also extends agricultural subsidies, totaling RMB 30 to 40 billion a year, but most of the funds are used for reclamation projects on major rivers. Unlike developed countries, China simply has too many farmers and cannot afford to give subsidies to them all. Alleviating the tax burden on farmers is equivalent to increasing their income. The Central Committee of the Party has also recommended 'turning fees into taxes,' and we are seeing initial results in this regard, which are useful as reference.

6. China's annual fiscal revenues come to more than RMB 1.6 trillion. If extra-budgetary revenue is included, the total approaches RMB 3 trillion. In contrast, taxes and fees paid by farmers total RMB 250–300 billion (or RMB 105 billion, if based on the statistical parameters of the State Bureau of Statistics). This five-year tax exemption is therefore certainly affordable in terms of State finances. We can retain the 'three deductions and five charges' (which come to about RMB 55.2 billion). Their ceiling amounts can be set by each province but absolutely must not be exceeded. Reduced local revenue that results from this action can be supplemented by transfer payments from the Central government. Within the five years, we should have formulated all regulations pertaining to implementing a rural personal income tax.

I respectfully submit this proposal to the Party Congress for its review and decision.

Note

* This is the recommendation proposed by the author at the 16th National Congress of the Communist Party of China (NCCPC).

31 The non-state-owned economy should be owned and operated by, and for the benefit of, the people*

(November 11, 2002)

The 'people-operated' sector is owned and operated by the people and benefits them directly. It is distinguished from the State-owned sector by being people based, self-reliant, self-created, self-operated, and self-developed.

In existence since ancient times, people-operated economies possess tremendously tenacious vitality. China's 'socialist transformation' of the 1950s transformed this sector into public ownership, but it returned in full force in the 1980s.

The people-operated sector is comprised of what is known as the 'individual economy' [ge-ti], private enterprises, partnership operations, and cooperative operations. The first three are all new incremental additions to the economy. In terms of its 'social nature,' the economy of private enterprises belongs to the category of capitalism. In 1989, there were a total of 90,581 private enterprises, a number that rose to 960,726 in 1997, at an annual growth rate of 34.3 percent. These enterprises employed 1.64 million in 1989 and 13.49 million in 1997, and their output rose during that period from RMB 9.7 billion to RMB 3.6923 trillion. Their output now accounts for more than one-third of the country's GDP. This is an economic variable that deserves close attention.

Overall, most private enterprises are family businesses. Despite the problems that come along with hiring relatives, family operations have irreplaceable advantages. At present, China has a mixed economic structure in which family economies will continue to be indispensable for a long time to come. Some enterprises have the underlying conditions to increase income, expand corporate scale, and move out of family control by embracing modern corporate systems. They have been able to separate their operations from ownership. This has been done in part to attract professional management from wherever it might be ['the five lakes and four oceans'] in order to raise their level of expertise. Most private businesses are small- and medium-sized enterprises that have been established through pooling 'idle social funds.' Small- and medium-sized enterprises have few fixed assets and, being 'small craft,' can tack with the wind more easily, update equipment and products, stimulate domestic demand, improve their own operations, and enhance their market competitiveness. Eight million small- and medium-sized enterprises are already registered with the 'industrial and commercial administration' in China. They account for 60 percent of China's gross industrial output and 75 percent of China's jobs.

People-operated enterprises have the chance to move into areas that were previously monopolized by the State-owned sector right now, as those are being
opened to them. Subject to State approval, they can also move into funding. In
light of these changes, the privately held sector must expand alliances, concentrate capital, and establish democratic supervisory and regulatory mechanisms to
ensure checks and balances.

The question on the table is why a socialist country, which previously espoused
full public ownership, should now allow and support a 'people-operated sector'
that includes private and individual [*ge-ti*] companies. The answer is simple: it is
necessary in order to deal with the objective situation in which we find ourselves.

The economic activities of humanity are constrained by objective laws, and
a given social system will not exit the stage until it does not accommodate the
development of the forces of production. It is true that small-time owners of
companies and private enterprises hire and exploit labor and are therefore are of
capitalist 'nature.' Marx said that exploitation is a crime, but he also said that it
was the engine for growth of a certain period, namely the capitalist period. The
people-operated sector of our own economy is able to meet increasingly diverse
needs of our people and also to absorb large amounts of our rural surplus labor
into the nonagricultural sector, and that is highly important right now. Historically, creating job opportunities for urban as well as rural labor has been a pressing task in China, and it is an urgent task now. Since the people-operated sector
has well-defined property rights, it enjoys a comparative advantage relative to the
State-owned sector since it is both self-restraining [in terms of reckless expendi-
tures] and willing to take calculated risks [in terms of going for profits]. It is very
strong in stimulating and creating business. Through use of capital that comes
from society at large, and taking advantage of different methods of ownership,
this sector can also attract the participation of citizens at large. It thereby enhances
the operating ability of capital and provides opportunities for equal enjoyment
of results. Every one of the developed countries in Europe, as well as America,
actively supports the development of small- and medium-sized 'people-operated'
enterprises with various policies and institutions. China is a developing country
and is pursuing industrialization to prepare the forces of production for developed
socialism. To that end, we absolutely must take advantage of the 'supply capacity'
of the private sector. People are going to have to liberate their old way of thinking
about 'whether it is called socialism or capitalism.' They must understand that
socialist countries must have forces of production that are superior to capitalism
before they can eventually replace capitalism. 'How to handle the relationship
between capitalism and socialism correctly' is the key question we face.

Some people are questioning the excessively high incomes of owners of private
enterprises. This issue has to be analyzed in terms of specifics. It is an undeniable
fact that private owners exploit the surplus value of their workers, but they also
contribute to the revitalization of the national economy. In addition, the work
they do in managing complex operations is a form of human labor as well and
should be compensated. They should also be compensated for such things as invested monetary capital, their knowledge and any patents, for being willing to

bear market risks and opportunity costs. It is rational to include all of these into their personal income.

The State should place high importance on the people-operated sector and support its smooth development. In particular, the State should ensure that it has equal opportunity in the market, equal access to capital, equal chance to participate in various kinds of production – it should be able to use capital, labor, and other factors on an equal basis. The government should transform its functions with regard to enterprises and streamline its duties. In particular, it should move away from the all-encompassing role of approving and administering every detail to a selective role of providing services, setting rules, and establishing systems so as to create a suitable environment for the development of the people-operated sector. One main problem the people-operated sector faces is lack of capital. When our State-owned banks are reluctant to extend credit, the strong inclination of citizens is to save rather than invest. This is a temporary phenomenon arising from systemic issues. Banks should adjust their loan-deposit ratios and lend, in appropriate amounts, to people-operated enterprises. The government should use a certain amount of its public-finance resources to establish a loan guarantee system, support legitimate transactions, and establish personal credit records. It can also experiment with allowing people-operated financial institutions to operate on a trial basis. It should improve the taxation system, reduce transaction costs, and enable the financing function of the capital markets to play a more vigorous role.

One scholar estimates that China's total social assets come to between RMB 32 and 35 trillion, of which personal savings totals about 11 trillion. These idle funds should be put to use as productive capital. After a period of experimentation, and once stock-market conditions allow for it, people-operated enterprises should be allowed to list on the market as a way to gain financing. The emergence of rural enterprises in the early 1980s was due to lending support from banks, and the results were quite good. We should make use of that experience.

The people-operated sector has grown as fast in rural as in urban areas. Fast-developing rural enterprises constitute an even larger sector than the farming done on the 2 billion *mu* of arable land that is contracted out to farmers. Under the leadership of the Party, our country's farmers have 'turned their lives around' not once but twice since the founding of New China. The first time was when 'land reform' got rid of the landlords' monopoly on land and thereby saved farmers 35 billion kilograms of grain that they were paying in 'land rent.' The second time was when we got rid of the people's commune system and started implementing contracting out collectively owned land to households for production. This enabled farmers to have sufficient food and clothing and even store up a surplus in the good years. Due to the fact that there are too many people on the land, however, per capita income of farmers comes to only one-fifth of what it is in cities. Farmers are currently facing a third great improvement in their lives as we restructure employment and facilitate the shift of the rural population into cities in order to participate in their industrialization. By the middle of this century, we aim to have 150 million rural people employed in nonagricultural sectors. To achieve this goal, we must develop people-operated industry and commerce to create more jobs. Not only will this facilitate urban development, but it will lessen the pressure of too many people on the land in the rural areas. We can increase the scale of farming operations, improve productivity, and raise incomes of farmers, all of which will serve to promote the modernization of agriculture. Our own experience tells us that a system that relies exclusively on public ownership is inappropriate for the primary stage of socialism. Instead, the State-owned economy should be 'primary' while other forms of ownership are allowed to develop in tandem. Within the sphere of public ownership, ownership by the State continues to be an indispensable tool by which the State regulates national income. The State must necessarily undertake a certain amount of public works and produce a certain quantity of public goods. If it does not, the legal standing of its own political power will be jeopardized. Taxes paid by citizens are meant to pay for the welfare of the general public and the expenses involved in State security. These include national defense, the building of basic infrastructure, culture, education, and such other endeavors that the private sector is either unable or unwilling to undertake. Given that the State's tax revenues are limited, while public works cannot be cut to nothing at all, they must be limited. The determination of exactly how much has to depend on what is necessary to preserve the leading role of the State in guiding the national economy. Opening up some sectors to competition will help in guiding capital investment in the direction of some major products.

The main problem that State-Owned Enterprises have to resolve is that of 'owner absence.' When nobody 'owns' resources, nobody is responsible for them. To deal with this problem, the entire country is moving to implement shareholding systems. In so doing, the rights and obligations of enterprises are made the specific responsibility of 'natural persons' and 'specified legal persons.' The Central government and local governments are setting up shareholding companies in which control shares are maintained by the government. They are also setting up Asset Management entities to oversee the evaluation of assets and to make recommendations on their disposition. We anticipate that the State-owned sector will become profitable after reforms. Under no circumstances should we think of simply abolishing it.

Our country must keep up with the times. On the one hand, the State should formulate policies, including the creation of a legal system, that lower barriers to entry into the market. It should support the development of the people-operated sector as an indispensable component of a market economy. On the other, it should reform existing State-Owned Enterprises and collectively owned enterprises by implementing shareholding systems. It should do all it can to establish a system in which public ownership is primary but other forms of ownership are encouraged to develop in tandem. The past 20 years serve as evidence that this kind of 'socialist economic order with Chinese characteristics' has already been quite successful and will have even broader horizons in the years to come.

Note

* This article was originally printed in *China Business Times*. Small changes have been made for this republication.

32   A nonpublicly owned
forest industry*

(January 22, 2003)

1. Forestry affects the security of the ecological environment. Rampant felling for many years has decimated our reserves of natural forests. Under the guidance of the Central Committee of the Party, the forestry sector has had some success with reforestation in recent years, but the task is truly enormous. The 'vegetation coefficient' is still low, and soil erosion is intense. Increasingly frequent dust storms indicate that our ecological environment has not received the consideration it requires. As a policy matter, it still is regarded as being secondary to economic growth. This is a mistake: we absolutely must not pursue economic development at the cost of jeopardizing our environmental security.

It takes a long time for a tree to grow. China must seize the moment and take every opportunity to further develop its forestry.

2. State investment funds are only sufficient to meet the needs of our major forestry regions in the northeast and Inner Mongolia, as well as several nature reserves. China's nationwide practice in ancient times was to rely on the people's own investments into local forestry, and there is plenty of room now for reviving that practice. Relying on communities and agriculture to develop the non-State-owned forestry sector has tremendous potential.

3. First, property rights must be clearly defined. The entity that plants is the entity that 'owns' and benefits. We must extend legal protection to this activity as a form of 'private property.' For reforestation being undertaken by cooperatives, we can experiment with using a shareholding system – that is, a form of mixed ownership.

A shareholding system has the benefit of making the 'physical' into an abstraction that then can convert all input values into shares. Labor, capital, and technology can all be regarded as inputs. The 'equity' as represented by shares incorporates the prices of the inputs; the earnings off the equity are distributed according to number of shares. Not only can this system enable very large-scale reforestation projects, but it can greatly increase employment.

4. Meanwhile, we must institute monitoring systems for our publicly owned forests. Digitized management systems should be set up that track not only the total numbers of trees but the numbers of specific species. Contracts, rules, and overall management should be unified, but there should be specific 'seats of responsibility' – i.e., individuals should be accountable, and the same goes with enforcement procedures: individuals must be held accountable. Any illegal felling must be punished.

5. We must focus on increasing survival rates when we carry out reforestation. When trees are planted in springtime in the north, they must receive timely irrigation or they simply dry out and die and all that effort is wasted. Various irrigation techniques are being used in some places and should be more widespread. They include water-retaining agents, water storage bags, and the digging of small water holes.

6. In the course of encouraging a people-operated forestry sector, the State should also provide financial support, including micro-loans. It should establish nurseries and offer technical guidance.

7. We have abundant labor resources. With the appropriate policy environment, we have the potential to transform our natural environment and, at the same time, make reforestation into sizeable and powerful industry.

Note

* This is a speech delivered by the author at a conference on nonpublicly owned forest development.

33 Systems innovation in rural communities

(November 6, 2003)

In developing their economies, rural communities are now facing the task of modifying a number of systems. I encourage you to consider the following in the process.

1. Clarify property rights. Specifically, the land-contracting right [the '*cheng-bao*' right] that a farmer has obtained must be a usage right that is both long-term and guaranteed. This is to ensure that farmers are motivated to invest sufficient inputs into the land to increase production. To enable mobility of the rural population, transfer of land-use rights, for compensation, should be allowed so as to develop a market for land gradually. Right now, some villages adjust land allocations among farmers every year: a small adjustment is done annually, and a major one is made every three years. This practice must be forbidden. We must uphold our existing policy that does not reduce land allocations on a person's death or grant them on a child's birth. We should encourage the industrialization of farming operations by allowing alliances among farmers, although these must still be based on households.

2. Protect civil liberties. Our Constitution bestows a variety of rights and freedoms upon the people that include, for example, the freedom of speech, the freedom to debate, the freedom to criticize government officials, and the freedom to pursue a life of well-being. No party shall encroach upon these rights in any way. The personal rights of every citizen are to be protected by law, and no government entity may detain a citizen without authorization, unless that person is being lawfully prosecuted by the judicial department. The principles of 'presumption of innocence' and 'suspicion of crime not being a crime' shall be upheld in the practice of our criminal law. Facts should be the basis for any action, and the law should be the determining criterion.

3. Extend humanitarian concern to others. All citizens within a community want to develop their own potential and maximize their own interests, which is quite natural. Income disparities inevitably accompany the process due to subjective and objective differences in people's situations. Rural communities, autonomous entities, and the grassroots level of political power must take care of the vulnerable in their midst, however – low-income groups of people that include the aged, the weak, the sick, and the disabled.

Rural communities should participate in the government's social security activities and establish social aid mechanisms so that the fruits of reform can be fairly distributed and polarization can be avoided.

These remarks were written on the occasion of convening the third national forum on 'village heads,' held in Kunming. I extend my congratulations.

34 Thoughts on poverty alleviation

(April 3, 2004)

1

China is not only a developing nation with a huge population but is in transition from being an agricultural to an industrial country. With resources that are scarce and unevenly distributed, we have poor people everywhere, but they are to be found in particular concentrations in rural areas. Land reform in the 1950s enabled farmers to pay less 'land rent,' which lessened, but did not eliminate, poverty. Before 1978, according to our own government-set standards, one-third of our entire rural population, or 250 million people, was living in poverty. [After 1978] the government promptly launched a poverty alleviation campaign aimed mainly at the problem of not enough food.

In the early 1980s, the Central Committee of the Party began formulating long-term programs to address such things as food shortages in poverty-stricken regions. These places were generally remote and lacked transportation, so getting grain to them was costly and wasteful. The system of contracting publicly owned land to individual households was already being tried in various regions. We recommended that it now be used to raise the self-reliance of poverty-stricken areas and reduce the amount of grain that had to be supplied. The Central Committee of the Party accepted this proposal, and the results were that per capita net income of farmers increased nearly three-fold, while the number of people defined as 'poverty stricken' fell to 125 million. During this period, our main poverty-alleviation strategy relied on systems innovation.

At the same time, targeted poverty-alleviation programs were aimed at specific areas. We submitted proposals for State Council approval that would allocate RMB 200 million for use in places where environmental damage had been most severe, the Dingxi and Hexi regions in Gansu Province and the Ningxia Hui Autonomous Region. Called the 'three western areas' poverty-alleviation program, the project had good results (wells bored in Gansu are still working, for example). Some people were relocated out of arid mountainous areas to places with better conditions, setting up life in new places, which could also be considered a form of poverty alleviation. At the initiative of Comrade Xiang Nan, various nongovernmental poverty-alleviation foundations and other social charitable groups, as well as such international organizations as the World Bank, made contributions.

2

In the mid-1980s, China's market-oriented reforms (at the time, the market was referred to as a 'commodity economy') began to address restructuring of entire systems. Urban–rural disparities and regional disparities were widening by that time, and uneven economic development was becoming apparent due to the constraints of social, economic, natural, and geographic conditions. It was inevitable that our policy of 'efficiency first' began to affect equitable distribution. Relatively 'poverty-stricken' low-income groups began to appear in both urban and rural areas.

On the eve of the 35th anniversary of the founding of New China, the Chinese government issued a Notice that mandated changing the 'face of poverty' in poverty-stricken areas. Based on the criteria of RMB 200 in per capita annual income, 18 poverty-stricken areas were designated as the focal areas. They included 592 'poverty-stricken counties' located in the Yimeng mountainous area; the southwest, northeast, and Nulu'erhu mountainous areas in Fujian Province; the Taihang mountainous areas; the Daba mountainous area; the Wuling mountainous area; the Jinggang mountainous area; the Gannan mountainous area; and the 'three western areas' in Gansu and Ningxia.

The government allocated RMB one billion as a poverty-alleviation fund. This was managed and supervised by entities that were set up for the purpose, 'leading groups,' and offices for poverty alleviation from the Central-government level down to county levels. Since that time, rural poverty alleviation has been officially included in line items of government budgets.

3

Our specific methods at that time were to design 'production and development projects,' then allocate funds and materials according to project. We focused on family planning and compulsory education (illiteracy dropped to 5 percent, and average life expectancy rose from 35.5 to 71.4 years). Educational levels of poor families rose in response, and people were able to rely on their own labor to provide for themselves.

Some sooner than others, all provinces and autonomous regions began liberalizing the household registration systems that discriminated against people from rural areas. This had the effect of stimulating a labor market and enabling people to move from one place to another for employment. Rural migrant workers who have properly found work in cities are now being given full 'citizenship' treatment, while discrimination of various kinds is prohibited.

4

1. A socialist country must always be human oriented. It must extend its greatest concern to the most vulnerable groups. Allowing 'some people, in some areas, to get rich first so as to facilitate growth of the forces of production' was a correct policy, but, at the same time, we must adhere to the goal of common prosperity.

2. While the fight against poverty should focus on increasing people's income, it should place even greater emphasis on social development, on improving people's community environments and living conditions, so as to carry forward the 'three civilizations.' At the same time, we must strengthen our ability to regulate the market economy in order to prevent the self-reinforcing spread of corruption. I note the following in this regard.

1. Returns from economic growth should provide universal benefits to poverty-stricken people through both primary distribution and redistribution of national income. The distribution of national resources should incline toward poverty-stricken areas to an appropriate degree.

2. We should focus on developing labor-intensive industries so as to provide more job opportunities to poverty-stricken people.

3. The State should invest in basic rural infrastructure and should implement a 'work for assistance' program.

4. Rural areas should continue to develop enterprises with diversified forms of ownership so as to increase in situ local employment.

5. People-operated enterprises should be allowed to enter certain capital-intensive industries that have, up to now, been monopolized by the State and that have been operating in the red. This should enable the government to improve its ability to make transfer payments to poverty-stricken areas for industrial development.

6. We should consider modifying our current tax-sharing system between Central and local governments in the case of poverty-stricken districts. The purpose would be to limit the need of local governments in these areas to impose illegal fees on people in order to make up for their own budgetary deficits.

7. We should set up a social security fund that provides direct subsidies to the aged, the weak, and the disabled.

8. The banks should establish micro-lending systems to help poverty-stricken families create the means for their own subsistence.

9. We should reintroduce and further develop the rural education and hygiene initiatives, and the State should increase its investment in human resources by realizing free compulsory education. (Educational expenses currently account for 10–20 percent of the total income of a rural resident and can be as much as 40–50 percent of disposable income.) Elementary education and health are determining factors for sustainable economic development and permanent eradication of poverty.

10. Poverty-stricken families should be guided to participate in vocational organizations as indicated. They should voice their needs and participate in the government's formulation of relevant policies and regulations.

3. Based on World Bank standards, China still has 120 million people whose per capita daily income is below one dollar. Calculated by the standards that China itself is currently using, we still have 30 million people living in poverty and a long way to go before poverty is eradicated. We are a developing country with few resources. The United States still has 34.99 million people living under the poverty line, even some 200 years after the country became independent, which goes to show the difficulties of the task before us.

Over the next 20 years, China will be in a strategically opportune period to realize its goal of becoming a moderately prosperous society. By 20 years from now, releasing the potential for our economic growth will lead to an increase in wealth. Within the scope of the State's financial resources, we must strive to do all in our power to reduce the absolute and the relative number of our population that lives in poverty. We should use fiscal transfer payments among other measures to achieve this goal. This is not only what we ought to do, but what we can do, and I have every confidence that we will achieve it.

The income disparity problem involves a host of factors and many variables. Existing statistical data are only good enough to reflect general trends and should only be used by the government for reference in policy making. The government must take responsibility for investigating the actual situation; it must maintain the existence of the Poverty Alleviation Department to assist it in this endeavor and should continue with centralized oversight of regional development.

35 Deng Xiaoping and China's rural reform*

(August 20, 2004)

REPORTER: You were an advocate in 1978 for China's rural reform. We'd like to ask you to look back for a moment and reflect on the extent to which Deng Xiaoping played a guiding role in this crucial reform.

DU RUNSHENG: In the Mao Zedong era, this whole subject of 'contracting output quotas to individual households' was 'forbidden territory' – it was taboo. I would say that the very first thing Deng Xiaoping did was to lift this taboo by affirming his support for the system.

In 1978, our rural areas began exploring the process of reforming the land system, which is what really drew open the curtain to China's reform as a whole. In the course of this change, Deng Xiaoping, as paramount leader, stood very firm in his support and enabled it to move forward.

In early 1980, the State began work on drawing up a long-term plan, which Yao Yilin was asked to handle. One very crucial part of this long-term plan was how to resolve the problem of grain supply to poverty-stricken areas.

At that time, China's poverty-stricken areas had roughly 250 million impoverished people who were relying almost exclusively on grain sent in from other areas to survive. Grain transport was a huge problem since there weren't roads into some areas, and grain had to be transported by human beings and domestic animals. Along the way, pretty much all the grain was actually consumed. In meetings, we therefore raised the idea that it would be better to have local households raise grain themselves rather than try to keep on transporting it through the old grain supply system. This was what we now call the 'family contracting [cheng-bao] system,' which allows households to contract directly for producing grain quotas. Yao Yilin took this proposal to Deng Xiaoping, and Deng said, 'This looks good. Let's try it. If it doesn't work, we can always do something different.'

REPORTER: We've all heard about the 'black cat white cat' concept – is this something he came up with during the rural reform?

DU RUNSHENG: That was much earlier. At the very beginning, what he actually said was 'black cat yellow cat,' not 'white cat.' Back in the latter part of June 1962, the secretariat of the Central Committee of the Party held a meeting to discuss the East China region. The economy was in extremely bad shape at that time, but people were not allowed to have households contract for output quotas. People who were for and against allowing the practice were roughly half and half at the meeting. Deng Xiaoping then quoted an old folk saying that went, 'As long as a cat can catch a mouse, black or yellow cat, it's a good cat.' Based on what he described as the experience in rural areas, he then said at the meeting, 'What's the best approach for production? We have to look at it this way: if the form we adopt, in terms of the "relations of production," is effective, if it restores farm output quickly, then that's the right form. If the people want to do it that way, that's the way to do it. If it's an illegal form, we simply make it legal.'

In reality, by the time we recommended to Deng Xiaoping that we should implement the system of contracting output quotas to individual households, farmers were already doing this in Zhejiang, Anhui, and Sichuan Provinces. And Deng Xiaoping already knew about it from local authorities. One could say that it really was the courage of farmers themselves to go out and try it that gave Deng Xiaoping the material on which to base his decision. Based on their actions, he began to adjust our rural economic policies and initiate the whole process of reform and opening up.

REPORTER: How could Comrade Xiaoping be so sure about this, when the *cheng-bao* idea was so in conflict with the system of the people's communes? The collective ownership system of the communes was part of a 'three-level ownership system' that used production teams as the basic unit, not the household. So how could he decide so firmly to allow the contracting of output quotas to individual households?

DU RUNSHENG: The people's commune system was in essence an expanded version of the Soviet Union's collective farms. Not only did these not provide people with sufficient food and clothing, but they created an economy of scarcity. People paid the price of that mistake with their lives during the three difficult years from 1959 to 1961. Farmers spontaneously started contracting production to individual households several times, and each time it was seen as taking the 'capitalist road,' and they were attacked in a very ruthless way. To turn this situation around at last, Comrade Xiaoping took the risk on himself, which really was the mark of a great man.

REPORTER: Why was it so very hard for China to contract output quotas to individual households?

DU RUNSHENG: The era of 'taking class struggle as the key task' was already over by the late 1970s, but people had not yet recognized that very clearly. Such major questions as 'what was socialism' and how to build it were just being explored. The difficulty in instituting the *cheng-bao* system mainly related to the way China was transitioning from the 'democratic revolution' to the 'socialist revolution.'

With Deng Xiaoping's reemergence, China entered a period of reform and opening up. At this critical moment, in which direction China's impoverished rural areas might turn became an issue of historic proportions. It stood right in front of all Chinese people but particularly in front of Deng Xiaoping, who had only just begun to take charge of things. Faced with all kinds of doubts and divergent views, he took the very wise and resolute attitude of proactively supporting this reform. He explicitly expressed his support in written form on many occasions. In his speech on rural policies in May 1980, he said, 'After the rural policies were liberalized, some places where conditions permitted began contracting output quotas to individual households and the results have been good. Change has come very quickly. Most production teams in Feixi County in Anhui Province contracted output quotas to individual households and their output went up sharply. In Fengyang County, famous for the *Drums of Feng Yang*, most production teams introduced an all-round responsibility system called *dabaogan*, and in one year alone they have turned things around. Some comrades are afraid this system will have a negative impact on our collective economies. My view is that these fears are unjustified.'

At another point, he made the comment: 'In the long run, China's socialist agricultural reform and development will go through two major "leaps." The first will be abolishing the people's communes and implementing a household contract system that links pay to output. This is a significant advance, and we are going to have to stick to it for a long time and not change our policy. The second will be for our agriculture to develop economies of scale and collective "economies" that meet the needs of scientific management and mass [socialized] production. This is another significant advance that is going to take a very long time.'

This kind of clear-cut thinking and way of speaking was extremely helpful in alleviating the misgivings of some people. It helped achieve consensus on the issue.

And in fact, the moment poverty-stricken regions began the household contracting system, the number of poor people declined sharply, and the State had less of a burden to cover. People were very motivated. What's more, not only did poor areas welcome the change, but people in average areas also thought it was better than people's communes. So it spread out across the country.

At that point, given the changes in the situation, the Central Committee of the Party decided to issue a 'policy document' on the agricultural production responsibility system. We were asked to draft the very first No. 1 Document on rural issues. Before we presented the draft to the Political Bureau for discussion, we sent it to Comrade Deng Xiaoping and Comrade Chen Yun. Deng Xiaoping wrote his approval on the spot: 'Fully Agree!' Comrade Chen Yun also indicated: 'Active Support.'

REPORTER: It seems that Deng Xiaoping's support was absolutely crucial to pushing through this reform.

DU RUNSHENG: That's right. Given the political environment at that time, there was extremely great resistance to adopting the system. This was due to historical conditions and ideological constraints. One can imagine that without Deng Xiaoping's visionary and powerful support, the system might well have been killed in the cradle, or at the very least postponed for a long time, which would have led to head-on conflict with the rural population. That would effectively have blocked China's socioeconomic development.

Deng Xiaoping attached exceptional importance to China's rural areas, and one reason was that he was very concerned about China's food security. That concern was thoroughly different from the old concept of 'taking grain production as the central task.' He was in favor of developing diversified operations.

REPORTER: Can you talk a little bit about 'diversified operations'?

DU RUNSHENG: In 1986, when [we were] presenting reports to him, Deng Xiaoping made a number of comments. He said, 'In agriculture, grain is the main problem. We should avoid a situation in which we again have to import quantities of grain in a few years. That would affect the speed of our economic development.' He also said, 'Agriculture cannot rely on grain production alone to double output. It must also rely on diversified operations. With the growth of diversified operations, specialized groups or teams will appear that will stimulate the development of a commodity economy in rural areas.'

This way of thinking tied together the whole concept of increasing farm output through diversifying operations. It linked 'diversified operations' to a division of labor in rural areas, the growth of different industries, and a commodity economy. This greatly opened out the space in which the rural economy could develop. It expanded the economic capacity of rural areas and enabled an increase in rural incomes. It played an extremely important role in guiding our policy.

REPORTER: The dynamism of rural reform in China can also be attributed to an important group that should not be overlooked – namely, rural enterprises ['town-and-village enterprises]. What was Comrade Xiaoping's attitude toward these?

DU RUNSHENG: He gave them full support and on many occasions referred to them as 'a new force.' Rural enterprises first emerged in the 1950s in China. They 'wavered' in the 1960s, revived in the 1970s, and finally really began to develop only after reform and opening up. Generally speaking, their growth over the nearly 30 years prior to 1978 was a tortuous process. Their precursors were enterprises run by communes and production teams.

To a degree, the development of rural enterprises adjusted the imbalance between rural and urban areas in China, though that development has not been strong enough to break out of our dualist economic structure. Deng Xiaoping said, 'Our experience over the past 10 years has proven that we will be able to resolve the issue of shifting surplus labor out of agriculture, so long as we mobilize grassroots units [of the Party] and the initiative of farmers and so long as we develop diversified operations and new rural enterprises. Right now, rural enterprises have already absorbed 150 million of our rural surplus labor force.'

Given the numbers of people in rural areas and the limited amount of land, 'hidden unemployment' has been going on for years but is now becoming a serious political, economic, and social issue. If this issue of shifting surplus labor is not properly solved, it will have a direct impact on China's economic development and social stability. This issue can only be addressed by further industrialization and urbanization in China.

REPORTER: How should we evaluate the impact of Deng Xiaoping's theoretical ideas about rural reform on the process of China's rural reform?

DU RUNSHENG: Essentially every step of China's rural reform has unfolded in a way that conformed to Deng Xiaoping's theoretical concepts.

Reforms initiated by Deng Xiaoping directly or indirectly helped modernize rural agriculture, benefit farmers in a material way, and fundamentally change our modes of production. His contributions included his theoretical innovations on the 'three-step development goals,' on 'one country, two systems,' on 'science and technology as the primary force of production,' on the establishment of 'special zones for opening up China,' and most importantly on taking into our conceptual framework the propositions of a market economy. However, reforms have not yet gone far enough. Given our scarce resources, China still faces many problems that cannot be ignored in developing agriculture and our rural economy, while new problems will continue to emerge in the future. Solving these problems will require the guidance of consistent theories and the emergence of new theoretical approaches. In reforms over the past 20-some years, Deng Xiaoping's theoretical innovations set a fine example that is worthy of our study and emulation.

Note

* This is an interview of the author with the reporter of the *Finance* magazine.

36 'Urbanized towns' are the result of economic development

(August 28, 2004)

Urbanized towns are the product of economic development, since urbanization moves forward in concert with industrialization. Transforming agricultural technology, and also distributing its products, requires the services of the secondary and tertiary industries. Developing those relies on the effects of concentration of resources and lowering of transaction costs, which in turn stimulates the growth of cities.

Looking back at our own history, when the State carried out unified purchase and marketing, cities were 'closed.' It was necessary for rural enterprises to locate themselves out in the countryside, which was not the best choice. It meant that our urbanization was slower than industrialization, and it blocked the mobility of people, which aggravated rural poverty. We must now pursue policies that strike a balance between our urban and rural development.

Cities must necessarily be linked in a network structure. Since large, medium-sized, and small cities have different functions, they should be organized in a way that is evenly spaced and that allows each one to benefit from the others. In contrast to [our current situation of] disorderly industrial growth, intelligently planned cities are able to conserve land. We now have around 50,000 urbanizing towns. As the terminals of city networks, they absolutely must focus on conserving land. In order to encourage land conservation [by putting a realistic price on its value], we should begin to develop a land market as soon as possible.

As cities expand, land prices in a land market will continue to rise, which should be beneficial in using land with greater efficiency per unit. China has an extreme scarcity of arable land. We must place the highest importance on protecting it. In the past seven years, our amount of arable land has been reduced by 100 million *mu* [0.1647 *mu* per acre, so over 16 million acres]. In general, cities should build high rises, and we should no longer allow any construction of one-story buildings. As time goes on, the existing one-story homes will be cleared away. It is to be expected that real estate will become a powerful industry. Building high rises consumes a tremendous amount of steel rods [rebar] and cement, and we should certainly make sure to maintain a balance between supply and demand. In developing urbanized towns, we should not simply pursue higher numbers.

Instead, we should cut the number of [government] personnel involved so as to lessen the burden on farmers and prevent a building 'fever.'

In carrying our work to a deeper level, we should emphasize actual accomplishments. Our strategy for development should be very concrete in terms of different types of urban concentrations – urbanizing towns and townships, satellite cities, strip cities along outskirts of other cities, and commercial towns.

37 The critical element in our overall planning for urban–rural development*

China's rural migrant workers

(February 19, 2006)

Rural migrant workers are currently a very major issue in China. In the course of modernization, the most fundamental and important vector of population change is the process of farmers coming into cities and becoming urban workers. Today's rural migrant workers represent an intermediate or transitional form of this process. When they arrive in cities, they participate in nonagricultural work in urban areas, yet their personal 'status' [*shen-fen*] as farmers remains unchanged: they are not incorporated into cities as full-fledged urban residents. They exist on the margins of industries, the margins of urban and rural areas, and on the margins of the systems. They represent a bundle of contradictions, full of hope and also fully challenged by their predicament.

There is little doubt that having tens of millions of farmers working in urban areas is a phenomenon unique to China. We have pursued a dual-structure urban-rural development policy for a long time now by keeping large amounts of surplus labor in rural areas. Once farmers have the freedom to choose how they operate, once cities have demand for labor, and once the administrative barriers to labor mobility are removed, the massive flow of the labor force will become one huge surging wave. Under our existing land system, most farmers working outside their native places can still retain their means of agricultural production and their residences. They do not have to move their whole families out of their native places, 'turn their backs on the old well and leave the homeland forever.' On the other hand, all the systems that cities undertake to provide their citizens are not yet ready to accommodate farmers, from household registration management, to social security, to systems for political integration. Cities cannot yet incorporate all these people as their urban residents. Farmers are working in urban areas, but their 'status' as farmers remains unchanged – hence the tremendous numbers of what we call 'rural migrant workers.'

In a sense, it is inevitable that rural migrant workers become a transitional form of population transfer as we undergo the process of urbanization and industrialization, and this phenomenon can be regarded as performing two positive functions. First, it brings direct benefits to the rural areas. Every year, rural migrant workers bring home not only hundreds of billions of RMB but information on the outside world, culture, new social networks. This stimulus to the development of poverty-stricken rural areas is something that cannot be accomplished by fiscal transfer payments. Second, it can help relieve pressures arising from overly rapid urbanization. As cities grow, jobs change with market cycles and industry substitution, particularly in the construction and labor-intensive processing industries. Other jobs are by nature irregular – in the service industries, for example. By being able to cope with these changes, rural migrant workers provide a more elastic labor supply to the cities. Labor can grow quickly when the demand is high; when it drops dramatically, workers have a place to go back to rather than having to stay in cities as an enormous body of urban unemployed.

We must recognize, however, that the failure of cities to incorporate rural migrant workers into their systems, indeed the discrimination against and neglect of these people, is bound to lead to gathering problems over time. Not addressing these problems has the potential to become a major destabilizing factor.

The Issue of China's Rural Migrant Workers, written by Comrade Liu Huailian (published by the People's Publishing House), is a very useful systematic study of this subject. The author collected extensive data and research results and, through a comparative treatment that looks at historical, domestic, foreign, and interdisciplinary data, builds a fairly comprehensive platform for understanding the problems. Considering the fact that he is still working as a regional leader in the central part of the country, his explorations of the subject are that much more valuable. The reason for this is that rural migrant workers are not just a theoretical issue. They are an issue that requires action as a key aspect of balancing urban–rural development. If we manage to steer this issue in the proper direction, the course of our modernization will be far smoother. I hope that more and more people will be focusing their efforts on the subject.

Note

* This article was published by the *People's Daily* on February 19, 2006.

38 Changing 'due consideration for equity' into 'a concerted focus on equity'*

(August 15, 2006)

1. Development is essential

'First increase the size of the cake so that everyone is guaranteed he will have some.' We must seek to develop China with one heart and one mind, change our mode of economic development, emphasize efficiency, realize the goal of bringing per capita GDP up to US $3,000.

However, development is a continuous process, and creating equity in the distribution of social wealth too has a process. It involves equity at the outset, equity in the course of events, and equity at the end.

'Equity at the outset' means equal opportunity. This can be decisive in determining the end result. It can be a very considerable motivating factor. We must firmly take hold of our work in the sphere of education, raise the caliber of our citizens, so that they themselves are aware that participating in the process of social endeavors can raise their own incomes.

2. Equitable distribution is an eternal subject

From ancient times in China, we have had that saying about 'people being more worried about unequal treatment than they are about the actual amount they get.' When our farmers rose up in revolt, it was generally over demands for equity. 'Production' arises from social behavior in the sphere of producing things, and therefore production always comes around to the question of distribution.

Marxism holds that if distribution is to be equitable and just, the first thing that must be done is to abolish the exploiting class. Under the socialist system, 'distribution according to work,' and 'more pay for more work' can stimulate efficiency. Conversely, 'same pay whether the work is more or less' causes people to 'get a free ride' and simply loaf. In the 1950s, when China introduced the labor-day and work-point systems, Chairman Mao criticized these as being unnecessarily tedious procedures. The moment we stopped using them, however, egalitarianism erupted, and we had a crisis in production that exacerbated the 'three difficult years.' Equitable distribution and egalitarianism are totally different things. In fact, equity was also important in the period when we were 'transitioning out of the difficult time.' Implementing a unified State purchasing and marketing system

[State monopoly], and using coupons for the distribution of food and other scarce products, allowed us to move out from the 'mistaken region' of egalitarianism and to maintain social stability at that time.

3. Adopting a market economy in the 1990s, with its attendant rule of giving 'priority' to efficiency and 'due consideration' to equity

During this period [the 1990s], China allowed some people to get rich first with the idea that they would help others to get rich and move together toward common prosperity. This arrangement was basically something that had to be done to conform to the realities we faced. The market economy is competitive, however, and the rule of 'survival of the fittest' can lead to polarization and a constantly widening disparity between urban and rural realities. In light of the new situation, the Central Committee of the Party is now adopting a number of different policies to focus preferential treatment on vulnerable groups. These include focusing on addressing the 'three agricultures' (problems of countryside, agriculture, and farmers), using a scientific view of development to formulate plans for overall development, emphasizing the building of a 'new socialist countryside,' and increasing State investment in the process. [We] are attempting to address the income problems of hundreds of millions of people by employing macro-regulatory adjustments and improving income distribution. We are trying to balance investment and consumption, change government functions, get out of State monopolies, and eradicate corruption. The next steps to be taken involve greater equity in distribution.

In light of the aforementioned, I recommend that we change 'due consideration for equity' into 'a concerted focus on equity.'

Note

* This is the outline of a speech delivered by the author at a forum on China's market economy.

39 Choosing how we go about 'building a new countryside'

(September 26, 2006)

The Central Committee of the Party has brought forth a major governmental policy on 'building a new countryside,' which is a measure of extreme strategic importance. It addresses the 'three agriculture' problems (countryside, agriculture, and farmers).

The question now is how to carry out this policy. It is going to be of fundamental importance to enable farmers to inform themselves with knowledge, take advantage of the intellectual fruits of modern civilization, make themselves into human capital. The key is not in such things as increasing investment, undertaking basic infrastructure, or reconstructing housing.

Our farmers have long depended on small-scale operations to farm their land. As a result, agriculture is disengaged from modern industry, and farmers are disengaged from human knowledge and progress. They are not able to take advantage of new technologies to improve their own condition. Technological advances driven by the ongoing wave of globalization have increased pressures on them rather than brought them blessings. How to enable farmers to benefit from technology? One good way is to allow them to organize themselves and enter into modern markets, allowing the markets to serve as a bridge in connecting farmers and knowledge. The market possesses a kind of linking-up function that can tie the knowledge of different individuals together. 'Building a new countryside' means building human capacity. [We should] guide farmers in the direction of studying hard, gaining scientific knowledge, integrating with markets, and being able to recognize price signals so as to make intelligent decisions themselves. They need to know, for example, how futures markets influence what they should be intending to plant. They should know how the price of vegetables affects what they grow. In addition, they should know how they themselves can affect the markets.

There are many implications to the policy of 'building a new countryside,' but one indispensable aspect is to enable farmers to engage with markets and learn all they can. As time goes by, traditional agriculture will move in the direction of a knowledge economy. Better qualified farmers and a more prosperous agriculture will inject new life into our drive to build a socialist harmonious society.

40 Transform agriculture into a 'knowledge economy'*

(February 15, 2007)

1. The document of the Central Committee of the Party calls for vigorously developing modern agriculture and promoting the building of a 'socialist new countryside.'

Modern agriculture must differ from agriculture in the old days in its entirety, not just in certain respects.

2. From industry to service industries to a knowledge economy is the trend of world development. Most developed countries have completed the transition from industrial to service societies and are in the process of transitioning on to knowledge societies.

While national strength of all different kinds is important, the State should look upon continuous advances in knowledge as the driving force of development. If we are not willing to remain backward in our agriculture, we must focus on increasing the knowledge content of agriculture and transforming it in a 'knowledge economy.'

3. 'Knowledge is power.' With knowledge, people become more intelligent, and with more intelligent people, a country develops. The most important part of the process is cultivating human resources, the people involved in farming. When we have generations of knowledgeable farmers coming to the fore, we will see agriculture evolve into a knowledge economy.

4. The United States has increased both the quantity and quality of its agricultural production, and increased its exports, by taking advantage of genetic engineering and specifically of recombinant gene technology.

5. China has not yet emerged from farming land in the way it has been done for generations. To transform our technologies, we should start by employing information technologies. Townships should be linked up in interconnected networks via computers; computer programming should be used for agriculture, forestry, fishery, and other occupations, while digital technologies of all kinds can be used to improve agriculture. Data about plowing, seeding, management, irrigation, fertilizer application, harvesting, and marketing should all be entered into computers and utilized through various software programs. By now, most governments at or above the township level are equipped with computers; the main problem is training people to use them effectively. Of course, knowledge can also be acquired from sources other than computers. We should be using a range of learning methods as we turn agriculture into a knowledge industry.

Note

* This is the outline of a speech delivered by the author at the Spring Festival Mass Greeting Meeting.

41 Selecting the proper path for economic development

(September 2007)

1. China's greatest change over the past 20 years was to abandon the Soviet model and introduce a market economy. We 'discarded the old in favor of the new,' bringing in a market-economy system that allows a variety of forms of economic entities to participate in competition, systems innovation, and technological innovation. As a result, China's GDP now ranks fourth in the world.

2. As a developing country, China should focus all its attention on pursuing development. By that, we mean preparing the conditions for sustainable development and not just immediate gain. If it is not sustainable, interrupting development down the line will cause tremendous damage.

3. The results of development must be equitably distributed and must benefit the public at large.

4. To prevent excessive income disparities and keep the gap that currently exists between urban and rural populations from widening too quickly, we should set up a social security fund that provides coverage for people in both urban and rural areas. It should be used to mitigate income differentials.

5. Socialism is a system that distributes 'according to work performed' and that still operates under the 'capitalist class' mode of defining equality. At a time when resources 'gush forth' in unlimited quantity, we can move toward 'distribution according to need.' That time is very far in the distant future.

6. No social system will quit the stage when it can still accommodate growth in the forces of production. A new social system cannot be brought into being when conditions are not ripe within the old system. Our country, currently at the primary stage of socialism, takes public ownership as primary with other economic forms of ownership developing in tandem, and this social system should be in effect for many generations to come, even dozens of generations to come, if not longer.

7. We must transform our mode of economic development and establish a conservation-oriented society. Right now, we are using four times the amount of energy to create every unit of GDP output that developing countries use per unit of their GDP output. This makes it hard for us to be globally competitive.

8. Our country's political-system reforms are trailing behind economic reforms in the course of setting up a market economy. This may well affect our transition from a society that 'provides enough food and clothing' to a society that is 'moderately prosperous.' Both inside and outside the Party, we must establish democratic procedures. First of all, we must protect the constitutional rights of every citizen. We must improve our system of electing the primary 'responsible persons.' Finally, we must encourage the public to shine the light of democratic oversight on corruption so that 'corrupt elements have nowhere to hide.'

42 Adhere to 'socialism with Chinese characteristics'

(April 2008)

The continuous advance of technology stimulates the ongoing evolution of social structures in human society. Each age has its different, and more advanced, mode of production. The slave society was supplanted by the primitive society, then the feudal society, and then the capitalist society. Existing capitalist wealth far exceeds all wealth accumulated throughout past history, which has led some to regard capitalism as the 'final stage of history' despite its retention of class exploitation. The salvoes of the October Revolution announced that socialism would be supplanting capitalism, however, which was a revolutionary breakthrough in the world.

Socialism represents human longing for a future that incorporates certain values of democracy, liberty, love, and equality. In the economic sphere, socialism is based on 'social ownership' and aims to eradicate poverty, realize common prosperity, keep polarization in check, and establish a just and equitable system for national income distribution. The socialist society abolishes class exploitation. It employs a system of 'distribution according to work' and 'more pay for more work' in order to stimulate initiative. It celebrates work, despises exploitation, and welcomes those who would keep exploiters from carrying out exploitation.

'Distribution according to work' is still a 'right' that belongs to the capitalist class system, however. It is different from distribution according to the needs of individual persons. When society as a whole continues to advance to the point that resources 'gush forth' in unlimited quantity, our mode of distribution will get rid of 'distribution according to work' and evolve to 'distribution according to need' as we reestablish 'ownership by the individual.' Current conditions do not permit that to happen.

Socialism is a product of highly developed forces of social production. It both inherits and builds on certain advantages of capitalism until the point that it is able to supplant capitalism. Historically, socialist concepts have evolved from 'Utopian' to 'scientific' socialism, the latter being a stage that we in China are still far from attaining. In the 1950s and 1960s, China's socialist transformation only modified 'ownership' while our level of industrialization and urbanization remained quite low. In fact, what we did was to expropriate various forms of private property for no compensation at all. We did not undertake any corresponding shift of people from rural areas, and without doing that it was very hard to realize any kind of common prosperity. We have a long way to go before attaining scientific socialism.

The 13th Party Congress evaluated the overall situation of economic development in China and defined the systemic 'nature' of the country as being at 'the primary stage of socialism, with public ownership as primary with diverse other forms of ownership developing in tandem.' It asserted that this fundamental economic structure would be ongoing for generations, perhaps dozens of generations, and perhaps even longer.

'Socialism with Chinese characteristics' differs from the Stalinist socialism of the Soviet Union in the following respects.

1. It allows diverse economic components and diverse operating forms to coexist.

2. Small- and medium-size enterprises exist in all sectors, including agriculture, industry, and service industries, which serves to concentrate capital that is held throughout society.

3. It utilizes abundant human resources to produce labor-intensive products that are exported in exchange for currency to those countries with smaller populations and more land.

4. Its socialist goal is 'common prosperity,' not 'common poverty.'

In short, the one and only path that China must choose to take is the socialist path. Only socialism can save China, and only socialism with Chinese characteristics can serve to develop China. These represent a kind of 'soft-power' way for China to move out into the world and be successful. Let us unify our intent so that we can fight together.

43　New options for economic development*

(June 3, 2008)

1. Farmers in China

A leading comrade once said that New China was paid for with the lives of countless numbers of people, and most of those were farmers.

When the country transitioned into the period of 'economic construction,' farmers got to work and lifted grain output from 320 billion to one trillion kilograms, which kept us from having to import massive amounts from other countries. Farmers conscientiously observed our family-planning policy and reduced births by 400 million over a period of time, thereby reducing population pressures. Farmers were also the ones to create the '*cheng-bao*' system for contracting public land to families, which enabled our entire society to have enough to eat and wear and move toward 'moderate prosperity.' Farmers are the 'main force' for building a new socialist countryside, and, once it develops, that countryside will have unlimited potential.

Our hard-working farmers face the extreme problem of too little land for too many people, but while we cannot manufacture more land, we can shift people. Industrial development requires higher levels of urban concentration: if we reach an urbanization rate of 50 percent, we should be able to have shifted enough people to enrich our farming population.

2. Sustainable development

China's greatest change over the past 20 years was to abandon the Soviet model and introduce a market economy. We 'discarded the old in favor of the new,' bringing in a market-economy system that allows a variety of forms of economic entities to participate in competition, systems innovation, and technological innovation. As a result, China's GDP now ranks fourth in the world.

As a developing country, China should focus all its attention on pursuing development. By that, we mean preparing the conditions for sustainable development and not just immediate gain, for interrupting development down the line will cause tremendous damage. The results of development must be equitably distributed and must benefit the public at large.

To prevent excessive income disparities and to control the gap that currently exists between urban and rural populations from widening too quickly, we should set up a social security fund that provides coverage for people in both urban and rural areas. It should be used to ameliorate income differentials.

3. Energy issue

We must transform our mode of economic development and establish a conservation-oriented society. Right now, we are using three to four times the amount of energy to create every unit of GDP output that developing countries use per unit of their GDP output. This makes it hard for us to be globally competitive.

China's industrialization requires the continuous supply of adequate energy. Our country's resource scarcity constitutes a bottleneck to development.

We now need to develop new energies: solar, tidal, and wind. Given our topography and year-round winds from all directions, wind energy should become a priority choice, and we should import mature foreign technology in this respect.

At the current stage, the cost for importing energy from abroad is too high. Besides, such method is unsustainable. We could build more nuclear power plants and learn the technology during the process. It is said that France mainly relies on nuclear power to push forward economic operations. We too should utilize nuclear energy on a larger scale.

Coal mines can serve as a backup resource, but too many coal-mine accidents have been occurring in recent years, killing many miners. Today's miners were yesterday's farmers. Some leaders are aiming for quick results by ordering miners to go into mines without regard for the safety of their lives. Mine disasters can be avoided. Casualties can be reduced with the proper precautions.

4. Establishment of democratic processes

Our country's political-system reforms are trailing behind economic reforms in the course of setting up a market economy. This may well affect our transition from a society that 'provides enough food and clothing' to a society that is 'moderately prosperous.' Both inside and outside the Party, we must establish democratic procedures. First of all, we must protect the constitutional rights of every citizen. We must improve our system of electing the primary 'responsible persons.' Finally, we must encourage the public to shine the light of democratic oversight on corruption so that 'corrupt elements have nowhere to hide.'

Gradually addressing these problems will greatly accelerate our ability to build 'socialism with Chinese characteristics.'

Note

* This article was first published by the *Yanhuang Cunqiu* magazine, Issue 6, 2008, and was revised when being included into this book.

Main works of Du Runsheng

1 *China's Rural Economic Reform*, China Science & Technology Publishing House, 1985.
2 *Choices of China's Rural Areas*, Rural Reading Materials Publishing House, 1989.
3 *China's Rural Economic Reform* (English version), China Foreign Languages Press, 1989.
4 *Collection of Du Runsheng's Works*, Shanxi Economic Publishing House, 1998.
5 *Du Runsheng's Works on China's Rural Reform* (Japanese version), Japanese Rural Culture Association, 2002.
6 *Evolution of China's Rural System*, Sichuan People's Publishing House, 2003.
7 *Chronicles of Major Policy Decisions on China's Rural Changes*, People's Publishing House, 2005.

Index

47–8; for land 95; for rural areas 7–15,
32–9; for water 121
education 152; for farmers 17–18, 28, 118,
163; in mountainous areas 76; poverty
and 76, 184, 185–6; prosperity and 61
efficiency 58–61, 81–2, 197
egalitarianism 1, 28, 115–16, 118–19, 196
Emperor's grain 42
employment 50–1, 86, 95, 159; for farmers
88, 164; poverty and 185; *see also* rural
work
energy 206; agriculture and 52; economic
policies and 153; grain and 108; in
mountainous regions 76;
Engels, Friedrich 27, 119, 149
environment 75, 107, 121
equal pay 9, 28
equity 58–9, 196–7
exchange rate 70
exports: of commodities 55; of finished
products 68; imports and 73–4; labor
surplus and 71; rural labor and 68

factor markets 83–4
factors of production 30
family operations 22–4; alliances and
117; commodities by 52; commodity
production by 117; in household
responsibility system 33; land
contracting and 114; large-scale
enterprises and 24; market economy
and 112–13; modernization and 24; in
private economy 175; private property
and 25; public ownership and 111–12;
remuneration for 33; in rural areas 102;
stabilization of 111–14
family planning 47, 110, 184
farmers 26, 98, 194–5, 205; capitalism
and 23; decision-making by 111, 118;
democracy for 117–18; diversification
by 136; division of labor and 88;
education for 17–18, 28, 118, 163;
employment for 88, 164; fees of 47, 113;
in feudalism 112; as free men 115–19;
income distribution and 173; income of
45; investment by 45, 88; land and 164;
land-use rights of 84, 89, 94, 111, 118,
181; large-scale agricultural production
and 170; loans for 165; means of
production and 28; national citizenship
for 163–6; organizations for 169–71;
private ownership by 23; private
property of 19; profits to 138; prosperity
of 56–7; public health for 164; savings

of 45; shareholding systems and 45;
subsidies to 42, 45, 65, 173; taxes of 47,
164, 172–4; tenant 22; *see also* family
operations; household responsibility
system
farmers' associations 165, 170–1
farm machinery 10, 24, 25
farm products: prices for 117; processing
of 51–2; *see also specific products*
feedstocks 44
fees, of farmers 47, 113
fertilizers 24, 37–8, 41, 105
feudalism 22, 23, 87, 112, 117
first: large, second: public 27
fishing, sustainable development and 106
fish ponds 42
five-guarantee households 10
fixed assets 195; in alliances 64; collective
ownership of 38; in shareholding
systems 95
floods 105, 109
food: industry 44; pollution in 71
forces of production: collective economy
and 9; in communes 9, 11, 102;
industrialization and 176; Marxism
and 23; Marx on 11; ownership and 23;
private ownership and 150; production
relationships and 9; prosperity and 61;
relations of production and 150; in
socialism 203–4; foreign debt 70
foreign exchange 64, 70, 167–8
foreign trade 70, 73; in GDP 71; labor for
68; *see also* exports; imports
forestry 38, 43, 47–8, 75; investment
in 179; labor and 180; water
and 108
freedom of speech 154
free men, farmers as 115–19
free will 19

Gang of Four 16
GDP: energy and 206; foreign trade in 71;
growth of 124; industry in 167
ge-ti (individual companies) 92, 126, 131,
142, 175
getting rich *see* prosperity
go-it-alone economies 33
government: communes and 29–30,
35; market economy and 82–3, 84;
private economy and 177; shareholding
systems and 93, 178; supply and
marketing cooperatives and 98;
township 47; Wenzhou economic model
and 142–3

For Product Safety Concerns and Information please contact our EU
representative GPSR@taylorandfrancis.com
Taylor & Francis Verlag GmbH, Kaufingerstraße 24, 80331 München, Germany

www.ingramcontent.com/pod-product-compliance
Lightning Source LLC
Chambersburg PA
CBHW050427280326
41932CB00013BA/2022

9 781138 595828